AIR WAR
SOUTH
VIETNAM

The US Navy's capabilities with carrier-based warplanes became exceedingly important as the machinery went into motion for an evacuation from South Vietnam. The F–4 Phantom was still the principal carrier-based fighter, although measures to replace it with the F–14 Tomcat were moving along nicely. (USN)

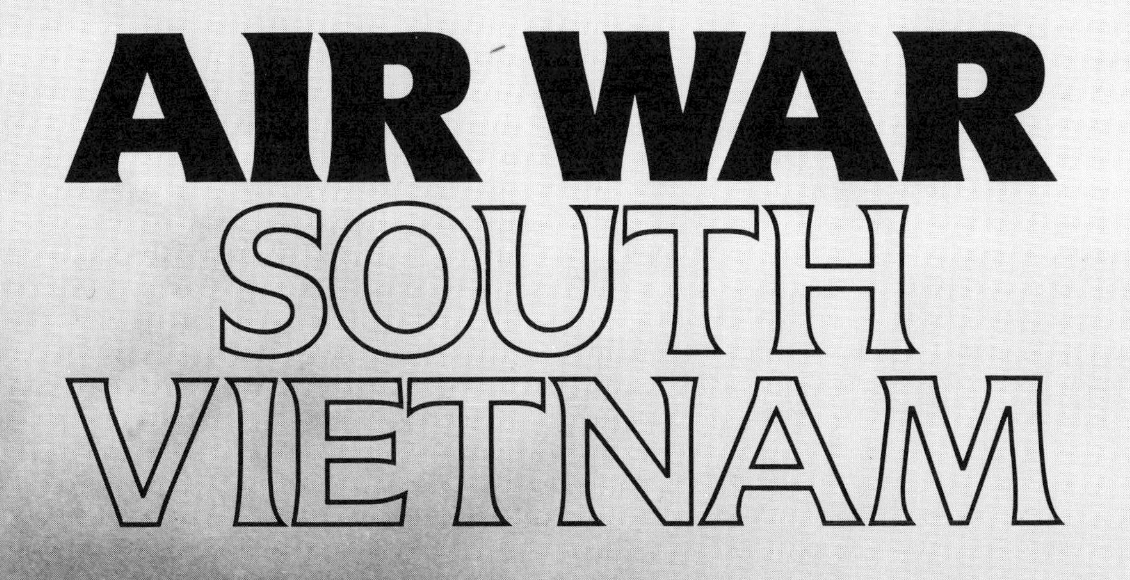

Robert F. Dorr

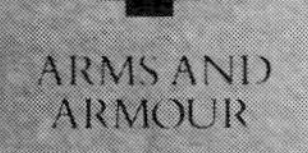

First published in Great Britain in 1990 by Arms and Armour Press, Villiers House, 41–47 Strand, London WC2N 5JE.

Distributed in the USA by Sterling Publishing Co. Inc., 387 Park Avenue South, New York, NY 10016–8810.

Distributed in Australia by Capricorn Link (Australia) Pty. Ltd, P.O. Box 665, Lane Cove, New South Wales 2066.

© Robert F. Dorr, 1990
All rights reserved. No part of this book may be reproduced or transmitted in any form or by any means electronic or mechanical including photocopying recording or any information storage and retrieval system without permission in writing from the Publisher.

British Library Cataloguing in Publication Data
Dorr, Robert F. *1939* –
Air war South Vietnam.
1. Vietnamese Wars. Air Operations, 1961–1975
I. Title
959.704348
ISBN 1-85409-001-1

Jacket illustrations: Front, an F–4B Phantom from USS *Midway* carrier-borne squadron VF–21, nicknamed 'The Freelancers', on an air-support mission for a US ground sweep against the Viet Cong in mid-1965. (US Navy via Phil Chinnery.) Back, Silhouettes of an American soldier and a Piasecki CH–21C Shawnee helicopter are seen against a sunset during the earliest days of US involvement in the South Vietnam conflict. Even in silhouette it is evident that the GI has an M–3A1 carbine and a blocked fatigue hat, which date the picture to the 1961–62 period. (US Army)

Designed and edited by DAG Publications Ltd. Edited by David Dorrell; layout by Anthony A. Evans; typeset by Ronset Typesetters Ltd, Darwen, Lancashire; camerawork by M&E Reproductions, North Fambridge, Essex; printed and bound in Great Britain by Butler & Tanner Ltd, Frome and London.

CONTENTS

The A–37B Dragonfly, like the F–5E Tiger, was essential to plans to bring the Vietnamese Air Force up to strength with a tactical force that was almost all-jet. The Nixon administration's plan was to have all VNAF equipment in place at the time of the cease-fire so that future deliberations would not hamstring Saigon's air arm. (CESSNA)

ACKNOWLEDGEMENTS

This account of the air war in South Vietnam begins with the first American participation in 1960 and ends with the fall of Saigon in 1975. Depending on how you look at it, this span of time covers the principal years of American involvement in the conflict – or, in a way to be understood only by those of us who lived through the time, the end of American innocence.

This history is told from an American point of view, but with considerable attention to the South Vietnamese outlook on the events of those years. It is typical for Americans to remember how the war changed them forever and to forget what it did to the Vietnamese. In due course, I hope one of my exiled Vietnamese friends will tell the story from his country's viewpoint. The purpose of this work is to provide a companion volume to *Air War Hanoi*, my history of the air war in the skies up north.

This book is dedicated to David Anderton, who assisted in its preparation but was not with us long enough to see it finished. I am indebted to Rod Dymott and Chris Westhorp who helped make it possible. Assistance was also received from the Department of State, the United States armed forces, and numerous people who were there.

I especially want to thank Hal Andrews, F. Clifton Berry, Jr, Michael A. France, Donald S. McGarry, David W. Menard, Peter B. Mersky, Robert C. Mikesh, R. J. Mills, Jr, Al Mongeon, Norman Polmar, the Gang at Roy's, Jim Sullivan, Norman Taylor, Minard Thompson, Stokes Tomlin, and Charles Zemple.

The views expressed in this book are mine and do not necessarily reflect those of the United States Air Force.

Robert F. Dorr,
Oakton, Virginia.
December 1989

MILESTONES IN SOUTH VIETNAM

(American dates; dates in Vietnam one day earlier)

Gulf of Tonkin	5 August 1964
Battle of Ia Drang Valley	October 1965
Tet Offensive	January–February 1968
Bombing Halt	31 October 1968
Easter Invasion	31 March 1972
Eleven-Day War	18–29 December 1972
Cease-fire	27 January 1973
Fall of Saigon	30 April 1975

GLOSSARY

AAA	Anti-aircraft artillery
AB	Air base
ARVN	Army of (South) Vietnam
FAC	Forward air controller
JCS	Joint Chiefs of Staff
LZ	Landing zone
MACV	Military Assistance Command, Vietnam
NVA	North Vietnamese (regular) Army
POW	Prisoner(s) of war
SAR	Search and rescue
TFS	Tactical Fighter Squadron
TFW	Tactical Fighter Wing
VNAF	(South) Vietnamese Air Force
VC	Viet Cong

1960
ELECTION YEAR

In that watershed year 1960, Vice President Richard M. Nixon and Senator John F. Kennedy locked horns in an incredibly close campaign for the American presidency. In public a few cautious voices – mostly veterans of the Second World War and the Korean War, neither of which had ended that long ago – were uttering a warning that Americans might have to go to war in the Belgian Congo. In secrecy, mostly for the purpose of keeping it secret from the American people, government spooks were bent on a plan to invade Fidel Castro's Cuba.

As there had been for two decades and would be for nearly two more, there was universal conscription – the draft. Every able-bodied young American was expected to serve in the Army, Navy, Air Force, Marine Corps or Coast Guard. It was taken for granted. Military service was honorable. Using force of arms in defense of freedom was not merely an acceptable course of action but, in this new era, an inevitable one.

If people thought about the prospects of being hurled into conflict – and they thought about anti-communism a great deal, as each candidate tried to be more anti-communist than the other – people worried mostly about the increasing size and number of atomic bombs being built by the Americans and Russians, about Premier Nikita Khrushchev's militancy. There was an excellent chance that Nixon might win the election and become president solely because he had once been photographed poking a finger into Khrushchev's face.

In a distant corner of Asia, brushfire wars spluttered and flared in the recently created nation, if it could be called a nation, of South Vietnam. This volume is about that war as it was fought in the air. The book is intended to give the reader a brief history of the American air war in South Vietnam and a look at the men and machines, the tactics and tribulations, of our fight to defend that embattled fiefdom. Intended to stand alone and to be read independently, the history which follows is also a companion volume to

The Grumman F8F Bearcat was used by the French in Indo-China and later by the South Vietnamese Air Force (VNAF). By the time Americans began trickling into South-East Asia in 1960, the Bearcat was very old and very weary. Nguyen Cao Nguyen, who became the VNAF's chief maintenance officer, described the Bearcat as a death trap which was kept in service for far too long. (MUSÉE DE L'AIR)

When American involvement in the Vietnam air war started in 1960, Saigon's President Ngo Dinh Diem (left), here receiving a visit by US Major General Matthew K. Deichelmann, was not yet well known or controversial. Diem gladly accepted early help for the Vietnamese Air Force (VNAF) but made it clear that he wanted Americans to avoid the capital's palace politicking. (USAF)

1960 was a difficult year for Dwight D. Eisenhower. The President had to miss a summit in Paris following the Soviet downing of a U–2 spy plane in May. The following month he had to curtail a visit to Japan because of anti-US demonstrations, though he successfully visited South Korea where he is seen talking to American Embassy personnel. Ike worried about the Russians and about the US military-industrial complex. The small, distant war in Vietnam did not enjoy a high priority. (US ARMY)

the author's *Air War Hanoi* (Blandford Press, London, 1988), a history of the very different air war against *North* Vietnam.

In 1960 people generally thought little about Vietnam and those with an interest in aviation thought about Vietnam no more than anyone else. In stateside garrisons the US Army and Marine Corps were making increasing use of helicopters in support of ground operations, but if anyone thought that the helicopter was going to revolutionize warfare, most people simply did not know it then. Aboard US Navy carriers, naval aviators practised their always-risky craft in a combination of propeller and jet aircraft, a few of them aware that the newly developed McDonnell F4H–1 Phantom was a kind of revolution in itself, but rarely did their 'area specific' exercises focus on South-East Asia. In the US Air Force they wanted more B–52s – they always wanted more B–52s.

That aircraft was typical of the era's strong emphasis on atomic warfare, the mighty eight-engined Boeing B–52 Stratofortress, with its 'chrome dome' silver-white paint scheme (the white on its bottom intended to help protect the crew from the heat of a nuclear blast), a machine that seemed enormous and was a breathtaking sight lifting into the sky with smoke trails fuming back from its water-injected J–57 jet engines. By 1960 the B–52 long-range atomic bomber was becoming rather old – nearly a decade old – but the Air Force was dominated by Strategic Air Command generals who wanted more B–52s capable of bombing the Soviet Union. In another two or three years, of course, it was understood that a new bomber would come along to replace the B–52 – but the nuclear confrontation with the Soviet Union would continue.

The USAF's Pacific component, PACAF, started the year with 61,876 people, 567 aircraft, six major subordinate commands, twenty-seven tactical squadrons and eleven bases, but none of them were in Vietnam. O'Donnell was more concerned with Korea,

The first American warplane to be supplied in numbers to the Vietnamese Air Force (VNAF) was the Douglas AD–6 Skyraider, a prop-driven attack aircraft which had been designed in 1944. Aircraft like these AD–6s could take enormous punishment and keep flying. They seemed ideal for a small, tough jungle war. (USN)

One of the South Vietnamese pilots being trained by Navy Lieutenant Ken Moranville is seen grinning from the cockpit of his AD–6 Skyraider at Bien Hoa in 1960. Years later Moranville returned and found that many of his students had been killed in battle. (USN)

Early pilots of South Vietnam's 1st Fighter Squadron (later re-designated the 514th Fighter Squadron) stand in front of the AD–6 Skyraider they flew against Viet Cong installations. Some Vietnamese pilots were very good. Some were not. (PERRIN GOWER)

where a TM–61C Matador missile launched on 26 February 1960 by the 310th Tactical Missile Squadron failed to destruct on command and had to be shot down by a chase plane, an F–100D Super Sabre firing a Sidewinder missile. In Korea, Syngman Rhee, at the advanced age of 85, was re-elected, then thrown out of office by a student uprising on 19 April 1960. USAF officers were nervous in a number of places in Asia. Vietnam was not one of them.

Indeed, PACAF's official history contains only two entries about Vietnam. The first says that in September communist North Vietnam announced the formation of the National Liberation Front (NLF) in South Vietnam. The second reported that, also in September, the US supplied South Vietnam with the first of twenty-five Douglas AD–6 Skyraider attack aircraft, taken from US Navy inventory, to replace ageing Grumman F8F Bearcats.

In fact, the Bearcats were still flying (of which, more shortly) and the communist guerrilla movement in South Vietnam was very real and not merely a device created by Hanoi. The NLF, which quickly became known on our side as the Viet Cong, was in every way a genuine uprising by natives of *South* Vietnam, some of whom were communists, some not. In the beginning, the Viet Cong were by no means under the complete control of Hanoi (although US policy was based on the notion that they were) and the opposition to a corrupt dictatorship in Saigon was neither entirely communist nor controlled from Moscow or Peking. Half-truths and untruths did not matter much to the American people as long as they were uttered about a place where not much was happening, but those same distortions – above all, the failure to understand that the uprising in South Vietnam was genuine – hampered American actions long after the Asian nation ceased to be a little-known backwater and emerged at the forefront of our consciousness.

Enter the Skyraider

If PACAF's history for 1960 says nothing about the USAF in Vietnam, the reason is that the American war in the air was begun by a young naval officer. And above all, by a naval warplane – a unique machine for a unique conflict.

With its huge, four-bladed propeller hanging out front and a tailwheel at the back, the Douglas Skyraider seemed less an aircraft than a collection of heavy iron, a kind of final tribute to the industrial age. In the jet era, it was not a jet.

The Skyraider's big Wright R–3350 Cyclone engine smoked, belched and wheezed, dripped oil, and dripped more oil. This was not a leak exactly, more like a programmed drip (pilots always had dirty flight suits). The joke was, if 'Charlie' didn't get you, you'd die by slipping on one of the oil slicks on any flightline where Skyraiders were parked.

The Skyraider had the fuel capacity to loiter over a Viet Cong force for an hour or more (while jets quickly gasped their fuel and had to leave). Jet aircraft had become so complex that they depended on everything from trouble-prone transistors to a steady flow of costly parts. The Skyraider, in contrast, could be, and was, put in the air with what one pilot described as spit, prayer and baling wire. When one jet pilot signed up for the job, they looked at him and wondered why a qualified jet jockey would want to fly the prop-driven 'Spad'. His answer: 'I want to fly low enough so I can see people on the ground.'

The first six Skyraiders for the VNAF (Vietnamese Air Force) were shipped aboard a former US Navy 'jeep' (escort) carrier now employed as a merchantman and arrived in Vietnam in September 1960. The old carrier came steaming up the Saigon River in full view of the Viet Cong on the city's outskirts, half the population of the capital, and the jet-set crowd who watched the war from the rooftop terrace restaurant at the Caravelle Hotel. The ship docked at the foot of Rue Vatinat, the road of revelry known in later years as Tu Do Street. For foreigners who could afford to travel a little out of the way, Saigon was still the 'Paris of the Orient', still offering a special ambience. The arrival of the warplanes doubtlessly seemed gauche. After all, it was only a small war, a little romantic, and it had little impact on the open-air cafes or the night life.

Navy Lieutenant Ken Moranville arrived that month, the first US naval officer in action in Vietnam. Moranville began training Skyraider pilots of the 1st Fighter Squadron (later redesignated the 514th). Soon he and fellow Americans were, in effect, flying 'on call' missions against Viet Cong guerrillas, often guided by a Cessna L–19 Bird Dog spotter plane.

During Moranville's time the war was constantly interrupted by coup attempts. On 11 November 1960 Moranville was at Bien Hoa when a coup was unleashed against President Diem by rebel paratroopers. The squadron's Vietnamese Skyraider pilots went aloft intending to bomb the coup leaders. The planes circled over the rebels' heads with full bombloads and intimidated them into surrendering. Later, Diem was assassinated, but the palace intrigue continued. VNAF Skyraider pilots were involved in several intended coups in Saigon.

At the end of 1960 Americans delivered eleven Sikorsky H–34 helicopters to the South Vietnamese forces. That year the US Army convened the Rogers Board to look at various aspects of aviation, and members of the board began to speak of a new concept called 'air mobility', in which helicopters would be used to transport infantry troops to and from the battlefield. Some officers doubted that this would ever happen. The helicopter was fast proving itself a valuable servant in many ways, but many had still to be convinced that the helicopter had a major role in warfare. There was much to learn.

In 1960 most people in the USAF were not thinking about Vietnam at all. Principal subject on the minds of most airmen was the strategic deterrent and the B–52 Stratofortress's nuclear mission. These B–52Bs of the 93rd Bomb Wing at Castle AFB, California, are typical. Few realized that in the decade to come the B–52 would acquire a conventional bombing mission in South-East Asia. (USAF)

RF–101C Voodoos were among the first US combat aircraft in South-East Asia. In May 1960 A/2C Robert F. Dorr stands beneath an RF–101C Voodoo of the 15th Tactical Reconnaissance Squadron, the 'Cotton Pickers', at Osan, Korea. By the following January these aircraft were in South Vietnam. (ROBERT F. DORR)

1961 KENNEDY ERA

As a new decade began, Soviet Premier Khrushchev announced that the Soviet Union would 'whole-heartedly' support 'wars of national liberation' such as 'the armed struggle waged by the people of Vietnam'. Despite the rhetoric, Soviet aid to North Vietnam was restrained and North Vietnam was not yet in control of the Viet Cong insurgency in the south.

On 20 January 1961, in a Washington blizzard, Americans inaugurated John F. Kennedy, 43, the youngest man ever elected President and a US Navy hero of the Second World War. Kennedy's inaugural speech boomed with Cold War sentiment about halting communism around the globe. It soon became apparent that Kennedy was intrigued by unconventional warfare and fond of the US Army's Special Forces, the Green Berets.

In private, Kennedy acknowledged that Saigon's Ngo Dinh Diem was not exactly the world's leading champion of democracy. The Kennedy administration's view of Diem

Apart from a few Sikorsky H–19s in South Vietnam's air arm, the first American helicopter in the country was the Piasecki H–21 Shawnee. The 8th and 57th Transportation Companies (the latter shown here) began to arrive in late 1961. (US ARMY)

Defense Secretary Robert S. McNamara, here talking domestic issues with the Pennsylvania governor in November 1961, was seen as the principal architect of American escalation in Vietnam. In fact, many others in the Kennedy administration joined McNamara (at left) in favoring steps to shore up Saigon's Diem regime. (US ARMY)

was characterized by an American diplomat who said, 'He's a son of a bitch but he's *our* son of a bitch'. Critics argued that the Viet Cong insurgency in South Vietnam – from its beginning, an uprising of people who *lived* in the south – gained support as long as Diem stayed in office.

Kennedy's choice as Defense Secretary was Robert S. McNamara, a former 'whiz-kid' of industry and an ideas man who believed that the US could assure survival of its South Vietnamese ally. McNamara insisted that the Viet Cong were infiltrators from the north, which they were not, and that the people of South Vietnam supported Diem, which they did not. Diem's failure to hold elections, his iron grip on the country through its police and military forces, and his tendency to line his own pockets were conveniently overlooked.

Critics of US escalation in Vietnam were to have no paucity of public figures to attack, among them White House aide McGeorge Bundy, military advisor General Maxwell Taylor, and Secretary of State Dean Rusk. But for some reason, especially after the Bay of Pigs fiasco in April 1961 when a planned invasion of Cuba went awry, the critics focused on the fact that Robert McNamara's middle name was Strange. Like it or not, McNamara was to be seen by many as the architect of a US build-up in South Vietnam.

The USAF was controlled in that era by bomber generals and its Chief of Staff, General Curtis E. LeMay, felt that strategic readiness was more important than some backwater of Asia. Still, LeMay picked up on President Kennedy's infatuation with unconventional warfare.

On 14 April 1961 the General established the 4400th Combat Crew Training Squadron, code-named 'Jungle Jim', at Eglin AFB, Florida. Airmen began training for a guerrilla conflict in old prop-driven C–47, B–26 and T–28 aircraft. Called Air Commandos (a name not officially adopted until the following January), they quickly garnered a reputation for inattention to military detail, unkempt appearance, and great courage.

As a result of visits to Saigon by Lyndon Johnson and Maxwell Taylor, it was decided to equip South Vietnam's air arm with a second fighter squadron of North American T–28s. This T–28 is at low level in an area held by the Viet Cong. The T–28 could land at unprepared airstrips which were unable to handle the first squadron's AD–6 Skyraiders. (US ARMY)

Laotian Problems

Kennedy and McNamara focused their early attention on Laos where the Soviets were supplying renegade troop leader Kong Le. The previous year the Boeing VC–47 of the US Air Attache in Laos had obtained photos of Soviet aircraft dropping supplies to the Pathet Lao forces in Laos but the aircraft was damaged by ground fire. In January a camera-equipped SC–47 began flying missions for the attache's office but on 24 March 1961, after 38 reconnaissance missions, it was shot down.

Lockheed RT–33 trainers were borrowed from the Philippine Air Force and, painted with Laotian markings, began flying

The H–21 was also the first American helicopter to have a door gunner, although he operated a .50-caliber weapon of Second World War vintage rather than the M–60 which came later. Rigs for door guns were made in the field and were not always well designed. (US ARMY)

Reflecting the fascination with unconventional warfare felt by everybody from President Kennedy downwards, the On Mark YB–26K was a 'new rebuild' of the Second World War Douglas B–26 Invader – intended for the kind of guerrilla conflict unfolding in South Vietnam. Readily distinguished from early B–26s by its wingtip tanks and enlarged propeller hubs, the YB–26K was being readied for combat when the future of the B–26 fleet in the war zone was questioned. (ROGER F. BESECKER)

reconnaissance missions over Laos on 24 April 1961.

In May 1961 twenty-five AD–6 Skyraiders arrived to join the six already serving with the VNAF's 1st Fighter Squadron at Bien Hoa. This effort was being handled by the US Navy although the Air Force, which had never operated the Skyraider, began looking at the plane for its Air Commando force. Ironically, the Skyraiders for Saigon's air arm were in better condition than AD–6s being flown by the US Navy. They had been through a stateside re-work facility and were the same as new.

The first member of the new administration to visit Vietnam was Vice President Lyndon Johnson, on 11–13 May 1961. The Texas politician, a respected figure but hardly a Kennedy intimate, reported that Diem was in control and that the US military advisory group, its strength now approaching 1,000, was doing well. As a result of the Johnson-Diem discussions, the US agreed to support an ARVN force increased in size from 170,000 to 200,000 men, to provide the VNAF with a second fighter squadron made up of North American T–28s, and to supply additional L–19 Bird Dogs to the VNAF's three liaison squadrons.

Plans were made to equip the VNAF's 2nd Fighter Squadron at Nha Trang with 44 T–28s and the liaison squadrons with fifteen L–19s. But first, T–28s flown by American pilots – the Air Commandos from Eglin – were to be brought over with US airmen who, on arrival, would be identified by the code-name 'Farm Gate'.

President Kennedy took office on 20 January 1961 and his interest in unconventional warfare soon became apparent. The USAF's Air Commandos were formed at Hurlburt Field, Florida, and began practising in the Douglas B–26 Invader. Known for a time as the RB–26 to indicate a reconnaissance mission, the B–26 was to be active over South Vietnam during 1962–64. (USAF)

35634

At first USAF Air Commandos intended to take a number of Curtiss C–46 Commandos with them to South Vietnam. They did not, however, and the airframe seen here remained stateside, but C–46s later turned up with civil operators such as Air America which was working for the CIA. (USAF)

The Vietnamese Air Force's second fighter squadron was equipped with the North American T–28. Carrying gun packs beneath their wings, the former trainers were a potent weapon against the communist Viet Cong insurgents, who were still being called the 'rebels' by many Americans early in the war. (US ARMY)

VNAF T–28 fighter-bomber flying off the coast of South Vietnam. (US ARMY)

First USAF Airmen

Beginning on 26 September 1961, the first USAF unit to arrive in South Vietnam on permanent duty status began its work. The detachment from the 507th Tactical Control Group at Shaw AFB, South Carolina, set up a command reporting post of 67 men plus MPS–11 search and MPS–16 height-finder radars. This was located at Saigon's Tan Son Nhut Airport, which was becoming busier and busier.

The first American combat aircraft in Vietnam were McDonnell RF–101C Voodoos of the 15th Tactical Reconnaissance Squadron (the 'Cotton Pickers') at Kadena, Okinawa, commanded by Lieutenant Colonel Earl A. Butts. A detachment of four Voodoos, code-named 'Pipe Stem', with six pilots and an intelligence officer and headed by Major Russell F. Crutchlow, arrived at Tan Son Nhut Airport on 18 October 1961.

It happened to be the day the Mekong River overflowed its banks and flooded hundreds of square miles of the countryside. The four RF–101Cs began photographing both the floods and the Viet Cong on 20 October. Another RF–101C detachment, known as 'Able Mable', positioned itself at Don Muang, Thailand, and performed photo-reconnaissance over Laos.

Captain A. Robert Gould was one of 'Pipe Stem's' RF–101C Voodoo pilots. In later years he remembered: 'It really came as a surprise when we got the order to go to Saigon for a Vietnamese Armed Forces Day. The general order indicated that there were [American] planes of all types going. We (the 15th TRS) were just part of the crowd. Then, all of a sudden, there was an announcement, in the newspapers yet, that the whole deal had been cancelled. Except we did not get orders to cancel. We and [our] headquarters thought we would get the order to cancel right up to take-off time.'

Gould liked the Vietnamese capital. 'Saigon in 1961 was wonderful. It was a little bit of Paris in the Orient. The food was wonderful, the girls beautiful, and the pace relaxed. We lived in the Caravelle Hotel, drove our Jeeps to Tan Son Nhut for our 0800 take-off, usually four flights per day, and were back at the hotel by 1500–1600 hours. We found we had to modify our sleeping schedule somewhat, however. Trying to find something to eat at 7pm was nearly impossible. Nightlife started at 10pm. But we had an 0500 wake-up. The solution was to come home in the afternoon, take a two- or three-hour nap, and then go out to eat at 10 or 11.

'We promptly started flying missions for the American Embassy [in adjacent Laos]. Our primary targets were airfields, bridges, and all the other normal military-type targets. A lot of area covers were flown using the Voodoo's 36in focal length split vertical cameras. We used French maps. There were no US maps of sufficient detail.'

Captain Dophus E. Guillotte, Jr, the intelligence officer accompanying the RF–101C detachment, found that there was little intelligence to be had. The Voodoos were tasked with reporting on what the Russians were doing in next-door Laos. 'We knew the Russians were dropping supplies in by parachute. We had pictures of the 'chutes on the ground. We even saw Russian twin-engine transports flying the area. But catching them in the act was tough.'

Taylor Visit

At President Kennedy's request, General Taylor went to Vietnam in October 1961. Taylor met Diem, reviewed the situation, and made note of the lack of mobility of the Army of the Republic of Vietnam (ARVN) troops.

The US Army's Rogers Board had been succeeded by the Howze Board which was studying air mobility. Board chief Lieutenant General Hamilton Howze contemplated the formation of an American air cavalry division. Howze also proposed to solve mobility problems in backwaters like Vietnam by equipping the Army with de Havilland Canada AC–1 Caribou cargo planes. For more than a dozen years the USAF had had sole jurisdiction over all fixed-wing aircraft except those used for administrative work, so Army officers liked Howze's idea and Air Force officers were enraged by it. Meanwhile, ARVN troops seemed paralyzed by Vietnam's poor road network, non-existent river transport, and clinging, clawing jungles.

Taylor recommanded advisors and helicopters. He did not, perhaps would not, point out that many of the ARVN simply did not want to fight. At his suggestion, the US Army's 8th and 57th Transportation Companies (Light Helicopter), equipped with the Piasecki H–21 Shawnee, embarked for South-East Asia. Like Skyraiders before them, the H-21s were brought up the Saigon River by a former jeep carrier – but unlike the Skyraiders, the H-21s retained their US insignia.

'Farm Gate'

On 11 October 1961 deployment began of the USAF's 'Jungle Jim' detachment. The unit, designated the 1st Air Commando Group and using the name 'Farm Gate' once in-country, included 151 officers and men with eight T-28, four SC-47 and four RB-26 aircraft. The 'R' for reconnaisssance prefix on the B-26 was the first of many deceits, intended to bely their combat role. The second came when Vietnamese markings were painted on the T-28s, which went into action on 26 December.

Both the command reporting post and the RF-101C Voodoos had preceded them, but 'Farm Gate's' airmen were really the first Americans in combat.

The markings on their T-28s were a fiction. They went through the pretense of carrying Vietnamese 'crew members' in their B-26 Invaders and T-28 Trojans, but they were doing the work and the fighting – beginning the long and painful US presence in a seemingly endless conflict. Their equipment, like their term for themselves, Air Commandos, came from the Second World War but their spirit reflected the youthful optimism of the Kennedy era. They wore ANZAC campaign hats, walked around toting tiny sub-machine-guns and bandoliers of ammunition, and spoke of completing their 'advisory' task within a few months.

The Douglas B-26 Invader, powered by two 2,400hp Pratt & Whitney R-2800-103W radial engines with three-bladed reversible propellers, had begun life as the A-26 during the Second World War and the original designation was at times resurrected in Vietnam. The B-26 could carry eight forward-firing 0.5in (12.7mm) machine-guns plus various combinations of bombs and rockets exceeding 10,000lb (4,500kg). At a time when the US insisted that the problem in Vietnam was 'Aggression from the North' (title of the State Department's White Paper pointing the finger at Hanoi), the B-26 was ideal for the real problem – Viet Cong guerrillas, themselves part of the population of the *south*, who operated in the bush and, being highly mobile, presented only a fleeting target.

Unfortunately, the Air Commandos found that the B-26 was not without its problems. B-26B and RB-26B Invaders were flown by American crews and with South Vietnamese markings. They were initially quite effective against 'Mister Charles', as the Cong came to be nicknamed, but their war was to be short-lived.

Although 'Farm Gate's' Americans were now flying around in T-28s with Vietnamese markings, this type of aircraft for the South Vietnamese began to arrive only in December 1961 when fifteen T-28B trainers were transferred to the VNAF from the US Navy. These aircraft were to be replaced later by T-28D fighter-bombers.

Wider War

Throughout the first year of the Kennedy administration, plans unfolded gradually to bring the US military presence in South Vietnam up to as many as 4,000 men. With hindsight, many close to Kennedy have argued that he never intended the presence to grow any larger, that he was comfortable with a few thousand and had no notion that the figure would one day exceed half a million.

Certainly, the kind of equipment reaching Vietnam was not yet new or modern and the US continued to focus its foreign policy interests elsewhere. But some say that Kennedy pushed a snowball from the top of a hill and that, as it gathered speed, it grew larger – until, in the period just ahead, it would grow out of control. If ever there existed an opportunity to restrain the escalation of the war, it was now. The opportunity was not seized.

A number of ageing US Army Sikorsky H-34 helicopters were being readied for transfer to South Vietnam at the end of 1961. The helicopter was identical to the HUS-1, which the US Marine Corps introduced to the conflict in its early days. (US ARMY)

1962

'FARM GATE', 'MULE TRAIN', 'RANCH HAND'

When Fairchild C–123B Provider twin-engined transports began landing at Tan Son Nhut airfield on 2 January 1962, no carpet was rolled out, no fanfare laid on. Lieutenant Colonel Floyd D. Shofner, the HMFIC (Air Force slang which translates loosely as 'Head Man in Charge') made no speeches, shook no hands. A simple one-liner for the press noted that the squat, high-winged C–123Bs belonged to 'Mule Train' – 'a temporary duty detachment designed to give logistic support to Vietnamese and American forces'.

The C–123Bs came from the 346th Troop Carrier Squadron at Pope AFB, North Carolina. Sixteen C–123B Providers made up the detachment, although only four arrived on the first day. In the period ahead the reliable but unglamorous C–123Bs were to be among the hardest-working machines in South Vietnam.

They were not, however, the only Providers in the country. At about the same time came 'Ranch Hand'. Three UC–123B Providers, each fitted with an internal 1,000-gallon chemical tank and removable spray bars attached under the wings, arrived at Tan Son Nhut on 7 January 1962. The cargo planes began spraying 200-meter wide swathes with chemical defoliant. This was to become one of the most controversial programs of the war.

President Diem was an ardent advocate of the use of herbicides both to destroy crops and to strip away foliage concealing enemy activities. President Kennedy's approval, however, came with severe limitations and called for carefully controlled defoliation flights along key roads and railways before attempting food denial.

Defoliation, to use the new word which entered the vocabulary when the UC–123Bs (and later UC–123Ks) carried out this macabre mission, satisfied almost nobody. In nine years of operations over South Vietnam and Laos, 'Ranch Hand' aircraft were to spray an incredible 2.5 million hectares (6.2 million acres) with herbicides, among them the notorious Agent Orange. What should have been foreseen, but was not, was that there would be devastating effects on the health of people who came in contact with chemical Orange, Vietnamese natives and American servicemen alike.

Meanwhile the conventional war went on. January was a month of tension along the Cambodian border – the demarcation line for what amounted to a Viet Cong sanctuary. When under pressure, the VC simply retreated across the line. On one such occasion, the South Vietnamese Army requested a dawn air strike on the VC-held village of Ba Thu in the Parrots Beak, the region of Cambodia which seemed to poke unnaturally into South Vietnam.

South Vietnamese pilots trained by the Americans were unable to handle pre-dawn take-offs, so American Air Commandos flew the strike. A number of C–47s happened to be along at the time. One of these flew along the canal which constituted the border at that location.

While eight T–28s and three B–26s bombed, rocketed and napalmed, everyone involved was certain that the mission was a success and that the border was properly respected. But a Cambodian complaint a few days later led to the US State Department pressuring the South Vietnamese to 'apologize' for the incident. It was exactly the kind of decision which was bad for the morale of both American and South Vietnamese pilots.

On 2 February 1962 a UC–123B Provider belonging to the 'Ranch Hand' defoliation people crashed on a low-level training flight. Enemy ground fire or sabotage was suspected, although it could not be certain

The US Army's De Havilland Canada U–1A Otter was operating with the 18th Fixed Wing Aviation Company at Da Nang, but Army officers pressed for introduction of the DHC CV–2 Caribou, a larger twin-engined transport. The Otter could carry ten fully equipped combat troops or a pilot and 2,000lb (910kg) of cargo. (DHC)

By 1962 Americans were beginning to locate Saigon on the map. Those in the city liked its amenities and its casual pace. This overhead view shows traffic at the intersection of Pham Hong Thai Gia Long, Le Van Duyet and Vo Tanh Streets. Some of the tongue-twisting names gradually became familiar to Americans. (US ARMY)

that the loss was not an accident. The three UC–123B crew members became the first USAF fatalities in South-East Asia.

In addition to its numerous helicopters, the US Army wanted to introduce its own fixed-wing aircraft to Vietnam. By inter-Service agreement, the Army was supposedly allowed fixed-wing aircraft only for 'administrative' purposes – such as the sixteen DH Canada U–1A Otters of the Army's 18th Fixed Wing Aviation Company at Da Nang.

Somehow, in spite of the USAF's exclusive claim to the mission, the Army had built up a fleet of DH Canada AC–1 Caribou twin-engined transports. Now, Army officers placed pressure on their superiors to permit Caribous in Vietnam. By year's end, the arrival of these transports was to be a certainty – although the Caribou's mission was very similar to that of 'Mule Train's' Providers.

New Command

On February 1962 the US created MACV (Military Assistance Command Vietnam), a curiously named headquarters which amounted to a combat field command in every way except name.

Lieutenant General Paul D. Harkins was named chief of MACV, which was roughly modeled after US-Taiwan Defense Command. After conferring with President Kennedy in Florida in January, Harkins was promoted to full general and took the helm in Saigon – supposedly equal to US Ambassador Frederick E. Nolting.

Neither man is remembered in later years for leadership or charisma. Nolting could have been a cipher and still have received more recognition than his predecessor, Elbridge Durbrow, who had mistakenly believed that Washington wanted him to be candid with President Diem. Durbrow had told the Vietnamese President to exile his unpopular brother and security chief, Ngo Dinh Nhu. Incredibly, Durbrow had even suggested to Diem that there should be elections in South Vietnam.

Frederick Nolting, nicknamed 'Fritz', was apparently expected to be nice to Diem rather than honest with him. A proper Virginia gentleman, Nolting was also a solid, sturdy, able man. Had he been given the authority to do so, Nolting might have prodded Diem to liberalize his rule. Nolting did report to Washington that Nhu and his wife, the notorious Madame Nhu, were widely hated for their authoritarian role in Diem's regime. He was told to maintain good relations with Diem and Nhu. He was also cautioned to be careful in his relations with Harkins, a general described by journalist David Halberstam as 'a man of compelling mediocrity'.

Harkins was an organization man, a staff man, who seemed to have no idea that the Viet Cong enjoyed considerable popular support – or even, indeed, that this was a political war. Under his leadership, reporting on Viet Cong strength was toned down. Each time South Vietnamese troops did anything other than turn and run from the battlefield, their action was reported as a great victory. *Time* magazine likened Harkins to General George S. Patton – surely the least accurate comparison ever to appear between that journal's covers. An optimist who reported to McNamara that he had no problems, Harkins never understood the appeal of the Viet Cong or the unpopularity of Diem and Nhu.

Nolting and Harkins were perhaps right for a generation of Americans little interested in Vietnam and preoccupied with other things – the Congo, Cuba, civil rights. The Vietnam war was unimportant. And Nolting and Harkins were just unimportant enough to run it.

There was plenty of action in the air, however. On 11 February 1962 US aircraft began loudspeaker work and leaflet drops in a program of propaganda – except that when the Americans did it, it was called 'psychological warfare' – which was sharply criticized by counter-insurgency specialist Brigadier General Edward G. Lansdale as being unfocused and unable to succeed.

Shortly afterwards, while on a propaganda mission, an SC–47 aircraft – the ubiquitous 'Gooney Bird' – took off in good weather for a routine leaflet drop south of Da Lat. The SC–47 crashed, killing eight Americans and one Vietnamese.

According to a statement from one of the mindless spokesmen who were fast becoming typical in this war, the flight had been conducted for the sole purpose of training the lone Vietnamese aboard. This kind of lie was, in time, fundamentally to alter the way Americans thought of their government. For now, however – 1962 was still a time of innocence – only one press item criticized this latest fiction that Americans were 'advisors' and nothing more.

The venerable Douglas DC–3, or 'Gooney Bird', became an early participant in the South-East Asia conflict, starting out in its traditional role as a transport and 'trash hauler'. This C–47 version belonging to the Vietnamese Air Force is seen at Saigon's Tan Son Nhut airport, with a US Army Piasecki H–21C Shawnee helicopter in the background. (USAF)

Another version of the 'Gooney Bird', the R4D–8 (redesignated C–117D on 1 October 1962) was the first aircraft brought into South Vietnam by the US Marine Corps. These Super DC–3s appeared in small numbers throughout the conflict, hauling supplies for both Navy and Marine Corps units. (USN/PHC KEN GEORGE)

Coup Time

On 26 February 1962 two mutinous South Vietnamese pilots in AD–6 Skyraiders attacked President Diem's palace. It was the sort of thing that was to happen again and again. Americans were instructed to avoid Vietnamese politics at all costs. One American who had come to train AD–6 Skyraider pilots even refused to give an affirmative answer when asked if he had heard of Madame Nhu, who was perhaps the most famous woman in Asia that year, in addition to being Diem's sister-in-law. 'Madame who?' he feigned.

The Cessna L–19 Bird Dog (which became the O–1 after 1 October 1962) was one of the most versatile and ubiquitous fixed-wing aircraft in South-East Asia. The US Army and Marine Corps and the South Vietnamese Army and Air Force were all among early operators of the two-seat Bird Dog, which was used throughout virtually the entire conflict. (US ARMY)

If the 'Dragon Lady' was a phantom to the Americans, equally elusive were the 'enemy airplanes' Americans had been led to suspect. Those who knew little about the region – Chinese and Vietnamese had fought each other for thousands of years – feared that Peking would introduce modern aircraft, perhaps Ilyushin Il–28 bombers, to the conflict. In fact, the Chinese Government was ignoring the war to its south, while North Vietnam had not yet begun to build an air force of its own.

Still, enemy aircraft were thought, somehow, to be connected with the upsurge in Viet Cong activity – so the 405th Tactical Fighter Wing despatched a part of its 509th Fighter-Interceptor Squadron from the Philippines to Tan Son Nhut. The three Convair F–102As (and one TF–102A two-seater) ran practice GCI missions (ground control intercept) but encountered no opposition in the air.

New Fliers

The first US Navy airmen given an operational role in Vietnam were the crews of the AD–5Q Skyraiders belonging to squadron VAW–13, brought to Tan Son Nhut to replace USAF F–102A Delta Daggers assigned under the 'Water Glass' deployment.

The AD–5Q was a radar early-warning and reconnaissance aircraft but was capable of functioning as an interceptor. Equipped with AN/APS–31C look-down radar to locate low-flying aircraft and armed with 20mm cannon – which had an unfortunate tendency to jam – the AD–5Q might have served as an effective counter had the enemy struck with propeller-driven warplanes. He did not.

Two North American T–28 Trojan fighter-bombers carrying under-wing gun pods fly over South Vietnam on 19 October 1962. The aircraft have South Vietnamese markings but the men in the front seats could well be Americans. (USAF)

The Fairchild C–123 Provider arrived in South Vietnam with the 'Mule Train' operation in early 1962 and remained throughout the war. An unpainted C–123B is seen leading a camouflaged aircraft over Vietnamese terrain. (USAF)

Advisors in Action

Apart from shooting down phantom enemies, the USAF was supposedly in South Vietnam to train. The record seems clear that Kennedy and McNamara wanted USAF airmen to train the South Vietnamese, with the goal of being able to withdraw at some future time.

Within Vietnam, far from talking of withdrawal, Harkins and other officers wanted to increase the size of the 'Farm Gate' operation. To help in the pretense that US fliers were *only* training, the VNAF supplied fifteen enlisted men who could fly with the Americans. They were merely providing a Vietnamese presence, however, not being trained. This seemed to undermine a request by General Harkins near year's end that 'Farm Gate' be supplied with additional aircraft – five T–28s, ten B–26s and two C–47s.

On 26 March 1962 the *San Francisco Chronicle* told readers that the two US Army Helicopter Companies in Vietnam were doing a little more than just 'advising' the South Vietnamese. 'How US Copters Face Red Gunfire,' the story was titled. Their low-level flying to get ARVN troops in and out of battle areas 'would frighten an instructor back in the States,' one H–21C pilot was quoted.

The paper did not publish what Army H–21C pilots called 'The Air Force Prayer' which read, 'God, grant me the eyes of an eagle, the stealth of a stalking tiger, and the balls of an Army helicopter pilot.'

Such was the impertinence of Army fliers, who felt that they were on the cutting edge of this war, a war which was dangerous and could result in death, but for Americans was still on a small scale and somewhat romantic in nature. One Army H–21C pilot told with pride his story of setting down in a landing zone only to see Viet Cong combatants pouring out of the trees and coming at him, rifles blazing. As the story is told, 'Charlie's' squad leader had instructed his troops that they could shoot down an American aircraft only by leading it with their fire. The H–21C pilot watched bullets thunking into the ground in front of his craft, took off without being hit, and escaped.

Men in the US Army's 57th Helicopter Transportation Company were, to put it mildly, envious of the relative comfort enjoyed by Air Force people. Coming ashore in Saigon with their Piaescki H–12C Shawnee helos, the men were told that they could sleep in their helicopters. The CO, Major Bob Dillard, felt differently and moved them into Saigon's brand new Rex Hotel. It was a shell when occupied – no electricity, no lifts, no water, no kitchen, not much but rooms. Still, with field ranges, blister bags, army cots and a PRC–10 radio, they made out all right for a while.

The helicopter company's vehicles were not licensed and they were ordered into civilian clothes while downtown. The men were cautioned to travel at least in pairs and no more than fours. They went to and from the war in 'blue and whites' – ageing Vietnamese taxis – lugging PRC radios and pistols. Although the Rex Hotel was never luxurious, men of the 57th missed it as soon as they were ordered into a tent city where conditions were worse.

These Piasecki H–21C Shawnee helicopters have temporarily settled on the beach where they have attracted the curiosity of local residents. In this 14 September 1962 view the crewmen performing maintenance on the H–21C are Sp5 Ralph F. Rigg and Pfc Robert Rogers. (US ARMY)

The Helio L–28A Courier, soon redesignated U–10B, arrived in South Vietnam in August 1962 when four aircraft joined the 'Farm Gate' detachment. One U–10B landed at a hamlet during a raging battle to remove a captured Viet Cong officer. The Courier had excellent STOL characteristics. (USAF)

One of the earliest helicopters employed in South-East Asia was the Sikorsky H–34 (the designation after 1 October 1962), used by the US Army, Navy and Marine Corps as well as South Vietnamese forces. This CH–34A at Fort Monmouth, New Jersey, is typical of helicopters which found their way to South Vietnam in the early days.

Major Emmett Knight, ops officer for the 57th, noted that two helicopter companies totalling 800 people had doubled the American population of Saigon. Knight felt that the 57th could be more effective using its H–21C helicopters in a constabulary way, to keep pressure on the enemy. The 57th might, Knight believed, keep the Viet Cong from winning – nothing more.

Knight felt that South Vietnamese security was poor. 'They'd take a map, number places of military interest, and drop troops into them indiscriminately.' There was no plan. Later on Knight went to the 120th Assault Helicopter Company, the 'Deans', in the UH–1 Huey, but even then he retained a healthy skepticism about what was going on around him. 'There were some fine Vietnamese troops and officers, but overall their army just didn't have the discipline or the will to fight.'

In April 1962 USAF Chief of Staff General Curtis E. LeMay visited Vietnam. LeMay noted improvement in the quality of South Vietnamese AD–6 and T–28 pilots, but doubted that the VNAF would be able to meet all its operational demands for some time to come. LeMay particularly wanted to improve the air transport situation in South Vietnam – although he did not care whether it was done with Army AC–1 Caribous or Air Force C–123B Providers.

On 27 April, en route for home, LeMay spoke in Los Angeles and publicly revealed the 'Farm Gate' program. 'This is a realistic training program. Those people, the Vietnamese, are at war. Our instructors occasionally accompany them on combat missions. Our pilots are armed. They will protect themselves if fired upon.'

On 9 April 1962 the presence of US Marine Corps aviation began with the arrival Colonel John F. Carey and a few good men who came into Soc Trang, in the Mekong Delta, in an R4D–8, the Corps' workhorse 'Super DC–3'. Situated 85 miles (137km) south-west of Saigon, the field had a remarkably good paved runway but little else in the way of amenities. The Marines' first problem was solved when the R4D–8 pilot removed the escape hatch atop his cockpit, stuck his head out into the open while talking on the radio, and announced that his 'Gooney Bird' had just become 'Soc Trang tower'. He gave landing instructions to a GV–1 Hercules bringing fuel, water and supplies into the airfield. Soon afterwards, the field became home for three Marine OE–1 Bird Dogs from squadron VMO–2 and twenty-four HUS–1 Seahorse choppers of HMM–362.

The Marines always seemed to get into the small, dirty wars at the beginning, and the marsh forests of the Mekong Delta were the ideal setting for the Corps' expertise in unconventional warfare. Not that the the men were enthusiastic about operating their ageing Sikorsky HUS–1 helicopters from the old Japanese base at Soc Trang in the southern extremity of the country. They were miles from the bars and bistros of Saigon, and the Delta was where 'Charlie' was strongest. The HUS–1s were needed near the river's mouth precisely because ARVN troops were faced with a real challenge from highly mobile, dedicated Viet Cong units, and helicopter mobility was supposed to turn things around.

HMM–362 was one of the first Marine units in country. Staff Sergeant Dave Remington wrote to his girlfield that the living conditions were abominable, maintenance was atrocious, and the HUS–1 just did not want to perform in the wet heat at sea-level elevation. 'We drop the ARVN. We pick them up. Sometimes they engage the VC. Sometimes they don't.' The Marines were not officially combatants but were frequently under fire, as if coping with cantankerous helicopters was not enough. One early HUS–1 crash was caused not by enemy gunfire but by fuel contamination, a persistent problem.

Second Lieutenant Steven Harding felt that they were accomplishing something. The advantage of helicopter mobility seemed to increase ARVN fighting spirits. 'The Viet Cong still control vast areas here, and we can't touch 'em at night. But we are beginning to deny them freedom of movement.' In fact, 'Shu Fly's' helicopters gave the relatively ill-equipped South Vietnamese Army an important boost in mobility and logistic support.

The Marines came to have a sense of belonging. When the decision was made to shift the 'Shu Fly' operation to Da Nang where the HUS–1 could perform better at higher altitude, some expressed disappointment. 'We'll be living better. But the Army guys who replace us in the Delta will be fighting the real battle with the VC.'

Two US Army units came to South Vietnam in May 1962, typifying the slow and gradual build-up which was taking place almost without notice. On 2 May came the Army's first medical aircraft – five Bell HU–1A Hueys of the 57th Medical Detachment (Helicopter Ambulance). Their mission, soon to be nicknamed 'Dust Off', brought to South Vietnam the first of thousands of what was to be a symbol of the war – the Huey helicopter. Indeed, with *Newsweek* taking the lead, in 1962 it seemed certain that the conflict would become formally known as 'The Helicopter War'.

Operation 'Shu Fly's' helicopters gave the South Vietnamese Army increased mobility. These helicopters are dropping troops for an assault on Viet Cong positions in a canal village near Dinh Tuong on 26 July 1962. The helicopters came under fire moments later. Known as the HUS–1 at this time and redesignated UH–34D as of 1 October 1962, these machines were already quite old when they arrived in the battle zone. (USMC)

ARMY
U.S. ARMY
64320
MARINES
YL 85
MARINES
YL 77
5805
MARINES
YL 75
HMM 362

U.S.ARMY
112711
ARMY

When US military aircraft designations underwent a change on 1 October 1962, the Cessna L–19 Bird Dog became the O–1. Many, like this O–1, were in the stateside training markings shown here when they were transferred to Vietnam. (US ARMY)

Three weeks later, on 23 May, the US Army's 73rd Aviation Company arrived with thirty-two L–19D Bird Dogs, two-seat observation machines which were quickly scattered all around the country. These were used for artillery adjustment, target acquisition, command and control, message pick-up and radio relay.

Kennedy Policy

Whatever else might be said as the commitment in Vietnam grew, Americans could rely on an officer corps as good as any in the world to lead their men in battle. Since the nation's earliest days, the 'Long Gray Line' at West Point had produced fighters, leaders, heroes. President Kennedy picked the occasion of a June speech to the West Point class of '62 – which would be decimated in South-East Asia – to disclose some of his thoughts.

His words, when read today, seem appropriate for the 1990s as easily as the 1960s.

Americans faced a new kind of war, Kennedy said, a conflict 'new in its intensity, ancient in its origin – war by guerrillas, subversives, insurgents, assassins, war by ambush instead of by combat, by infiltration instead of by aggression, seeking victory by eroding and exhausting the enemy instead of engaging him. These are the kinds of challenges that will be before us in the next decade. If freedom is to be saved, we need a new kind of strategy, a wholly different kind of force, and therefore a new and wholly different kind of military training.'

Kennedy and his lieutenants seemed confident that they could face the new style of warfare spreading on the earth, but it was widely understood that Kennedy intended a limit on the number of US troops in South Vietnam – which reached 6,419 on 30 June 1962.

On 23 July the US Army's 1st Aviation Company with AC–1 Caribou transports began operations in Thailand. Within a year two companies of the cargo aircraft were to be in Vietnam.

On 25 July fifteen more HU–1A Iroquois helicopters reached South Vietnam with the US Army's Utility Tactical Transport Helicopter Company (UTTHCO). These Hueys, equipped in the field with gun and rocket armament, began flying from Tan Son Nhut airfield, which was becoming more and more crowded.

By mid-August the number of Americans in South Vietnam had risen to 11,412. In every area things were slowly expanding. The Air Force decided to send four Helio L–28 Couriers to 'Farm Gate' for forward air controller (FAC) duty. In addition 'Mule Train' acquired a second C–123B Provider squadron.

The Helio Courier was a single-engined high-wing aircraft with space for four passengers or 70cu ft of cargo. The four L–28s served the 'Farm Gate' operation in a variety of ways, hauling people and packages and landing at unprepared strips. In one instance, an L–28 pilot landed at an outpost during a night battle to remove a captured Viet Cong officer for immediate interrogation. Some air commandos claimed that their own L–28 Courier pilots were willing to carry out risky medical evacuations when Army H–21C pilots were not.

A new type of Army aircraft arrived in the war zone in September 1962 when six Grumman AO–1 Mohawks of the 23rd Special Warfare Aviation Detachment were sent to Nha Trang to support ARVN forces in the area. The twin-turboprop Mohawk proved highly effective at visual and photo reconnaissance in direct support of troops on the ground. Like their Air Force brethren, Army pilots of the two-seat Mohawk were required to carry a Vietnamese observer. They were supposed to conduct their surveillance of the Viet Cong without shooting at anyone unless fired upon. In fact, the AO–1 had been designed from the outset to carry guns and rockets, and soon they were being used.

Aircraft Designations

The story is told that McNamara testified before Congress about the Lockheed C–130 Hercules and then proclaimed that he would move on to his next subject, the Lockheed GV–1 aircraft. Worried and puzzled, an aide whispered in McNamara's ear that the C–130 and GV–1 were, in fact, the same aircraft. Why then, fumed McNamara, were they not called the same thing?

Another version of the story has it that the US Navy's McDonnell F4B–1 Phantom and the USAF's McDonnell F–110A Phantom touched McNamara off. Whatever the case, the Defense Secretary ordered a uniform designation system.

The separate systems used by the US Army and US Navy were dropped. All Hercules aircraft were to be known as the C–130, all Phantoms as the F–4 – the Navy's

The 'Ranch Hand' operation came to South Vietnam flying Fairchild UC–123B Provider transports which had been fitted with special equipment to spray defoliant. It was not known then that one of the chemicals being sprayed by the UC–123B, Agent Orange, had harmful effects on people and was unable to distinguish between friend and foe. (USAF)

In another change of aircraft designations, the Grumman AO–1 Mohawk became the OV–1. Various models of the Mohawk served in Vietnam from 1962 through 1973. (US ARMY)

The Cessna O–1 Bird Dog was built to take punishment, but even it could not hold up when left out-of-doors to cope with the tropical storms for which South Vietnam was well known. This devastated O–1 is listed in Army records as having been assigned to the 57th Transportation Company (Light Helicopter), better known for its Piasecki CH–21C Shawnees. (US ARMY)

F4H–1 becoming the F–4B version, the Air Force's F–110A becoming the F–4C.

Put into effect on 1 October 1962, this change applied to almost every aircraft in the Army and Navy, and to some in the Air Force. In addition to standardizing service designations, the new system made some other changes – for example, dropping the 'L' for liaison category and instituting a new 'O' for observation category. The change applied to aircraft so far cited in this narrative in the following manner:

the Navy's Douglas AD–5Q Skyraider became the EA–1F;

the Navy's Douglas AD–6 Skyraider, also used by the VNAF, became the A–1H;

the Army's Grumman AO–1 Mohawk became the OV–1;

the US Marine Corps' Cessna OE–1 Bird Dog became the O–1B;

the US Army's Cessna L–19D Bird Dog, also used by the VNAF, became the O–1F;

the Air Force's Helio L–28A and L–28B Courier became the U–10A and U–10B;

the Army's Bell HU–1 Iroquois ('Huey') helicopter became the UH–1;

the Marine Corps' Sikorsky HUS–1 Seahorse became the UH–34D;

the Army's DH Canada AC–1A and AC–1B Caribou became the CV–2A and CV–2B (and much later, on 1 January 1967, under-went a further name change to C–7A); and the Marines' Douglas R4D–8 Skytrain transport became the C–117D.

The Grumman F8F Bearcat had been retired from service and did not acquire a new designation under McNamara's new system. Unchanged were the following aircraft mentioned so far: B–26, RB–26, B–52, C–47, F–100D, RF–101, H–21C, RT–33 and U–1.

On 6 October 1962 the co-pilot and crew chief of a UH–34D from squadron HMM–162 were the first naval aviators killed in action in Vietnam when their helicopter crashed.

Not long after the creation of MACV under General Harkins, in October 1962, the USAF command in Saigon became the 2nd Air Division, under Major General Rollen H. Anthis. Still a two-star slot, command of Air Force personnel in South Vietnam in later years was to become a four-star posting and the headquarters was eventually to be renamed Seventh Air Force.

Missile Crisis

Any American old enough to remember will easily recall the events of October 1962 as President Kennedy revealed the presence of Soviet missiles in Cuba and quarantined the island. The USA and the USSR moved towards confrontation. Never before, never since, has nuclear war been so close. Finally, to quote Secretary of State Dean Rusk, 'The other guy blinked,' and conflict was averted. That month, even the few people who had begun to think about Vietnam had their attention turned elsewhere.

It has often been said that the US 'backed into' Vietnam. There is a considerable body of evidence to suggest that President Kennedy always had the war in perspective and had no intention of increasing the American presence much further. But the American presence in Vietnam seemed to have a momentum all its own. In a way it almost did not matter what the President wanted. Once turned loose on the American psyche, Vietnam grew and grew.

Figures showed that at the end of 1962, the US Army had 199 aircraft in Vietnam, the Air Force 61. The number of Army helicopter companies increased from two to five. To many, the US seemed to be achieving its goal of propping up the Vietnamese Government which had been shakier and threatened by coups early in the year.

The Viet Cong, or National Liberation Front as they wanted to be known, were not getting noticeably stronger, were not yet 100 per cent controlled by Hanoi, and in 1962 were still willing to accept a partial victory in the form of a neutral state in the south. In 1959 Ho Chi Minh had predicted victory within a year. In 1962 he was saying with remarkable prescience that victory might take fifteen to twenty years. Foreign observers in Hanoi conjectured that Ho was in fear of a development few Americans were thinking about – a US bombing campaign north of the 17th Parallel in North Vietnam.

1963

END OF A SMALL WAR

As the new year began, the war in Vietnam was still not receiving much attention from the American public. The question of what was being accomplished in that distant Asian land was not receiving much scrutiny either. While an authoritarian regime in Saigon attempted to control countryside which seemed to belong to 'Victor Charlie' at night and, perhaps, to the ARVN by day, the number of US advisors slowly increased.

Elswhere in the region other Asian cities were becoming holiday spots for American servicemen on R & R (rest and recuperation) leave, which was jokingly referred to as I & I (intoxication and intercourse). Americans on leave were being seen on the sidewalks from Sydney to Seoul – and not a few were traveling all the way home to be with wives and girlfriends. In Hong Kong the local expatriates gathered at a Kowloon Bar where civil aviator Wally Gayda liked to drink with the men and try for the women. Gayda had flown C–46s and C–47s in the 'Big War', the one everybody remembered from just eighteen years ago, and had even shot down a Japanese fighter with a Browning automatic rifle stuck out of his 'Gooney Bird's' window. The author of this volume wondered if Gayda was prescient. 'They say this thing down in Vietnam is a small war,' he intoned. 'It ain't going to be that way much longer.'

'How do you know? probed Dutch Hemmel, and Air America pilot who was flying C–46s and C–47s in *this* war.

'I'll tell you how I know.' Gayda later made this sentiment a letter to the editor in a local journal. 'It's because of the girls in the bars, is how I know. The girls in the bars say the war is going to get a lot bigger.'

Dutch was ferrying a C–46 down to Vientiane where it would join the CIA/Air America war in Laos.

'And I'll tell you what else,' Gayda insisted. 'You talk to these American Special Forces guys who come up here. These Green Berets. The say the ARVN won't fight. They say the ARVN can't fight. That's how the hell I know.'

A sign of how things were going to be was the 2 January 1963 battle at Ap Bac where ARVN troops and their American advisors were soundly defeated. A UH–1B Huey was shot down, an H–21C damaged. Friendly troops lifted into battle by helicopter were overwhelmed and overrun. In an about-face from their earlier performance, the Viet Cong showed themselves unafraid of helicopters, especially 'slick' (transport) helicopters when they were not properly escorted by gunships.

The Viet Cong were becoming much better informed about aviation. Helicopter LZs (landing zones) were covered by fire, or

The first jet aircraft in South Vietnam (if temporary-duty RF–101C Voodoos are not counted) were two Martin RB–57E Canberra photo-reconnaissance bombers belonging to the 'Patricia Lynn' program. Using the call-sign 'Moonglow', these aircraft were soon painted a sinister black. Eventually five RB–57Es were assigned and the program continued from May 1963 to August 1971. (JERRY GEER)

The OV–1B version of the US Army's Grumman Mohawk introduced a SLAR (side-looking airborne radar) mounted asymmetrically in an 18ft (5.48m) pod under the starboard side of the fuselage. In Vietnam SLAR provided army ground commanders with rapid information about enemy movements. (ROBERT F. DORR)

booby-trapped by means of spears planted in the ground to puncture the bellies of helicopters. A captured document showed how the Viet informed their personnel: 'The [helicopter] type used to carry troops is very large and looks like a worm [H–21C]. It has two rotors and usually flies at an altitude of 200 to 300 meters. To hit its head, lead by either one length or two-thirds of a length when it flies horizontally. The type used by commanders and casualties looks like a ladle [UH–1]. Lead this type one length when it is in flight . . .'

At Ap Bac many other things went wrong – effective communication between US and ARVN personnel was the first casualty – but helicopter people in particular felt that their performance and their tactics had to be reviewed. A gunship escort was to become routine with helicopter insertions.

In later years Vietnam would be a word denoting a trauma to the American psyche, but in 1963 it was still the name of a divided country in South-East Asia. Don Harris, a young soldier heading to Qui Nhon to join a US Army helicopter company, tried something most Americans had not tried: he looked up Vietnam in an encyclopedia.

Harris read of a long thin slice of geography which ran 1,200 miles (1,931km) from north to south, varying in width from 25 to 200 miles (40 to 360km), divided at the 17th Parallel between communist North Vietnam, capital Hanoi, population 17 million and South Vietnam, population 14 million plus. Ninety per cent of Vietnamese, read Harris, derived their livelihood from agriculture. His encyclopedia did not say so but Harris, who knew a little of military affairs, wondered whether bombing an agricultural population would do any good.

North and South Vietnam were similar in area, each about 64,000 square miles. Both were created in July 1954 as the result of a conference at Geneva, ending the war between French and native Viet Minh forces, which had begun just after the Second World War. North Vietnam, with Hanoi its capital, was headed by communist Ho Chi Minh, perceived by many as a long-time fighter for independence from outside forces. South Vietnam, the gem of Saigon its capital, boasted Emperor Bao Dai until a referendum in 1955 deposed him and established a republic with authoritarian Ngo Dinh Diem as president.

The trappings of a republic, including a legislature, did little to hide the fact that South Vietnam was rigidly controlled by Diem and his ruthless brother, Ngo Dinh Diem. Authoritarian was the accepted word for the regime; corrupt was the word used by many. Middle-grade army officers, many of them trained in the United States, privately told their American contacts that no progress could be made against the Viet Cong until Diem was booted from office. Domestic plotting against Diem rose and fell in cycles. 1960 had been a big year for it. 1963 was to be another. Some of those officers friendly to the West felt that if they did not get Diem out, the Viet Cong would.

When he arrived at Qui Nhon, Harris discovered that most of his Army buddies had no interest in even these rudimentary facts. 'I spent a year doing admin work which supported out helicopter operations. The South Vietnamese troops, the ARVN, got carted around the country by our choppers. When they were in a combat situation, they froze up. They refused to take advantage of air mobility. They didn't want to fight. And we just sat there and counted the number of days we had left . . .'

One of the earliest American aircraft to serve with South Vietnam's forces was the Sikorsky H–19 helicopter, a veteran of US service in the 1950–53 Korean War. These VNAF H–19s are temporarily off the flying schedule at Bien Hoa air base in September 1962. (USAF)

Originally designed for the US Marine Corps, the Army's H–37A Mojave helicopter (and the similar CH–37B version) seemed ideal for the medium- or heavy-lift mission in South Vietnam. Far from pretty, the helicopter was powered by two 1,900hp Pratt & Whitney R–2800–50 Double Wasp engines and could reach 130mph (209km/h). By the end of 1963 plans were firming up to station a few H–37s in South Vietnam the following year. (US ARMY)

Viet Cong Strength

Viet Cong attacks on villages and government outposts were on the increase. The communist guerrillas in the south were poorly equipped for a prolonged war – most of their infantry weapons in 1963 were captured from ARVN troops, not supplied by Hanoi or Moscow – but the insurgents were receiving more and more arms from the north. And the Viet Cong clearly had the will to fight, which the ARVN lacked. Most American decision-makers charged that Hanoi was controlling the VC – this became a self-fulfilling prophesy – but none wanted to say that the VC were winning the war.

There were no front lines, no rear areas, so progress could not be measured by drawing a map. Thus, White House and Pentagon experts could say that the good guys were winning, even if no one knew how to measure this. In time the standard of measure became the 'body count', the idea being that more dead Viet Cong meant more progress towards winning. No one seemed to understand that in an insurgency, an increase in enemy corpses also meant an increase in the enemy's numbers as more Vietnamese were lured to the other side.

It was a strange time for Diem's regime to make arrangements for legions of disaffected

Few Army aircraft were as capable, or aroused as much Air Force ire, as the De Havilland Canada CV–2 Caribou which, by late 1963, was operating in several locations in Vietnam. A versatile heavy lifter which could get into airfields not even reached by the C–123B Provider, the CV–2 was unquestionably an asset. The USAF's problem was the word 'Army' painted on the side. (US ARMY)

enemy to come over to Saigon's side in the war. April 1963 saw the inception of the Chieu Hoi ('Open Arms') amnesty program aimed at rallying Viet Cong defectors to the government's side. Air Commando U–10Bs were to drop leaflets urging the VC to come over. Army UH–1B Hueys with loudspeakers were to broadcast the same message. The program was to continue throughout the war – but in 1963 many rural Vietnamese in a country which was 90 per cent rural were going in the opposite direction.

There were actually plans to remove some American units by the end of 1963. These plans are often cited as evidence that President Kennedy wanted to keep the US commitment to a modest scale. Still, more and more Americans were arriving and many of them were exponents of the 'new' unconventional warfare of which President Kennedy was so enamored. The Army's Special Forces, or Green Berets, sometimes seemed to have carte blanche in their efforts to support Saigon's army in the hinterlands. Air America, the airline carrier which was essentially owned by the CIA, was flying plain and unmarked aircraft in Laos and South Vietnam.

In those days certainly the most-traveled aircraft in South Vietnam was the Fairchild C–123B Provider, used for transport and defoliation.

In January 1963, to improve the Provider's take-off characteristics, the USAF sent the sole YC–123H prototype (a standard C–123B fitted with two General Electric CJ610 turbojets in underwing pods) for combat trials in South Vietnam.

This jet-augmented prototype had been tested some years earlier. Then and now it proved of limited interest. Yet a few years later the jet-augmented C–123K and UC–123K versions (introduced in May 1967) were to become standard throughout South Vietnam. The C–123 was an extremely versatile design which would reach its pinnacle in May 1969, when C–123 monthly combat sorties peaked at 9,707. The transport was to remain in service with the USAF until June 1972, and with the VNAF until the end.

Airdrop

On 24 March 1963 USAF C–123s and VNAF C–47s dropped 1,150 ARVN paratroopers on to drop zones in Tay Ninh province in Operation 'Phi Hon II'. It was not clear whether this airborne assault surprised or outwitted the Viet Cong. Most US Army leaders acknowledged that the helicopter was replacing the parachute as a means of

Well liked and exceedingly useful, the De Havilland Canada U–6A (formerly L–20A) Beaver was not quite the size of its big cousin, the U–1A Otter, but could handle liaison and transport duties larger than those accommodated by the O–1 Bird Dog. Beavers were few in number in South Vietnam, but ranged widely throughout the country. (US ARMY)

inserting troops into the combat zone.

In April 1963 the 777th Troop Carrier Squadron arrived at Da Nang with sixteen C–123Bs to augment the twenty-nine at Tan Son Nhut. Other increases in US aircraft strength in Vietnam consisted of Army aircraft, eight U–1A Otters, sixteen O–1A Bird Dog observation planes, ten UH–1B Iroquois (Huey) helicopters, and four additional CV–2 Caribous.

US Army aviation focused principally on the helicopter – in 1963 many were still calling Vietnam the 'Helicopter War' – but the success of the Army's mission depended heavily on fixed-wing aircraft, either as part of a ground unit or for general utility duties. As has been said often, for it was much on men's minds in those days, the 'rules' stated that the Army could operate fixed-wing aircraft for 'administrative' purposes only. In fact, fixed-wing aircraft were employed for reconnaissance and logistics duties.

The Grumman OV–1 Mohawk was becoming an increasingly familiar sight from one end of Vietnam to the other. This twin-engined aircraft, which had originally been developed as an Army-Marine Corps joint venture (although in the end the Marines purchased none) was a handy machine when only short, rough runways were available and ground units needed almost instantaneous photo coverage.

Gradually, increasingly effective sensors and radars were being produced for use with the Mohawk. The OV–1B variant carried a side-looking aerial radar (SLAR) in a long pod mounted under the starboard side of the fuselage. The Mohawk had been seen from the outset as living a simple, rugged life up near the front line with the ground infantryman, but the added burden of SLAR and other sensors degraded the performance of the aircraft and took it out of the category of low-cost, front-line warplane.

Nevertheless, the Mohawk soldiered on, and although supposedly unarmed, it carried machine-gun pods under the wings for defense and support missions. Officers took due note of the Mohawk's ability to carry not merely self-protection but offensive armament. This caused Air Force commanders to complain that the Army was violating the 'rules'. They argued that if the Army needed gun or rocket support, the USAF could supply it. The Army knew perfectly well that the Air Force had no assets with which to provide Mohawk-style support to the dogface on the ground and, furthermore, with its own aircraft the Army would be able to respond almost instantaneously rather than go through an increasingly cumbersome chain of command.

The debate about close air support had raged for years – in 1960-61 the Army had tested the Italian-built Fiat G.91 in the close air support role, in defiance of the rules – and Air Force leaders really fumed when responding to calls for close support from formations on the ground in preference to USAF (or VNAF) support. In due course the dispute was resolved in typical fashion. The Army could keep its Mohawks but went on

By mid-1963 there were no fewer than 233 aircraft from four services using Tan Son Nhut airfield just outside Saigon. Included were a number of US Navy Douglas EA–1F Skyraider early warning aircraft, similar to the one shown here. The EA–1F was not intended as an interceptor, but Navy officers felt it could be used to intercept any enemy night intruders which might appear. None did, and hostile aircraft were never a problem within the borders of South Vietnam. (US NAVY)

record as assuring that henceforth they would be unarmed. The Mohawks continued to fly with gun and rocket loads. The Air Force took comfort from the agreement, while the Army was encouraged by the reality of the situation.

There were those in the Air Force who did not even want the Army to have large helicopters. One of their targets was the Sikorsky H–37, not a new craft by any means but in 1963 the Army's largest load-hauling rotary-wing aircraft. Plans were being formed to despatch a number of these heavy-lift helicopters to South Vietnam (they were to arrive in 1964). Once it was pointed out that there was no reasonable alternative, not in Army khaki and not in Air Force blue, this portion of the ongoing inter-Service dispute evaporated.

A heavy-lift helicopter was one thing, a large transport quite another. While experts searched for clear direction in Vietnam, the USAF became increasingly vocal about an irritant to which it kept returning – the Army's CV–2 Caribou. This exceptional cargo plane had been procured by the Army to bridge the size gap between its largest helicopters and the Air Force's C–130 Hercules four-engined transports. Capable of lifting almost 3 tons of supplies or 32 passengers, the Canadian-built CV–2

Tan Son Nhut grew like topsy. The air base outside Saigon was perhaps the most important airfield from the beginning of the conflict until its end. Da Nang and Bien Hoa were also important, but being at the capital Tan Son Nhut was symbolic of all the installations that were gradually being taken over by the Americans. (USAF)

Caribou was able to get in and out of small unimproved airstrips – including some which even the C–123B Provider could not reach. In 1963 the USAF continued to argue – not yet successfully – that if anybody was going to operate Caribous, it should be the Air Force.

To return to the Army's UH–1 Huey helicopter – a flying 'ladle' as the Viet Cong called it – UH–1A and UH–1B models were proving their worth with the Utility Tactical Transport Helicopter Company (UTTCO), which had set up shop the previous year. This unit was to test the role of the helicopter as a 'gunship' or 'hog'. The escort mission required a particular kind of flying during its three stages – the en route phase, the approach phase, and the LZ (landing zone) phase. En route to their objective the Hueys were encouraged to fly high, out of reach of 'Victor Charlie's' small-arms. During the approach, they were to descend to treetop level while some miles from the objective. At the LZ, of course, they were in combat – supporting the 'slick' (transport) helicopters inserting troops into the battle zone. Rather remarkably, despite extensive exposure to Viet Cong gunfire, UTTCO lost only one gunship Huey in combat between 16 October 1962 and 15 March 1963.

The Army's Bird Dog became perhaps the most ubiquitous fixed-wing aircraft in the war zone. The tandem, two-seat high-wing liaison craft could land almost anywhere and was no easy target to hit from the ground, making it a good candidate for observation duties in Viet Cong territory. As the US Army shifted toward an airmobile concept making increased use of helicopters, and training of fixed-wing pilots declined, the Army decided that its O–1 Bird Dogs were needed more in Vietnam than at training bases.

Vietnamese children. Always they left an impression on the minds and hearts of the Americans who traveled to little-known Vietnam to fight in a little-publicized war. The children seemed to know no politics and to belong to neither side. If any of these are still alive today, they should be in their late 40s. (DAVID W. MENARD)

A significant number of TO–1D Bird Dog trainers (formerly TL–19Ds) were sent back to Cessna to be modified for combat duties. In addition to other improvements, underwing racks were installed, enabling the machine to carry smoke/marker rockets. Most of the aircraft were returned to the Army as O–1Ds but twenty-two were loaned to the Air Force for forward air controller (FAC) duties as the O–1F.

The first Army O–1Ds to reach the battle zone belonged to the 73rd Aviation Company commanded by Major John S. Kark. This unit became the latest of many tenants at Saigon's Tan Son Nhut airfield, beginning in May 1963. As reported by historian Al Adcock, Kark's unit logged some 30,000 combat hours in its first year, performing resupply of forward troops, medical evacuation, flare drops, spotting and forward air control.

Busy Tan Son Nhut

The number of aircraft operating from Tan Son Nhut was getting out of hand. The figure reached 233, including Convair F–102s and Douglas EA–1F Skyraiders brought in to guard against an imagined enemy air offensive. In due course the interceptors were deemed unnecessary and were withdrawn.

To cite one further fixed-wing aircraft which was employed to good result by the US Army – and, in time, by the South Vietnamese – the de Havilland Canada U–6A (former L–20A) Beaver was a large, high-wing liaison ship, not as large as its cousin the Otter but substantially larger than the Bird Dog. U–6A Beavers shuttled men and materiel around the country, dodged the occasional stream of Viet Cong gunfire, and suffered very light casualties.

While air and ground combat operations continued – the T–28s and B–26s of the 'Farm Gate' detachment were in action daily, supporting ground operations against the VC – politics in Saigon took an ugly turn.

Train Cover

As 1963 drew on, Vietnamese and American pilots discovered that the mere presence of an aircraft overhead was often sufficient to keep 'Victor Charlie' away. Vietnamese O–1 Bird Dogs escorted truck convoys and trains, occasionally accompanied by an A–1H Skyraider or T–28 fighter-bomber. Experience showed that the Viet Cong usually would not launch one of their typical ambushes if an aircraft was on the scene – even an unarmed O–1.

Recce Canberras

In May the 6091st Reconnaissance Squadron, USAF, flew two RB–57E Canberra reconnaissance aircraft to a temporary site at Tan Son Nhut. Part of a program called 'Patricia Lynn', the Canberras were the first jets in Vietnam. Like so much that happened in the ever-expanding war, 'Patricia Lynn' was billed as a brief, temporary program; instead it was to be one of the longest, its aircraft remaining until August 1971.

These particular Canberras, originally built as target-towing aircraft, were fitted with reconnaissance systems by General Dynamics at Fort Worth. Initially the forward nose was redesigned to house a KA–1 36in forward oblique and a low panoramic KA–56 camera. Mounted in the inside of the bomb bay door was a KA–1 vertical camera, K–477 split-vertical day-night camera, and a KA–1 left oblique camera. The RB–57E Canberras were so badly wanted that ferry pilot Captain Bill Scott and navigator Lieutenant Bill Sung were pressed into service – combat service, it might be added – to fly the first mission on 7 May 1963, using aircraft 55-4243.

Soon afterwards, new crews arrived from the States and the 'Patricia Lynn' RB–57Es became permanent residents. They used the call-sign 'Moonglow'. Their photography of Viet Cong installations proved invaluable.

There were problems, however. When equipment worked properly, which it often did not, the US intelligence apparatus was frequently unable to exploit the information gained. No courier aircraft were available to deliver reconnaissance film rapidly throughout Vietnam until the arrival of two Cessna U–3 aircraft (militarized versions of the Cessna 310) later in May. Intelligence information from Air Force RB–57Es was seldom compared with information from Army OV–1 Mohawks, so there was a duplication of effort.

On 11 June 1963 an aged Buddhist monk burned himself alive in public. Encounters between Saigon police and demonstrating Buddhist leaders constituted only one aspect of growing discontent against President Diem, his brother Ngo Dinh Nhu and the latter's 'Dragon Lady' wife, the diminutive but spiteful Madame Nhu. The Diem government was harsh, authoritarian and corrupt. Congressman Otto Passman

The ubiquitous Huey. The US Army's Utility Tactical Transport Helicopter Company (UTTCO) managed to lose only one in combat during a six-month period ending in March 1963. Here, in next-door Thailand, US and Thai soldiers rappel from a UH–1B Huey during 13 June 1963 demonstration for Thai Premier Sarit Thanarat. Throughout the South-East Asia conflict, Thailand supported US efforts to bulwark South Vietnam. (US ARMY)

reflected the views of many when he said that Americans did not want to prop up an unpopular regime which was lukewarm about its struggle against communism. President Kennedy reiterated that some Americans would be withdrawn from Vietnam by the end of the year.

In July 1963 the USAF's 19th Tactical Air Support Squadron, or 19th TASS, began arriving with O–1 Bird Dogs. The Air Force Bird Dog pilots were to train Vietnamese in forward air control, visual reconnaissance and observer procedures.

Opposition to President Diem was mounting from several quarters. American leaders were apparently unaware that a major plot against Diem was being mounted by Generals Duong Van Minh, Tran Van Don, and others. In a kind of general response to unrest at the end of October, a US naval task force was positioned off Vietnam and three F–102s were flown in to Tan Son Nhut. There was no role for either when the coup began on the morning of 1 November 1962.

Some reports have it that several ARVN generals approached the new American ambassador, Henry Cabot Lodge, asking how the US would respond to a coup. Lodge, new to his role as President Kennedy's envoy but experienced in such matters, sent 'immediate' cables to the State Department warning that Diem was losing support.

Troops took over key installations and surrounded Diem and Nhu in the palace. Four A–1H Skyraiders and two T–28s flew overhead, joining in the uprising. An occasional splutter of rifle fire was heard in that area of Saigon but resistance to the coup was scattered and weak.

Fighting continued into the next day when Diem and Nhu – after attempting to escape via an underground tunnel from the palace –

Saigon, seen from 3,000ft (914m). It was more than a capital; it was a gem, a pearl – the 'Paris of the Orient', replete with cozy sidewalk cafes from which patrons could watch the war in the distance. By 1963 the gem was beginning to lose its luster. In later years, whatever else a massive influx of Americans may have done – good and bad – there was no denying that Saigon was never the same again. (NORMAN TAYLOR)

Without airlift, the massive infusion of men and materiel into South Vietnam would have been impossible. In 1963 the airlift arm was called Military Air Transport Service (MATS), soon to be renamed Military Airlift Command. The Douglas C–124 Globemaster II was nearing the end of a long and successful career as one of the USAF's real workhorse transports. (ROBERT F. DORR)

were captured. Placed inside a vehicle near the palace, the pair were murdered – although some versions of the event say that Nhu was given an opportunity to commit suicide. The rebels established a Military Revolutionary Council headed by General Minh.

The war did not slow down for the coup. Viet Cong attacks on government installations increased. At one point, 'Farm Gate' pilots had to fly close support for a beleaguered outpost without having the requisite Vietnamese crew member aboard. The Vietnamese fliers were too busy with the coup.

The US supported the new rulers in Saigon and continued its activities throughout South Vietnam. A small number of Americans were withdrawn before year's end, reflecting President Kennedy's wish to bolster Saigon's forces and reduce the US presence. Some of Kennedy's supporters claim that he wanted to have a larger and more visible withdrawal of US troops from Vietnam in time for his re-election campaign in 1964. It can never be proven, however, whether Kennedy would have continued the withdrawals.

The President was assassinated in Dallas on 22 November 1963 in one of those wrenching historical moments which affect everyone, everywhere, and the question of what to do in Vietnam passed into the hands of Lyndon B. Johnson.

While the world reacted with shock to the loss of the American president, a battle unfolded that showed that the Viet Cong were increasingly ready for larger-scale actions. Before dawn on 24 November 1963, the Viet Cong launched a well-planned ambush at an outpost named Chu La and a strategic hamlet on the Ca Mau peninsula, both in An Xuyen Province. Defending South Vietnamese troops were overrun while the VC shot down a US Army H–21C Shawnee.

As the battle continued with US and South Vietnamese aircraft overhead, VC gunfire damaged ten H–21Cs and UH–1 Hueys. American and VNAF A–1Hs, B–26s and T–28s attacked at low altitude, returning again and again to hit the VC within a short distance of friendly troops.

In another of the rare airborne assaults of the war, C–47s and C–123Bs dropped a battalion to cut off the VC line of withdrawal. The 'Mule Train' C–123Bs put most of the paratroops on the wrong side of the Cai Nuoc River, enabling most of the VC to escape. At the same time, the VC seriously damaged a B–26 which went down with the loss of its crew.

Some Americans flying overhead observed that the South Vietnamese troops did not seem very interested in fighting and, on at least two occasions, broke off encounters with the VC when they had a good prospect of inflicting harm. The loss of two aircraft, coupled with severe damage to two Vietnamese A–1H Skyraiders, made it clear that winning the war was going to be a long and hard struggle at best.

Included among withdrawals from Vietnam under decisions which remained from the Kennedy presidency, the USAF's 'Dirty Thirty' unit of transport pilots and support personnel left South Vietnam on 3 December 1963. These Air Force people had logged more than 20,000 hours in Vietnamese C–47 'Gooney Birds' in what one history called 'one of the oddest cargo operations of the time'. By day the American pilots had hauled cargo ranging from live animals to primitive tribesmen. By night they dropped paraflares to illuminate battlefields at remote outposts.

VNAF Progress

Progress by Saigon's own air force was an important sign of hope as 1963 neared its end. So fast was the VNAF growing that it had to redesignate all its units – the 1st Fighter Squadron became the 514th, the 2nd the 516th, and so on. Now, the VNAF had five wings located at Da Nang, Nha Trang, Pleiku, Bien Hoa and Tan Son Nhut. Included in this force were two squadrons of A–1 Skyraiders, two of T–28 Trojans, two of H–34 helicopters, three of O–1 Bird Dogs and two of C–47 Skytrains. The VNAF was not only bigger, it was better: training received strong emphasis. In later years the quality of VNAF pilots was to deteriorate, but in 1963 most were very good.

Earlier in the year Defense Secretary McNamara had announced that the Vietnamese would soon be able to fight their own war and that it would become possible to withdraw the remaining 15,640 US military personnel. The US role in Vietnam would end during 1965, said McNamara. Some of what McNamara said was taken seriously by the people involved, who thought they would be going home soon.

President Johnson sent McNamara to Vietnam for a 19–20 December visit. McNamara found the Minh government shaky and indecisive. Publicly he exuded optimism. Privately he advised Johnson of a dilemma. If the US poured too many men and weapons into the country to prosecute the war, it might hurt rather than help South Vietnam's goal of defending itself. McNamara also found that infiltration from North Vietnam was increasing. He authorized flights by Lockheed U–2 reconnaissance aircraft to cover infiltration routes. U–2s were quickly moved to Bien Hoa for this purpose.

The end of 1963 was, to US Navy Captain Deke Thatcher, the last juncture at which Vietnam could be called a small war.

The number of Americans committed was still small enough for the citizenry at large to be little affected, and even some of the men in the combat zone could continue viewing the war as small and romantic. Thatcher, part of a Fleet evaluation group examining the size and structure of carrier air wings, sat through a three-hour meeting at the Pentagon and noted that Vietnam was not mentioned once. The Navy was making progress integrating its new McDonnell F–4B Phantom into carrier air wings and would soon begin looking for a replacement for the proven Douglas A–4 Skyhawk lightweight attack craft. Thatcher observed that in looking at future readiness needs, Navy planners skipped around the world, imagining a conflict off the Soviet Union's Kola Peninsula in one exchange of words, talking about the threat in Korea moments later. Looking back later, there seemed to have been something terribly unreal about all this. The Phantom and Skyhawk had some fighting ahead of them, but not where the Navy thought.

At the oft-mentioned Tan Son Nhut air base on New Year's Eve, USAF Airman Walter Todd took a smoke break by propping himself in a seating position on loading docks that were under construction. He drew in on a Marlboro, savoring the odd hues under the night's sodium-vapor lamps.

Like most airmen at the base, Todd had noticed men and materiel being brought into South Vietnam by the marvel of long-range airlift. The Douglas C–124 Globemaster was a frequent sight and people at Tan Son Nhut were beginning to see the occasional Lockheed C–130A Hercules. 'You know,' Todd told a pal, 'they're bringing an awful lot of stuff in here. They say we'll be finished here in the near future. You know what? I don't believe it.'

Wally Gayda, Deke Thatcher and Walt Todd did not survive the decade of the 1960s, but back there at the dark beginning – back when only a few of us saw it coming – they might as well have been clairvoyant. At Alameda, on the American west coast, the USS *Bon Homme Richard* (CVA–31) was preparing to put to sea in January. As Thatcher knew, even if no one else did, the war which included the US Army and Air Force was about to have an increasing role for the carrier Navy as well.

Henry Cabot Lodge (in tropical suit), an unsuccessful candidate for Vice President in 1960, became the US ambassador to Saigon in 1963. In the latter capacity, New England patrician Lodge was closely linked to Defense Secretary Robert S. McNamara (at microphone) and General Maxwell Taylor. These men saw the American presence in Vietnam gaining strength at the very time that the Viet Cong were also gaining strength. Not only was McNamara still saying that US troops would be able to withdraw soon but, at this juncture, he was still being believed when he said it. (USAF)

1964 WIDENING WAR

It felt like the Second World War, flying with the USAF in South-East Asia in 1964. Men walked around bare-chested, carrying sub-machine-guns and bandoliers of ammo slung over their shoulders. Bush hats were popular. The sound of aircraft engines on an airfield in the early morning was evocative of that early era. The wheeze of a propeller turning over, followed by a gnashing and then the cough, cough, and finally the roar of a reciprocating engine coming to life. It was like a time that many of the men remembered from their own experience, long before jet engines had come along.

Operating their ageing fleet of B–26 and T–28 aircraft at Bien Hoa, 200 USAF Commandos made up the 'Farm Gate' detachment which, by 1964, was rapidly swelling in size. The 34th Tactical Group was established to give Air Force people in Vietnam a unit which sounded more appropriate for their growing size – reporting, of course, to 2nd Air Division in Saigon. At first there was a clandestine aura to the presence of the airmen. They wore civilian clothes and kept in the background. They used a term that had become fashionable – COIN, meaning counter-insurgency. Some of them scarfed up black-market weapons, of which the most popular was the Swedish K sub-machine-gun.

Up through November 1964 – which meant through the Diem regime and for the year that followed – it still was a counter-insurgency air operation. Men and aircraft, working in small numbers, were effective against the Viet Cong insurgents. Throughout this period, combined VNAF and USAF efforts mounted up to 35 sorties per day. The intent was to enable Saigon's forces to function more effectively in the bush, and it worked.

Apparently in the belief that the war was being won, the 19th Tactical Air Support Squadron equipped with Cessna O–1F Bird Dogs was deactivated in August 1964. It was one of many signals to the airmen that the war was almost over. Indeed, if they did not know the war was almost over, Secretary of Defense Robert S. McNamara told them it was over with each new public utterance.

That same month, the North Vietnamese attacked US ships and retaliatory air strikes were flown, but for participants of the 'in-country war', it felt as if things were winding down. When the 19th TASS was reactivated a few months later, everyone assumed that this was just another of the many changes that kept occurring. Everyone said the VC were being licked and the guys would soon be able to go home.

Coup d'Etat

On 30 January 1964 Major General Nguyen Khanh led a coup against the indecisive Minh regime and installed yet another new, military government in Saigon. Khanh had

The Bell UH–1 Iroquois helicopter, fast becoming known as the Huey, was not yet a familiar sight on American TV screens but an increasing number were reaching the few thousand American advisors in Vietnam. On 12 February 1964 Staff Sergeant Bill Crow is loading 2.75in rockets aboard one of the early armed Hueys. (US ARMY)

power but not popularity. Americans quickly indicated their support.

On 11 February 1964 all B–26 Invader bombers in South Vietnam were grounded after a wing had failed on an aircraft in the US. It became clear that the B–26 could not handle the 750lb (227kg) bombs it had been carrying without suffering structural damage. Colonel Benjamin S. Preston, Jr, head of the 34th Tactical Group at Bien Hoa, struggled to keep his B–26s in the air but every aircraft had cracked stress plates and loose rivets throughout its wings.

On 1 April the last B–26 was flown out of South Vietnam. Plans to bring in the On Mark B–26K variant were shelved. To provide an interim strike capability, the 1st Air Commando Squadron borrowed nine T–28s from the VNAF in April.

Then disaster struck the T–28s. On 24 March one aircraft lost its wing on a bomb run. This was followed by another T–28 wing loss on 9 April. Major General J. H. Moore, 2nd Air Division chief in Saigon, lamented that, '[We are] practically out of business'. American T–28s were replaced in May 1964 by the A–1E Skyraider, the 'wide-body' version of the versatile attack aircraft which had side-by-side seating up front.

At times the requirement for the Americans to carry a Vietnamese passenger – who was ostensibly being trained – became ludicrous.

During yet another visit to Saigon in May, Secretary McNamara reiterated the administration's policy that all US airmen should be out of combat within a matter of months. American fliers were told to limit their activities to providing genuine training only, and apparently McNamara meant it this time.

To make up for the loss of USAF strike aircraft, four VNAF squadrons would receive A–1H Skyraiders and another two squadrons would be added, the aircraft coming from US squadrons slated for withdrawal. McNamara touted this as a continuation of withdrawals which had begun the previous year with the 'Dirty Thirty' transport personnel.

Also in May the 1st Air Commando Squadron which had been operating the T–28 received its initial increment of six A–1E Skyraiders. Nine more came the following month. The eventual plan was to have sixty Skyraiders in country.

The press and public were focusing not on Vietnam but on Laos. A detachment of the 1st Air Commando Squadron had moved to Udorn, Thailand, in March with a force of four T–28s, its mission to train the Royal Laotian Air Force in operations and maintenance. Few Americans knew who was who in Laos – or for that matter in Vietnam – enabling the *San Francisco Chronicle*'s Arthur Hoppe to write hilarious columns about the dreaded Vietnarians, the Loyal Royal Army, and a princely leader named Ngo Manh Ngo. In fact, the T–28s, known now by the program name 'Water Pump', were helping the royal Lao regime against the Pathet Lao guerrillas. By June F–100 Super Sabres located at Da Nang were also striking Pathet positions in Laos.

New Commander

A major change of command took place on 20 June 1964 when the lackluster General Harkins was replaced by General William D. Westmoreland. The new senior American officer had served in the 9th Infantry Division during the Second World War and had distinguished himself as a paratroop leader with the 187th Airborne Regimental Combat Team in Korea. He was also a former superintendent of the United States Military Academy, West Point, which produced so many of the nation's heroes and leaders. 'Westy', those who were friendly called him. In due course, those who were not would nickname him General 'Waste More Men' because of his repeated calls for increased troop strength.

Shortly afterwards, on 2 July, Henry Cabot Lodge was replaced as American

The Huey helicopter was fast demonstrating that it could be extremely useful in a variety of roles. This UH–1B, with eight loudspeakers mounted on the starboard side of its fuselage, is dropping leaflets and broadcasting messages designed to support the Saigon regime. This kind of 'psyop' (psychological operations) rarely had much effect and this one, ironically, is taking place on 5 August 1964, the day that the Gulf of Tonkin incident spread the war to North Vietnam. (US ARMY)

Steaming westward in the Indian Ocean in early 1964, the USS *Bon Homme Richard* (CVA–31) was a holdover from the Second World War. '*Bonnie Dick*' became one of the most-used aircraft-carriers in the Vietnam era, making combat cruises in 1964, 1965–66, 1967, 1968, 1969 and 1970 before being finally decommissioned on 2 July 1971. The carrier's Crusaders and Skyhawks flew in combat in North and South Vietnam and in the unacknowledged war in Laos. (USN)

A DH Canada CV–2A Caribou ready to take on soldier passengers at Saigon's Tan Son Nhut airfield in February 1964. At about this time most Caribous acquired a thimble-like nose radome, not seen on this aeroplane. Caribous joined USAF C–123Bs in taking care of the in-country airlift mission, visiting remote landing strips sometimes not far from enemy troops. (US ARMY)

A Viet Cong mortar attack on the flight line at Bien Hoa on the night of Hallowe'en, 31 October/1 November 1964, destroyed five Martin B–57 Canberras and damaged thirteen. In this overhead view two B–57 Canberra parking spaces are marked with the charred, blackened remains of what were once twin-engined jet bombers. (USAF)

Major Charles Vasiliadis arrived at Bien Hoa in November 1964 to join the First Air Commando Squadron and to fly the first of 493 combat missions in the A–1E Skyraider. Here Vas checks the 'daisy cutter' extended fuse designed to detonate bombs above ground level. (USAF)

Ambassador by General Maxwell D. Taylor, another paratrooper and war hero. Taylor had been Kennedy's man and had survived the transition to become Johnson's man. He was distinguished by a total lack of experience in diplomatic affairs.

Some in South Vietnam continued to feel that they should be prepared to cope with an air threat from up north, whether North Vietnamese or Chinese. On 26 June 1964 three F–102 interceptors were deployed to Da Nang for ten days under the program name 'Candy Machine'.

Door Gunners

In 1964 the Bell UH–1 Iroquois helicopter had all but replaced the earlier Piasecki H–21C in US Army units. Up at Qui Nhon, on the coast where beautiful beaches faced aquamarine sea, the 117th Aviation Company painted its Hueys in an unusual blotched camouflage scheme. Carl Vogel, a young private first class in the 117th, noticed that nobody was referring to the Iroquois by its official name. First called the XH–40, then the HU–1, and now the UH–1, the helicopter was now, and always would be, the Huey. The name Huey was used so widely that most people never knew it was called anything else.

Pilots of the UH–1B Hueys now operating in the country were concerned that the Viet Cong seemed to control the war at night. An early attempt to provide night illumination from Hueys in Vietnam was a field modification owing its existence to the creative mind of CWO–3 Kenneth La Monte. La Monte used 4ft (1.2m) lengths of steel pipe mounted on the universal gun mounts on each side of a UH–1B Huey. Six bomb shackles secured to the bottom of each pipe enabled the helicopter to drop up to twelve flares. This was not enough to wrest the nocturnal battlefield away from 'Charlie', but as the war progressed further improvements were made with flares, searchlights, xenon lights, Starlite scopes, and other devices.

By 1964 Strategic Air Command Boeing KC–135 tankers were operating from neighbouring Thailand and were beginning to support US warplanes throughout South-East Asia. The tankers employed either the 'flying boom' or the probe and drogue refueling system. In this view the probe from the right wing of an F–100D Super Sabre is visible in the foreground on a flight taking place near Da Nang. (DAVE SANDS)

Back home, the helicopter – only now beginning to win acceptance in the Army – was receiving more attention than ever. The Howze Board had recommended that at least one Army unit be equipped entirely with helicopters. The 11th Air Assault Division was formed for this purpose, reviving the colors of an airborne division which had won honors in the Second World War. Helicopter tactics were tested, refined, and in the fall of 1964 the division participated in 'Air Assault II', a massive exercise in the Carolinas with 35,000 men participating. The 11th Air Assault was only a test division but a time was coming when its men, machines and tactics would be moved into a future unit with an even prouder name – the First Cavalry Division.

In the US Army a new species was being bred to go with the helicopter – a door gunner. Army aviation was serious about the role this gunner played in protecting the other members of his crew and issued some advice which seemed to make sense. With hindsight, this instruction tells us much about how helicopter crewmen were regarded at the time. To quote:

'Learn the way of a tiger.

'That's the theme of the program for training "Shotgunners" – or officially Aerial Door Gunners – those tough, skilled soldiers who, in the tradition of their counterparts on the stagecoaches of the old West, are protecting their UH–1 "Skycoaches" while flying over South Vietnam.

'The Shotgun training program began early in 1963 when the US Military Assistance Command, Vietnam, requested combat-trained men to take over from the helicopter crews and mechanics the job of manning automatic weapons that protect the Hueys on operational missions.

'The 25th Infantry ("Tropic Lightning") Division in Hawaii responded swiftly. Thus far more than 2,000 officers and men from the division have completed this training and have seen action across the sights of their machine-guns. Thirteen of them have given their lives. More than 100 have been wounded.

'From its inception the Shotgun program has been entirely volunteer. Shotgun I was organized into five platoons, each with 20 men commanded by a lieutenant. These platoons were attached to the Aviation Companies requesting assistance.

'Spiced with the imagination and initiative of the assigned officers and non-commissioned officers, the training has become centralized and sophisticated. Reports filed by teams returning from combat enable the 25th Aviation Battalion, which is charged with the Shotgun training program, to update its instruction continuously.

'Because demands on the men serving as shotgunner are severe, each candidate must pass a class III flight physical examination in which vision, color blindness, hearing and other physical conditions are closely checked. If the individual displays any inability to operate under the many pressures that will face him, he is thanked for his interest but cut away from the program. There are always plenty of volunteers to fill vacancies.

William C. Westmoreland became the senior American officer in South Vietnam on 20 June 1964. He had distinguished himself in Korea and at West Point but was to be criticized for appearing to believe that the war could be won if only more American troops were made available. (US ARMY)

'Training is primarily with the M–60 machine-gun, but the soldier also must be an expert with the 50-caliber machine-gun, M–79 grenade-launcher, .45-caliber pistol, M–3 machine-gun, the .30-caliber M–2 carbine and the new M–16 rifle. Always present is the basic infantry weapon, the M–14 complete with bayonet.

'The four-hour course in the function, care and maintenance of the M–60 is an important part of the schedule. To test reaction of men in a tense situation, platoon leaders frequently pull rounds from ammunition belts to cause weapon stoppages. At other times a weapon may be incorrectly reassembled to force the next man to spot the error.

'Recently it was decided that because of an increased number of night missions being reported from Vietnam, added emphasis would be placed on night weapons firing training. Additional emphasis also has been placed on familiarization with the various types of helicopters, and on offensive and defensive flying tactics in South-East Asia.

'The training platoons are first introduced to helicopter flight from a mock-up. They are orientated in the various gun mounts and also in free firing with the "Bungee cord", a resilient strap slung in the door of the craft to support the weapon.

'As training progresses the men learn techniques of aerial observation and firing at various altitudes and how to respond with instantaneous but planned reactions. Accuracy is constantly emphasized, especially in the descent-to-a-landing-zone phase. While supplying suppressive fire, the shotgunners must keep an eye on accompanying support helicopters as they continue to assist troops from the craft – all in split seconds.

'Constant re-evaluation, updating and evolution of the program is stressed. Reports from men returning from Vietnam provide experience in formation flying and gunnery. Artfully camouflaged, human-sized dummies recently replaced the old 50-gallon drum targets to provide greater accuracy in gunnery practice.

'In addition to training in weaponry and tactics, the already jungle-trained 25th Division men receive a thorough re-orientation in jungle survival. They also are taught to swim fully clothed and to maneuver in treacherous waters against the chance of being forced into such a situation. Intensive training also is given by the Division surgeon's office to prepare men to meet and overcome the health hazards of disease-infested jungle regions.

'Today, the Shotgun X platoons in Vietnam are all trained by their parent Lightning Division to strike from the sky. Each is composed of three eight-man squads and a platoon sergeant, under command of a company grade officer.

'As did their counterparts of old who fought off robbers and Indians in the wild and wooly West, they have learned the ways of a tiger in order to kill a tiger; and they prove every day that they can meet the guerrilla forces of what has become a wild and wooly East.'

At this point, the document from this period concludes with a plug for one of the best-known US Army divisions: '[Door gunners] prove every day that men of the 25th Division are "Ready to Fight, Anywhere! Any time!"' This final note reflected the kind of innocent confidence that still possessed Americans at this early juncture. It would take more time to teach the lesson that Lyndon Johnson's America was not nearly as ready as everyone believed to fight and win a prolonged and brutal Asian land war.

War up North

Following North Vietnamese attacks on US Navy vessels in the Gulf of Tonkin on 2 and 4 August 1964 – what became known as the 'Gulf of Tonkin incident' – the US sent carrier-based aircraft on a one-time strike against targets in North Vietnam.

In 64 sorties, A–1 Skyraiders, A–4 Skyhawks and F–8 Crusaders from two American carriers bombed and rocketed North Vietnamese bases, sinking or

The 'Roadrunners', otherwise known as attack squadron VA–144, were in the war early, starting with the Gulf of Tonkin strikes on 5 August 1964, and kept returning until the squadron was disbanded in 1970. Several versions of the Douglas A–4 Skyhawk, including the A–4E shown here, were flown by 'Roadrunner' aviators. (USN)

Aircraft 555 was given high visibility when the 555th ('Triple Nickel') Tactical Fighter Squadron went to Asia in the first Far East deployment of USAF F–4C Phantoms, though 444 is also there in the background. At this juncture USAF Phantoms are still painted in gull gray and white, with FJ 'buzz numbers' on the fuselage sides. Soon the demands of the war would cause them to be camouflaged. (USAF)

seriously damaging twenty-five PT boats and destroying a major portion of Hanoi's petroleum stores and storage facilities.

Pilots reported that fuel oil tanks were burning profusely at Vinh as they left the area and intelligence analysts concluded that 90 per cent of Vinh's fuel installation had been destroyed. There was a strong possibility that the analysts were over-estimating the effects of airpower on a largely rural Third World country which lacked tempting industrial targets: such wishful thinking was to recur often over the next nine years. The out-country war – which is outside the scope of this narrative, about the war in the south – had begun.

The war up north is the subject of a companion volume, *Air War Hanoi*. In the south, on 5 August 1964, B–57 Canberra light bombers were brought in to Bien Hoa and F–100 Super Sabres deployed to Da Nang. In addition, F–105 Thunderchiefs were brought in to neighboring Thailand.

Carrier Operations

The US now began to maintain a fleet presence off the Vietnamese coast. In September 1964, to provide for any eventuality, the carrier *Ranger* (CVA–61) was despatched to the Gulf of Tonkin, arriving on the 18th. This coincided with the movement of several Air Force units into South Vietnam. In the event there was no immediate call for naval forces. Many believed that the Viet Cong threat remained a less serious matter than the internal struggle and bickering within the Saigon regime.

In another of the seemingly endless changes in the Saigon regime, on 26 October the former mayor of the capital, Tran Van Huong, was installed as premier of a provisional civil government. Huong was to prove unable to bring order to his administration or to be right about significant victories over the Viet Cong.

The Viet Cong staged a mortar attack on busy Bien Hoa air base during the night of 31 October/1 November 1964. Four Americans were killed and thirty wounded. A large number of aircraft were damaged. Included in the casualties were five B–57 Canberras destroyed and thirteen damaged.

On the first Tuesday in November, Lyndon Johnson defeated Barry Goldwater at the polls and was elected for a four-year term of office. Johnson would be eligible to run for a second four-year term in 1968 and it was widely assumed that he would do so. He had promised Americans a 'Great Society', built with government aid to broad sectors of the economy. He had also convinced many that Goldwater – a Reserve general in the USAF and a military pilot – would have solved the Vietnam problem by launching a bombing campaign against North Vietnam. While there were few direct quotes on the question, most voters believed Johnson would not do such a thing.

Skyraider Pilots

The A–1 Skyraider was perhaps the most numerous warplane in South Vietnam at the time, being operated by the VNAF's 514th, 516th and 518th Fighter Squadrons and by the USAF's First Air Commando Squadron. Armorers at Bien Hoa realized that the A–1 – or 'Maytag Washing Machine' as someone christened the aircraft – had carried numerous varieties of underwing ordnance over the years. Each time a new bomb or rocket was introduced, the Skyraider was re-wired to carry it. One crew chief remembered finding some of the aircraft with up to 500lb (227kg) of wire inside the wings. 'Nobody could remember which wires were connected to what. So we had no way to remove the excess, and our pilots paid a penalty in extra flying weight.'

Communications were poor. Faulty bomb fuses caused a premature mid-air detonation of 500-pounders which killed a squadron pilot near Rach-Gia in the Mekong Delta. The old 20mm cannon on the Skyraider were so worn out that they sometimes exploded and threw shrapnel in all directions, on one occasion narrowly missing a pilot's head.

Major Charles Vasiliadis, known as 'Vas' for short, arrived at Bien Hoa in November 1964 to join the First Air Commando Squadron and promptly racked up the first of no fewer than 493 combat missions in the

This US Army Bell UH–1B Iroquois, better known by now as the Huey, is a 'hog' or gunship, armed with an M–6 machine-gun system. This 12 February 1964 view of the Huey was taken before most Army units began using toned-down colors. (US ARMY)

Somewhat like the guard who rode 'shotgun' on the Old West's stage coaches, the door gunner of the US Army helicopter became a familiar sight. This gunner of a UH–1 Huey gunship is holding the Army's standard-issue M–60 machine-gun. (BELL)

A–1E, the 'wide-body' version of the Skyraider, or 'Spad' as it was now being called. One day, leading a flight while using the call-sign 'Norm 61', Vas bombed a Viet Cong tunnel complex in a densely wooded area 8 miles (13km) west of the Ben Cat US Special Forces camp. A few days later he was carrying 500-pounders (227kg bombs) against a VC-occupied village a mere 20 miles (32km) north-west of Bien Hoa.

On this mission, Vas forgot to throw a switch to change from the Skyraider's external fuel tank to internal fuel. Pulling away from a bomb run, his requisite Vietnamese passenger sound asleep beside him, Vas applied full rudder to cope with the very strong torque characteristic of the Skyraider and was climbing over flat paddy fields when the big R–3350 engine began to splutter and groan. His passenger snapped awake, thought it was time to bail out, and began to climb over the side.

Vasiliadis had sharp memories of once finding a downed VNAF crew mate after the Viet Cong had castrated him. He did not want his own crewman to suffer a similar fate. At the same time, he had to get control of his aircraft. He released the stick long enough to grab the Vietnamese and the Skyraider's nose plummeted downwards. He released the Vietnamese long enough to grab the stick and the man tried to bail out again. 'No, no, no!' Vas shrieked above the spluttering of the engine and the roar of the airstream blasting into the open canopy. Rice paddies spun crazily in front of them as Vasiliadis belatedly remembered the fuel switch, flipped it, and felt the engine belch back to life. The Skyraider settled into a gentle climb. The Vietnamese nodded, grinned sheepishly, and sat back in his seat.

December saw the first overseas deployment of the USAF's F–4C Phantom fighter – the Navy F–4B had reached the

US Navy F-4B Phantoms from the USS *Constellation* (CVA-64) were in the air during the Gulf of Tonkin air strikes on 5 August 1964, but they encountered no air opposition and did no fighting. The Phantom was widely in service throughout the Fleet by the end of 1964 and would soon be seen in Vietnam dropping bombs – like this F-4B, striking Viet Cong targets in South Vietnam. (USN)

Gulf of Tonkin aboard the USS *Constellation* (CV-64) earlier in the year – when the 'Triple Nickel' 555th Tactical Fighter Squadron arrived at Okinawa and prepared for a temporary deployment to Thailand. Within weeks there were to be F-4s in South Vietnam at Da Nang and Cam Ranh Bay.

Christmas Eve Bombing

Nobody ever claimed that the Brink Hotel in Saigon was any great shakes, The old, colonial style building had been taken over as a US Army officers' billet and was replete with all the little pleasures Americans always needed to fight a war, including a shoeshine stand, a small PX selling nylons, make-up and cosmetics to our all-male force, and a dining area nicknamed 'the Pit'. Prices being low everywhere, most of the men preferred to eat up the street where several joints offered hamburgers and other amenities.

On the afternoon of 24 December 1964, tinsel hung from the ceiling in the dining area and a plastic Christmas tree was alight in a corner. With Army officer-advisors preparing to celebrate Christmas Eve, a Viet Cong sapper on a bicycle hurled a 250lb (113kg) *plastique* (explosive charge) into the place and the Brink Hotel exploded, throwing flames and debris out into the street and collapsing upon itself. Two Americans and 51 South Vietnamese were killed.

Unknown then, of course, was the fact that Ambassador Maxwell Taylor had urged that there be swift and powerful retaliation against North Vietnam for any such VC provocation. Taylor had been consulting in Washington during the week of 27 November 1964, and found himself caught between policy-makers who wanted to withdraw and those who wanted to retaliate. He had suggested a compromise under which the US would strike back for specific VC provocations, but only with South Vietnamese participation to preserve the 'native' character of the war. That did not happen this time, however. The latest South Vietnamese government under General Nguyen Khanh was in turmoil, seeking to cope with protests by Buddhist agitators, and was in no condition to participate in a credible joint response. The Brink Hotel bombing came and went.

A week later, in a furious action at Binh Gia, VC troops overwhelmed the ARVN and killed 177 South Vietnamese soldiers and six Americans. Unlike the Saigon hotel bombing, it scarcely made the newspapers. At Binh Gia a Special Forces advisor sat in the grass looking at burned-out huts and destruction. He inserted a blade of grass between his teeth, turned to a buddy, and shrugged. 'When the hell are we going to be able to hit these bastards back, anyway?'

Fixed-wing Gunships

For some time the USAF had been experimenting with the notion that a large fixed-wing aeroplane flying in a pylon turn could bring side-mounted guns to bear on a ground target with great intensity. Although there were doubters, among them Tactical Air Command's General Walter C. Sweeney, Jr, who felt that a gunship could not survive the gunfire expected in Vietnam and fulfill its mission, Air Force General John P. McConnell was impressed by stateside test results with a Convair C-131 and Douglas C-47. McConnell noted in particular that a gunship might be effective in defending hamlets and outposts under night attack. He was determined to test the idea under live fire.

On 2 December 1964 a test team headed by Captain Ronald W. Terry arrived at Bien Hoa airfield not far from Saigon and were quickly followed by gun kits to convert two C-47s, gunsights, and ammunition. Terry began a series of test flights, some of them over-water, to teach C-47 pilots how to acquire a target, roll in on it, and commence the turn.

The ancient 'Gooney Bird' now had a 'fighter' version, as the FC-47 gunship was initially named. The aircraft flew the first of several day combat missions on 15 December 1964. Captain Terry and crew worked with a forward air controller (FAC), firing successfully on Viet Cong sampans, buildings, trails and suspected jungle staging areas. From the beginning the FC-47 had been seen as a night weapon – one of a number of ways the US sought to take command of the night from 'Victor Charlie', or the Viet Cong – and was capable of dropping flares while orbiting overhead to relieve a beseiged encampment.

The FC-47's first night mission on 23-24 December 1964 seemed to prove that this new role for the 'Gooney Bird' could blunt the ever-increasing night attacks on South Vietnamese outposts. Once again, the gunship 'Gooney Bird' showed itself to be very effective in hosing down formations of enemy troops. In due course the aircraft was to be redesignated AC-47 and known to many as 'Puff the Magic Dragon'.

On 31 December 1964 the number of American troops in South Vietnam was 23,000.

1965

THE BIG BUILD-UP

It was the single event that most altered the perceptions of Americans – those on the scene, and those at home – about what was happening in Vietnam. On 10 April 1965 two battalions of United States Marines landed, the first of many.

Before the Marine landing, those first weeks of 1965 were unique. It was the last time Vietnam was far down on the list of topics which concerned most Americans. Other events, at the time, captured more attention. Congressmen Jerry Ford launched a successful attempt to replace Charles A. Halleck as the House Minority Leader. Egypt's fiery Gamal Abdul Nasser spouted off against the US and one of his MiGs shot down an unarmed cargo plane belonging to a US oil company. When Robert F. Kennedy was sworn in on 4 January to serve in the same chamber as Edward M. Kennedy, it marked the first time brothers had served in the United States Senate in 162 years. In London the absence of Vice President Hubert H. Humphrey from the 31 March funeral of Sir Winston Churchill was viewed by many Britons as an affront. In New York city Mayor Robert F. Wagner was being sorely criticized because his city was said to have reached an intolerable state with its strikes, slums, crime, traffic snarls and racial tensions. Vietnam? At the outset of 1965 a black person was still called a negro, and sometimes worse, and the struggle for racial integration received more headlines than the storming ashore at Da Nang of United States Marines.

The Marines could have arrived by stepping off a commercial jetliner, as other US servicemen did. Instead, they waded out of the sea, M–14 rifles at the ready, field packs and pit shovels clanking – the same way that they had landed on Tarawa, Saipan and Iwo Jima. But on this beach no one was shooting at them.

To PFC James L. Waple, the worst thing about it was being seasick and retching all over the inside of the LST [landing ship, tank] that took them from Okinawa to Da Nang. 'They decided to put us ashore Hollywood-style, replete with amphibious landing on the beach near Da Nang. Unfortunately, there was no enemy entrenched on the beach so we got wet for nothing. We came ashore drenched with salt water and were greeted by a few Marines, who were mostly curious, and a couple of children with flowers.'

Other Marines grumbled about getting wet while carrying the 100lb (44kg) of gear a Marine needed to live. The Da Nang area and the Chu Lai peninsula were hot and dry in April, but the Marines stepped on to solid ground soaking wet.

The converted escort carrier USS *Core* approaches a berth in Saigon harbor on 17 June 1965, carrying more than 70 warplanes to be turned over to the Vietnamese Air Force. Visible on deck are Douglas EA–1F Skyraiders. (USAF)

The air war would have been of no importance if it did not help the fighting man on the ground. Taking cover on 31 July 1965 while his platoon is fired on by the Viet Cong, Marine Corporal Ronald S. Newman typifies the Americans who joined the big build-up in South Vietnam. (USMC)

In March during the feverish post-monsoon weather, 3,500 Marines had put to sea aboard the vessels *Mount McKinley*, *Henrico*, *Union* and *Vancouver*. These four ships of Amphibious Task Force 76 took six weeks to reach the Vietnam coast and spent the last few days pitching up and down in vile seas. Exhausted, muggy, seasick, Major General Frederick J. Karch's Marines made a full-fledged landing, assaulting an empty beach. There *were* Viet Cong in the area – an entire regiment were to confront the Marines soon – but at the time of landing there was no enemy.

It was the beginning of the build-up. It was the end of a small and distant guerrilla war which had seemed romantic and a little dangerous but not very important. The sight of regular Marines storming ashore was played across TV screens in America and no one believed – nor should they have – the official explanation. The official story was that Marines were in Vietnam solely to protect American airfields. In fact, they were going into combat. Although the fiction of an air base defense role was to be maintained stalwartly, the truth was that Americans were advisors no longer.

Looking back at 1965 (and at events which preceded the Marines' arrival), it hardly seems possible that the year began with US troop strength in South Vietnam at a mere 23,000.

Lyndon Johnson, inaugurated for a new term on 20 January 1965, followed up his election victory by appointing an inter-agency working group to examine all alternatives available to him in Vietnam. Such groups rarely arrived at unpopular conclusions but Johnson's lieutenants did report that the latest Saigon regime headed by Major General Nguyen Khanh was tottering, that the communists were pouring men and materiel into South Vietnam, and that the very survival of a valued American ally was in danger.

At this worst possible juncture, *US News & World Report* revealed that the new US Ambassador, Maxwell Taylor, had gotten off on the wrong foot with Khanh and even worse with Khanh's powerful wife. *Life* magazine said that Johnson's first priority was 'to come to grips with the badly deteriorating situation in South Vietnam'. Critics warned Johnson against a bigger investment of blood and treasure, pointing out that the South Vietnamese often lacked the will to fight and that no number of Americans, not even ten times those now in country, could prop up a corrupt regime and faltering army. Johnson's decision, it seemed, was clear: he should withdraw US forces and waste no men or weaponry in a faraway land that few Americans could find on the map.

Ironically, ten times 23,000 was less than half of the eventual American commitment. Even in early 1965, Saigon-based General Westmoreland was saying that he needed more US troops. It was the beginning of a

They started calling it Johnson's war. Lyndon B. Johnson (here with wife Lady Bird) was in charge. The President had promised Americans a 'Great Society' and was annoyed that Vietnam kept distracting his attention from social programs, but he believed his advisors when they argued that more American troops were the solution to the problem. (USAF)

A Guam-based Boeing B–52F Stratofortress (57–0144) loaded with 750lb (340kg) bombs crosses the South Vietnamese coastline en route to a target in October 1965. B–52 'Arc Light' missions began earlier in the year. The huge bombers struck from high altitude, raining down bombs by the mile amid Viet Cong jungle areas. (USAF)

Typical of the way the Viet Cong operated right in the midst of their enemies, in mid-1965 they planted a bomb in the American Embassy chancery (left). A number of people were killed and wounded and damage was spread along the street for more than a block (right). (USAF)

prolonged period in which the general would repeatedly increase his estimate of the number of men he required.

To be fair, Westmoreland was repeatedly provoked by a determined and relentless enemy. For years Pentagon officers had told anyone willing to listen that the US could fight effectively only by carrying the war to North Vietnam. An excuse for just such action occurred on 7 February 1965 when, in the latest of a continuing series of provocations, the Viet Cong mortared and assaulted the American compound at Pleiku in the central highlands, killing eight Americans, wounding dozens, and destroying five helicopters.

Johnson ordered American dependants out of the country. He authorized the first sustained air strikes against North Vietnam, known initially as 'Flaming Dart'. By 7 March 1965 Johnson had authorized the ongoing campaign of air strikes against North Vietnam known as 'Rolling Thunder', destined to last more than three years with intermittent breaks aimed unsuccessfully at prompting negotiations.

Amid all this, stability was still lacking in Saigon. General Khanh, leader of the Armed Forces Council, had agreed to support Premier Huong, but at the end of January he ousted Huong from office. There followed a period of unrest and turmoil, ending in the exile of Khanh later in the year.

The South Vietnamese Air Force had been growing slowly and, for a brief time, participated in air strikes up north, flying A–1 Skyraiders. In fact, on the first raid above the 17th Parallel, USAF Captain Al Bache, advising the VNAF's 514th Fighter Squadron, watched in awe as Air Marshal Nguyen Cao Ky led his Skyraiders to Vinh only to attack the wrong target. Ky was a popular and charismatic figure on the Saigon scene, not only in the Air Force but also in the volatile world of South Vietnamese politics. Originally a transport pilot who transitioned to the Skyraider, Ky has been described by men who flew with him as a superb leader but, at best, an average pilot.

The air war over North Vietnam was now under way in earnest. In South Vietnam there was much debate about what to do next.

It had long been evident that this war would never have traditional front lines or

The McDonnell RF-4C Phantom began operating from Tan Son Nhut airfield in October 1965. The first aircraft to arrive were painted in the same gull gray and white paint scheme already illustrated. Later they were to be camouflaged. RF-4Cs flew photo-gathering missions throughout South Vietnam while RF-101C Voodoos did much of the reconnaissance work over the north. (USAF)

rear areas. One could get killed at Tan Son Nhut airport as easily as on combat patrol. Westmoreland and other commanders no longer liked British expert Robert Thompson's idea of establishing 'strategic hamlets' – this notion seemed to relinquish rural areas and nocturnal hours to the Viet Cong without a fight – but were hard put to come up with a better idea. American and ARVN troops had long been carrying out 'search and destroy' missions, but these seemed increasingly irrelevant as the size of ground battles grew. While Americans poured into the country and experts searched for a coherent strategy, airpower was used to hit the enemy in the north and south.

Naval Air War

With the widening of the war, the US Navy temporarily had four aircraft-carriers on station in Vietnamese waters. 'Yankee Station' was the dot on the map in the Gulf of Tonkin where carriers launched missions against North Vietnam. Increasingly, however, 'Dixie Station' in the South China Sea – springboard for air strikes on *South* Vietnam – gained importance.

With the USS *Hancock* (CVA–19), *Coral Sea* (CVA–43), *Ranger* (CVA–61) and *Midway* (CVA–41) operating in the combat zone, the Navy was very busy, north and south. Flying a pre-planned air strike or an impromptu close support mission in South Vietnam was no picnic, and one frustrating aspect was not being able to see ground fire when the enemy was shooting from jungle cover in broad daylight. Studies showed, however, that carrier pilots were more nervous about making a hook-arrested landing on the pitching deck of the flat-top than about being shot at.

An aircraft-carrier had a crew of 3,000–5,000 men, of whom perhaps 300 were pilots or aircrew members. Life aboard ship was no picnic, either, especially for the ship's company and the men in the Carrier Air Wing who routinely clocked 14- or 16-hour days simply to 'keep 'em flying'. Men worked when exhausted. They worked at night in the eerie glare of sodium lamps. They worked amid wrenching claustrophobia. By virtue of its very purpose, the aircraft-carrier had everything stuffed into the minimum space needed to contain it – bunks and bombs, food and fighters, refrigerators and rockets. Back home, self-appointed experts in economics might scold Lyndon Johnson for seeking guns and butter at the same time; the aircraft-carrier had both, but in the most cramped space possible.

Although there were differences based on size and age, a typical Carrier Air Wing had two fighter squadrons (Vought F–8

The Vought F–8 Crusader was the principal fighter of the US Navy and Marine Corps as the war widened. The Crusader is best remembered for its role as an air-to-air fighter, but both Navy and Marines operated the F–8E fighter-bomber version, shown here on a combat mission from Da Nang with the 'Death Angels' of VMF–235. (USMC)

Defense Secretary McNamara and MACV chief General Westmoreland confer with Vietnamese General Tee, I Corps commander in the Da Nang area, during an August 1965 fact-finding trip by McNamara. (USMC)

Crusaders or McDonnell F–4 Phantoms), two or sometimes three light attack squadrons (Douglas A–4 Skyhawks), and a medium attack squadron (Douglas A–1 Skyraiders). At this juncture some carriers had a detachment of a heavy attack squadron (Douglas A–3 Skywarriors). Most had reconnaissance detachments (Vought RF–8 Crusaders), airborne early warning craft (Grumman E–1B Tracers or EA–1E/EA–1F Skyraiders) and helicopters (Kaman UH–2 Seasprites). Operating with a mixture of jet and propeller-driven aircraft, which needed different fuels, was a tough proposition and some Navy planners were already looking to an all-jet Carrier Air Wing in the future.

Because of budgetary constraints prior to the big build-up, the Navy suffered from serious shortages of aircrews, aircraft, ordnance and carriers as soon as the war expanded in 1965. Intake and preparation of new personnel was increased at Naval Air Training Command bases back home, but some things just could not be done quickly.

Design, development, purchase and construction of a new aircraft-carrier was a major political, fiscal and physical effort and very time-consuming. Throughout the entire war in fact, only two carriers were commissioned, the USS *America* (CVA–66) in January 1965 and the USS *John F. Kennedy* (CVA–67) in September 1968 – and the latter vessel never reached the war zone.

Several other carriers were of Second World War vintage and were near the end of their useful lives or due for major refit. This was true of the USS *Midway* (CVA–41), which is usually remembered as the vessel which got the first and last Navy MiG kills of the war. *Midway* departed the combat zone in 1965, went back to Alameda, California, for a major refit, and was not in service again until five years later.

Weather over the South China Sea and the Indo-Chinese land mass infuriated every man who flew, but particularly angered the carrier-based naval aviator who faced the full range of nasty conditions over sea and land. During a 'good' day in 'clear' weather, every nook and cranny beneath the Vietnamese ridgelines was shrouded beneath patches of cloud.

The winter north-east monsoon season between December and May brought violent storms with cloud cover which often extended from 2,000 or 3,000ft (610 or 915m) to 40,000ft (12,196m). Long periods of dismal visibility and the almost complete absence of all-weather strike aircraft (save only the Grumman A–6 Intruder) meant that pilots were almost always flying in the worst conditions. Meanwhile the wet murk formed a protective cloak over the massive influx of men and materiel being sent to the Viet Cong from North Vietnam.

The Grumman A–6A Intruder arrived in South-East Asia with the 'Sunday Punchers' of attack squadron VA–75 aboard the USS *Independence* (CVA–62), flying its first combat mission on 1 July 1965 against targets 'up north'. The twin-engined Grumman product was decidedly subsonic, with a maximum speed of perhaps 684mph (1,102km/h) at sea-level and a combat radius of around 600 miles (960km). If it worked right – the 'Sunday Punchers' had been sent

The Republic F–105 Thunderchief became perhaps the best-known US aircraft in the 'out-country war' against North Vietnam. F–105s were stationed in neighbouring Thailand and were not generally employed within South Vietnam. By the end of 1965 most USAF warplanes were acquiring camouflage paint schemes like that shown here. (REPUBLIC)

The Lockheed F–104C Starfighter put in short tours of duty in the combat zone twice. The first F–104Cs in Vietnam belonged to the 435th Tactical Fighter Squadron at Da Nang between April and December 1965. The F–104Cs returned to South-East Asia in July 1966, based at Udorn in Thailand. This 1965 view taken in South Vietnam shows the 'Zip 104' with a load of two 750lb (340kg) bombs. The fighter did not have the range to carry these bombs very far. (USAF)

to war to find out – the Intruder would almost certainly be the Navy's antidote to the scummy weather.

The key to all-weather operations in the Intruder was the computerized internal system known as DIANE (digital integrated attack and navigational equipment). The acronym had been created because Diane was the name of Grumman engineer Bob Nafis' daughter. But DIANE was no lady in 1965. There were maintenance and reliability problems. 'Down' time was unconscionable. At first there was real doubt that the A–6 Intruder would be successful.

A two-man, side-by-side cockpit straddled the nose of the distinctly ungainly Intruder. Humorists looked at the oddly shaped aircraft and insisted that the pointed end was supposed to be at the front.

Elegant or not, the Intruder was soon flying missions over South Vietnam where, increasingly, American troops directly engaged the Viet Cong. Aboard the USS *Kitty Hawk* (CVA–63) the 'Black Falcons' of VA–85, the second medium attack squadron to fly the Intruder in the war zone, saw action from 'Dixie Station', beginning in November 1965. After a vicious land battle and the virtual slaughter of the ARVN 7th Regiment, *Kitty Hawk*'s Carrier Air Wing 11 bombed, rocketed and strafed VC positions in the Michelin plantation, a scant 45 miles (70km) north of Saigon, inflicting heavy casualties and providing relief to beleaguered ground forces.

Marine Air

The April 1965 arrival of US Marine ground forces was accompanied by an impressive show of Marine airpower. Captain John D. Cummings, a back-seat F–4B Phantom RIO (radar intercept officer) with the 'Gray Ghosts' of Squadron VMFA–531, found conditions at Da Nang incredibly crude when the Marine Phantom crews arrived:

The first Phantoms to fly in Vietnam, as distinguished from those operating in neighboring Thailand, were brought by the US Marine Corps in April 1965. The 'Grey Ghosts' of squadron VMFA–531 were the first to fly from Da Nang. One squadron which came soon after was the 'Crusaders' of VMFA–122 headed by Indochina veteran Lieutenant Colonel John Verdi. One of the latter squadron's F–4B Phantoms is seen here. (USMC)

At Cam Ranh Bay on 29 July 1965, General William C. Westmoreland and Ambassador Maxwell D. Taylor, both former paratroopers, join a reunion with members of the 'Screaming Eagles', the 101st Airborne Division. (USAF)

Air Force F–4C Phantoms arrived in South-East Asia looking like this, in the peacetime gull grey finish with white undersides with a peacetime 'buzz number' just ahead of the national insignia on the fuselage and a Tactical Air Command badge on the tail. By late 1965, they were being camouflaged. This Phantom carries a strike camera beneath its port inboard wing pylon. (USAF)

'I remember choking clouds of dust, everywhere. The only other guys at Da Nang were the Marine UH–34 helicopter guys from the "Shu Fly" operation which dated to 1963, and we harbored a little resentment because they lorded their combat experience over us and were living in old, cool French colonial buildings while we had tents or slept beneath the wings of our Phantoms. We'd arrived in Vietnam with our toilet bags, our flight gear, and our socks. We were dusty and gritty, waiting for portable showers to arrive. I found the only flush toilet on our side of the base and I kept the location secret from most of the guys.

'In those days nobody knew much about flying air-to-ground missions at night. It was true that "Charlie" rules the night. The VC had almost complete freedom to run patrols, set up ambushes, and reposition their units. We did fly some night missions, including one with a C–123 orbiting over some VC, dropping million-plus candlepower flares which just about burned our eyes out.

'We flew all sorts of missions in the Phantom. I flew one all the way down by the suburbs of Saigon. We had the newer, low-drag bombs rather than the box-finned World War II stuff the stateside Marine units were equipped with, but we never had enough of the bombs, not ever. Our guys would go out with a six-bomb MER [multiple ejector rack] with only three bombs. This was during the "non-bomb", as McNamara called it.' Throughout the conflict, there would be instances when the number of bombs available was insufficient for the aircraft committed to battle.

While Marine Phantoms operated from Da Nang, across the airfield from Air Force F–100s and F–104s, more Marines moved into Chu Lai to build an airfield where none had existed before. The air base resulted from the expanding Marine presence; by July 1965 ground combat Marines were pitted against the Viet Cong in Operation 'Starlite' and it was publicly acknowledged that they were taking offensive action. Initially Chu Lai was home to two squadrons of A–4 Skyhawks, the same lightweight, single-seat attack craft serving aboard Navy carriers offshore.

Carnage at Bien Hoa

At Bien Hoa, where a VC mortar attack had destroyed five B–57 Canberras and damaged thirteen the previous Hallowe'en, it was time for a debacle which would forever evoke unpleasant overtones to men in the B–57 community – and this time, the communist guerrillas had nothing to do with it.

On Sunday morning, 16 May 1965, Captain Charles Fox was about to start engines to lead 'Jade' Flight, a formation of four B–57s, on a strike mission. Fox was carrying a typical bombload – nine 500lb (227kg) bombs in his Canberra's internal bay and four 750-pounders (340kg) under the wings.

One moment, there was no hint that anything was wrong. The next, Fox's aircraft exploded with a brilliant flash and a concussion that sent shrapnel and debris raining along the Bien Hoa flight line. Captain Howard Greene, pilot of the nearby B–57 using the call-sign 'Jade 4', led his back-seater in abandoning their aircraft. Greene, his seat parachute flapping against his hind side, sprinted past fuel storage bladders, leapt over concertina barbed wire, and took cover in a ditch – just as new explosions reverberated. For more than a minute new explosions shook the Bien Hoa ramp as B–57s went up, bombs exploded, and 20mm cannon shells cooked off.

Fox and six other members of 'Jade' Flight were among those who died in the gaseous, flaming carnage. The reverberations sent an entire J65 engine flying for half a mile. In all, 28 men were killed, 105 wounded. Among aircraft totally destroyed were ten B–57s, eleven VNAF A–1H Skyraiders and a Navy F–8 Crusader which had landed only moments earlier.

Army Aviation

On 7 May 1965 the first full-scale combat unit of the US Army, the 173rd Airborne Brigade, arrived from its peacetime garrison on Okinawa and took up positions around Bien Hoa and Vung Tau. Again, the Johnson administration flogged the fiction that the troopers' purpose was to provide airfield security. This final attempt publicly to deny an American combat role evaporated on 27 June when the 173rd spearheaded the largest airlift of the war, with 144 Army helicopters carrying men into War Zone D in an area where Allied forces had not operated for a year.

Strategic Air Command's giant B–52 Stratofortress bombers, built to carry hydrogen bombs, flew the first of countless conventional bombing missions under the program name 'Arc Light' on 17 June 1965, with twenty-eight B–52Fs striking Viet Cong concentrations in Binh Duong Province. A stupid tactical mistake caused two of the B–52Fs to collide while marshaling off the coast, killing all aboard both aircraft.

On 18 June 1965 yet another change in the Saigon leadership occurred. Major General Nguyen Van Thieu was installed as president and Nguyen Cao Ky, the VNAF commander, as premier. Ky, it will be recalled, had started his flying career in transports and moved to the A–1H Skyraider. He and his beautiful wife liked to tour military installations in matching flight coveralls. Some American critics, already

For a time Saigon's air arm operated a few B–57 Canberra bombers, including the aircraft shown here being taxied out on a mission. The Canberra proved too complex for the Vietnamese, however, and in due course their few B–57s reverted to the USAF. (USAF)

torpid from the seeming endlessness of the conflict, questioned whether Thieu and Ky would provide any more leadership or stability than their hapless predecessors.

In July 1965 Secretary of Defense Robert S. McNamara made one of his periodic visits to Saigon, but now McNamara was no longer uttering the previous year's language about American withdrawals. Now McNamara spoke of a 'phased build-up' of US forces in Vietnam, as if there existed a master plan and everybody in Washington was of one mind.

Phase I, said McNamara, was defined as the period when the US would 'stop losing the war'. Phase II would be the period 'in which we intend to start winning'. In fact, the American footsoldier was going to begin winning on the battlefield almost immediately. Winning the war was another proposition.

As if to confirm that Americans really were being killed and wounded, the Internal Revenue Service, for purposes of establishing an income tax exemption, reached a finding that Vietnam had been a combat zone since the beginning of the previous year.

In a move just as fitting, Pacific Air Forces (PACAF), the Hawaii-based headquarters for the USAF in the region, proposed that aircraft in the combat zone be dressed in war paint. A three-color camouflaged scheme was created, and is usually known as the T.O. 1–1–4 paint scheme after the technical order which created it. Forward air controller (FAC) Cessna O–1 Bird Dogs retained their uncamouflaged finish to enhance visibility against the jungle background. The first aircraft in-theater to receive camouflage paint was a C–130 Hercules transport.

On 6 August 1965, after more than two years of combat flying in South Vietnam, the 'Patricia Lynn' RB–57E Canberra detachment suffered its first casualty. On a night infra-red reconnaissance mission in aircraft 55-4243, pilot Captain Dick Damon and navigator Lieutenant Dick Crist were hit by small-arms fire. The aircraft was set afire. The crew ejected and the aircraft crashed a short distance from Tan Son Nhut.

Landing by parachute in the darkness,

In the Battle of Ia Drang and from then on, American soldiers arrived by helicopter. September 1965 marked the introduction of the Boeing CH–47A Chinook when fifty-six helicopters began flying from the First Cavalry's base camp at Anh Khe. The Chinook, inevitably nicknamed 'Shithook', was a battlefield mobility replacement for the piston-driven Sikorsky CH–37 Mojave and was powered by two Lycoming T–55–L–7 turboshaft engines offering 4,400shp. (US ARMY)

Crist came face-to-face with a Vietnamese. Drilled to cope with the enemy, Crist grabbed the man by the collar and pressed his cocked .38 service pistol into the man's stomach. Seeing others gathered around, he belatedly realized that he was in a group of friendly South Vietnamese. Embarrassed, Crist put his pistol away. His story was later widely told among flight crews to make the point that a quick trigger finger could cause a friendly group to become suddenly very unfriendly. The 'Patricia Lynn' detachment, which had grown from two Canberras to five, now had four aircraft left.

Now the build-up of American forces gathered momentum. On 27 August 1965 the 1st Cavalry Division (Airmobile) – derived from the 11th Air Assault Division which had pioneered helicopter operations in the US – began to arrive Anh Khe. A shoulder patch with a silhouette of a stallion's head was the mark of the historic First Cav. Now the Cavalry rode helicopters instead of horses. The First Cav had 15,787 men, 1,600 vehicles and 428 helicopters, plus six Grumman OV–1 Mohawk spotter aircraft.

The spirit of the Cavalrymen was typified by their first commander, Brigadier General John Wright, Jr, who bounded out of a Huey with machete in hand and ordered the scrub to be cleared until it was as close-cut as a 'Golf Course', the nickname quickly applied to the Anh Khe base.

In October 1965 the air cavalry was called into action when the largest unit of North Vietnamese regulars yet seen laid seige to the Special Forces camp at Plei Mei. There followed a series of fire fights and maneuvering engagements with numbers of American soldiers inserted on the battlefield by air for the first time. The expanding battle between Cavalrymen and NVA regulars lasted thirty-one days. It marked the first time a division had fought a continuing action using helicopters for virtually all troop movements.

The Battle of Ia Drang Valley, it was called. Ia Drang was the first test of the helicopter in a division-scale battle. It was also the first challenge to a citizen army, the first ever maintained by the US in peacetime through universal conscription. Most important, at Ia Drang for the first time the American soldier came face-to-face not merely with Viet Cong guerrillas but with the NVA (North Vietnamese Army), Hanoi's seasoned regulars, the same fiercely motivated troops who had booted the French out of South-East Asia. In 1965 the NVA regular was the best-trained and most experienced fighting soldier in the world. At Ia Drang, over the length of two fortnights, he was defeated by the American Air Cavalryman in a battle so decisive that there should never again have arisen any question about who would prevail on the battlefield.

The Battle of Ia Drang Valley saw the use of all helicopters then in inventory. The Bell UH–1B Huey was used as a gunship or medical evacuation ('Dust-off') ambulance, while the longer, more powerful Bell UH–1D Huey was the usual 'Slick', or troop transport. The bubble-topped Bell OH–13G Sioux ('Possum') and the Hiller OH–23 Raven were standard LOH, or light observation helicopters. The Sikorsky CH–54 Tarhe or Flying Crane carried freight, artillery pieces and supplies in a detachable cab beneath its fuselage. The twin-rotor Boeing CH–47 Chinook – which Americans unavoidably named the 'Shit-hook' – became another carrier of freight, artillery, or men.

At Ia Drang 434 aircraft flew 54,000 sorties carrying 73,700 personnel, delivered 5,048 tons of cargo to the troops and brought an additional 8,216 tons into Pleiku from port cities like Qui Nhon. Artillery batteries were re-located 67 times by Chinooks.

Air Force Operations

The USAF had begun the year with four principal bases in South Vietnam, Saigon's Tan Son Nhut airfield (used since October 1961); Bien Hoa air base (since November 1961), Da Nang (January 1962) and Pleiku (July 1962). Binh Thuy air base was opened in May 1965 and Cam Ranh Bay in November 1965. The latter, built in tidal marsh and mudflats on the coast, was an engineering miracle, a marvel of the excesses of American technology. F–4 Phantoms flew from Cam Ranh Bay in operations over

In April 1965, Brigadier General Frederick J. Karch led the Marine amphibious landings which began the massive build-up of American forces in South Vietnam. On 4 September 1965, Karch had lunch with New York attorney and former Vice-President Richard M. Nixon in an expeditionary tent at Chu Lai. US forces numbered only 23,000 at the beginning of the year, but the arrival of Karch's Marines marked the end of the American role as advisors and the beginning of openly acknowledged combat. (USMC)

South Vietnam. (Most missions up north were mounted from airfields in Thailand.)

On 18 February 1965 Americans were relieved of the requirement to carry a Vietnamese crew member while flying combat missions. This removed the fiction that USAF pilots were advisors. At Bien Hoa, where the 1st Air Commando Squadron was flying the A–1 Skyraider, Major Charles C. Vasiliadis threw up his hands with joy. On a recent mission the sleeping Vietnamese beside him had been having nightmares and began talking to himself.

Public attention throughout 1965 was focused on the air war up north where Phantoms and Thunderchiefs were attacking heavily defended targets and fighting MiGs. There was planty of action in the south, however, with the same Phantoms and 'Thuds', as well as many other types. On 23 October the 4503rd Tactical Fighter Squadron (Provisional), with its twelve Northrop F–5A Freedom Fighters, arrived and set up shop at Bien Hoa air base. These were the only F–5s in US inventory, having been diverted from production for foreign F–5 purchasers. As part of Operation 'Skoshi Tiger', to test the suitability of the F–5 as a potential first jet for the VNAF, the American squadron flew its first combat mission five hours after arriving from the States.

The F–5A had been designed as an inexpensive lightweight tactical fighter. At the very time the F–5A was being blooded, Northrop was beginning worldwide sales to Third World air forces, which were to continue for nearly two more decades and result in over 3,000 sales of the F–5A and subsequent versions. The twin-engined configuration offered extra insurance against hits from low-level VC ground fire. The first supersonic fighter to reach many of the air forces which used it, the F–5A could fly at Mach 1.4 and could be dived at 818mph (1,315km/h).

Fixed-Wing Gunships

An experiment the year before, the fixed-wing gunship lost its novelty and became a guardian angel to beseiged combatants at isolated outposts. On 8 February 1965 the FC–47 gunship with its array of side-firing 7.62mm miniguns was sent to the Bong Son area in the face of the Viet Cong offensive in the central highlands. For 4½ hours, the gunship poured 20,500 rounds of

'Puff the Magic Dragon', also known as the 'Dragonship' or 'Spooky', was a nocturnal saviour to American and South Vietnamese troops at beseiged outposts deep in Viet Cong country. The Douglas AC–47, originally designated FC–47, had a row of 7.62mm miniguns mounted along the port side of its fuselage and could fly overhead in a pylon turn, bringing torrents of gunfire raining down on the enemy. (USAF)

The 4503rd Tactical Fighter Squadron (Provisional) tested the Northrop F–5A Freedom Fighter in low-level bombing sorties against the Viet Cong insurgents. In-country operations in 1965–6 proved that the F–5A was an effective, low-cost fighter suitable for a less developed country's air arm and the type was chosen for the VNAF. Here, aircraft 63–8428 is bombing a VC emplacement. (USAF)

SP6 Sidney S. Reeder was one of the Air Cavalrymen who came to their new domicile at the Anh Khe 'golf course' to unleash a new form of air warfare on the world. Crew chief on a Bell UH–1B Huey helicopter gunship, Sid was shot down twice while fighting in the Battle of Ia Drang Valley, where the First Cavalry Division engaged North Vietnamese regulars and inflicted a stunning defeat on Hanoi's best. (REEDER)

ammunition into a hilltop where the Viet Cong had dug in. The strike killed about 300 VC troopers.

General Joseph H. Moore, Jr, was the top Air Force officer in Vietnam, heading what was known at the beginning of the year as Second Air Division, although it was soon to be renamed Seventh Air Force. Moore was impressed with 'Puff the Magic Dragon', the FC–47 or military DC–3 which was able to bring gunfire to bear on the enemy with withering accuracy. Moore requested a squadron of sixteen gunships and noted that, because of the FC–47's small size, it would be more effective to use the C–131 (or the similar T–29) as the gunship airframe.

As it turned out, the Douglas aircraft was the only transport then available and by year's end it had been re-christened AC–47

Saigon was the only American embassy in history to have a deputy ambassador, the slot occupied in 1965 by seasoned diplomat, U. Alexis Johnson (right). At Bien Hoa, Johnson presents an American presidential unit citation to the VNAF's 514th Fighter Squadron, which operated Douglas A–1H Skyraiders. Looking on (at left) is Air Vice Marshal Nguyen Cao Ky who, only weeks later in June 1965, became head of government as the Saigon regime underwent one of its frequent leadership changes. (USAF)

Douglas A–4E Skyhawk (151096, coded CF–17) of attack squadron VMA–211 lands at the new Marine Corps airbase at Chu Lai. Skyhawks flew in direct support of Marine ground troops who went on the offensive in July 1965 in Operation 'Starlite'. (USMC)

The Republic F–105D Thunderchief carried the brunt of the war 'up north' when Rolling Thunder operations against North Vietnam commenced in 1965. All were based in Thailand, and there was supposed to be an agreement precluding their use against Viet Cong forces in South Vietnam. But Thuds appeared from time to time for close air support work in support of US troops in the south and sometimes were forced by battle damage to divert to bases there. (USAF)

to mark its 'attack' role. In rather hurried fashion, the Air Force put together the 4th Air Commando Squadron with twenty AC–47s (sixteen plus four for command support and attrition). The 4th arrived at Tan Son Nhut air base near Saigon on 14 November 1965. Because of delays in receiving miniguns, the squadron was only beginning to ready itself for operations at year's end.

Throughout 1965 the American build-up continued, the air war widened, and worries persisted about the stability of the Saigon government. In mid-year the never-popular General Khanh was replaced as premier by Nguyen Cao Ky, better known until then as a VNAF A–1H Skyraider pilot. Although flamboyant, Ky was also a consummate politician and some hope began to emerge that he and his supporters might be able to put South Vietnam on a stable keel.

Shortly after the beginning of combat missions over North Vietnam, it became clear that the Vietnamese Air Force (VNAF) A–1 Skyraider couldn't survive against Hanoi's heavy defences. In South Vietnam, however, the Skyraider was a workhorse in combat against the Viet Cong. This A–1H belongs to the VNAF's 520th Fighter Squadron, 74th Wing and is using the new runway at Binh Thuy in the Mekong Delta in 1965. (VIA ROBERT C. MIKESH)

Naval Air

In December 1965 the nuclear-powered aircraft-carrier USS *Enterprise* (CVAN–65), carrying the largest air wing ever deployed, brought the newest in warfighting technology to the Gulf of Tonkin. *Enterprise* had made a highly unusual Indian Ocean crossing and gotten supplied by air from Tananarive, Madagascar, where the author of this volume recalls seeing the ship's COD (carrier on-board delivery) aircraft kicking up clouds of red laterite dust at Ivato airfield.

Arriving in the combat zone, *Enterprise* conducted combat operations very briefly from 'Dixie Station', sending its F–4B Phantoms and A–4C Skyhawks against Viet Cong guerrillas, before moving north to join *Kitty Hawk* and *Ticonderoga* on 'Yankee Station' flying missions into North Vietnam. Two aircraft from the nuclear-powered carrier were downed over the south, an F–4B Phantom (151409) on 2 December 1965 and an RA–5C Vigilante (151633) on the 15th, though all crew members were rescued. After moving to the north, *Enterprise* suffered four more aircraft losses in the final days of December – an unusually high toll.

As the year drew to an end, a number of aircraft types had seen combat for the first time. The RF–4C Phantom began flying reconnaissance missions from Tan Son Nhut in October. The F–100 Super Sabre and F–104 Starfighter flew from Da Nang from early in the year. The introduction of the B–52 Stratofortress in May, with the first of many 'Arc Light' missions, was, of course, an event of major significance.

A new ally joined in the war when the first South Korean combat troops began taking up positions in South Vietnam near the end of 1965. At the end of the year, anti-war demonstrations were widespread in the US and the number of American troops in the country had risen in a year's time from 23,000 to 181,000.

In late March 1965, Douglas A–4C Skyhawk (149574) of the 'Blue Tail Flies' of attack squadron VA–153 settles to a tailhook landing aboard USS *Coral Sea* (CVA–43). Commanded by Captain George L. Cassell, *Coral Sea* spent the year of the American build-up flying missions primarily against North Vietnam but also over the south. A–4 Skyhawk pilots were often called upon to provide close air support to American troops on the ground. (USN)

Grumman A–6A Intruder of the 'Black Falcons' of VA–85 with a full load of Mark 82 250lb (114kg) bombs. The second US Navy squadron to introduce the problem-plagued Intruder to combat, VA–85 mounted operations from USS *Kitty Hawk*(CVA–63) against targets in South Vietnam in November 1965. A year or more followed before serious difficulties with the Intruder's 'black boxes' were resolved. (USN)

1966

LYNDON JOHNSON'S WAR

Over the holidays President Johnson halted the bombing campaign against North Vietnam, known as 'Rolling Thunder'. It was micro-management. Even small decisions – what time of day to launch a mission, what ordnance to carry – were being made not by commanders on the scene but in the White House situation room.

After a 37-day halt, bombing was resumed on 31 January 1966. Stopping and starting an aerial campaign in this fashion was supposed to send signals. The signals were supposed to persuade the enemy to engage in peace talks. Instead, the US appeared to broadcast its own confusion and crossed purposes. A halt to the bombing did not bring peace. Bombing did not win the war.

The number of Americans in South Vietnam was on the increase, of a magnitude no one could have thought possible even a couple of years previously. The Americans were going to take the countryside back from 'Charlie', take the night back from 'Charlie'. Maps began to appear in military journals 'proving' that portions of the country were being reclaimed after being controlled by the Viet Cong. It all had very little to do with reality. Even an official document of the period made note of the absence of clear purpose:

'The lack of a comprehensive plan for South-East Asia which clearly stated US objectives and outlined the steps to reach those objectives was a major obstacle to sound planning and achievement,' said an Air Force report. This was a polite way of saying that nobody knew what the hell they were doing. In Vietnam and Laos, where the situation was dire, absence of clearly stated goals contributed to failure to stabilize the

When the Grumman A–6A Intruder went to war from US Navy carrier decks, there were growing pains with its DIANE electronics system. By 1966 the Intruder was a force to be reckoned with and bolstered the striking power of carriers off the coast of South Vietnam (USN)

military and political situations. Comprehensive inter-agency planning for overall US objectives and policy in the region was long overdue.

Presidents Johnson and Thieu and Premier Ky met in Honolulu for a two-day conference beginning on 7 February 1966. The war's political, social and economic aspects were the subject of the talks.

The Marine Corps introduced a new aircraft type on 8 March 1966 when twenty-seven Boeing-Vertol CH–46A Sea Knight helicopters of squadron HMM–165 flew ashore and landed at the growing Marine helicopter field at Marble Mountain near Da Nang. With a crew of three, the tandem-rotor transport helicopter could carry 24 troops or 4,600lb (2,087kg) of cargo.

The CH–46A was generally a tough, capable machine but it soon demonstrated a serious allergy to the powdery white sand of the Vietnamese lowlands. Its engines gobbled sand, then went on the blink. Sand was getting into the fuel system, clogging the works. It was not the last time Americans were to have difficulty with helicopters that did not agree kindly with sand. In the case of the CH–46A, the problem was fixed only to have the Marines discover structural problems with the helicopter.

HMM–265 became the second Sea Knight squadron in South Vietnam with a further twenty-four CH–46As, but the fleet had to be grounded for a time until a structural change could be incorporated. A better 'fix' was the improved CH–46D model which did not arrive until the following year. The CH–46E followed soon after.

Forward air controllers (FACs) drew the risky job of identifying and marking targets for artillery and for jet fighters. Until newer types came along, the FAC aircraft was the dated but reliable Cessna O–1 Bird Dog. In late 1966 Captain Stokes Tomlin, wearing standard Air Force fatigues and gripping the O–1's propeller, was a part of a four-plane detachment from the 20th TASS working under rough conditions at the Marine base at Khe Sanh. (STOKES TOMLIN)

Army Aviation

With its huge fleet of helicopter and fixed-wing aircraft scattered everywhere in South Vietnam, the US Army had difficulty finding a way to standardize training, operational methods and combat procedures. An

US Marines line up to clamber aboard a Boeing-Vertol CH–46E Sea Knight helicopter. The original CH–46A model arrived in March 1966 but had structural problems. In time the CH–46A, CH–46D and CH–46E Sea Knights proved to be important servants of the Marine Corps and greatly improved their mobility. (USMC)

An F-4C Phantom on a combat mission in South-East Asia, its camouflage paint beginning to wear. Depending on who was at the controls, the superlative Phantom was usually not the best warplane for close air support of US and ARVN troops in combat in South Vietnam. Only the most skilled pilots could bring this 'fast mover' in on a bombing run and deliver its ordnance with precision. (USAF)

attempted 'fix' was the formation of the 1st Aviation Brigade on 1 March 1966. Although units in the field retained operational control over their aircraft and helicopters, the brigade offered a centralized focus and helped assure that 'lessons learned' were learned everywhere.

To the American television viewer back home, who rarely went an evening without observing the beat of UH-1 Huey rotors, it was almost impossible to understand what progress was being made in the war. After 1965's Battle of Ia Drang Valley – the turning point; the American soldier never again had to fear losing on the battlefield – some public affairs expert in Saigon came up with the idea of naming military operations with American terms.

The TV audience could hear about Operations 'Attleboro', 'Irving', 'Thayer', 'Paul Revere' (and later 'Cedar Falls', 'Junction City', 'Pershing', 'Pegasus' and 'Delaware') without learning a thing about Vietnamese geography – and never did. Spokesmen at the evening press briefing in Saigon – the famous 'Five O'Clock Follies' in the jargon of correspondents – used the arithmetic of body counts to make the point that the war was being won without ever describing the size or shape of the Viet Cong and NVA enemy.

These operations, most of them helicopter insertions of large numbers of troops over days, were in fact wearing down the Viet Cong and NVA. In Operation 'Paul Revere IV' in late 1966 the newly arrived 4th Infantry Division, supported by elements of the 25th Infantry Division and First Cavalry, was lifted into mountainous, jungle-covered terrain near the Cambodian border of Pleiku Province to search out regular NVA units and their base camps. Six weeks of campaigning netted almost a thousand enemy dead along with tons of captured weapons, equipment and supplies. Had the operation been given a name based on geography, TV watchers and correspondents alike might have had a better feel for what was going on.

As 1966 drew on, the Douglas AC-47 fixed-wing gunship proved to be one of the most potent aerial weapons available to friendly forces. In a war without sharply defined front lines and rear areas, defeat or victory – however temporary – was often determined by how US and ARVN troops handled an enemy assault on one of their outposts. If the Viet Cong or North Vietnamese reached the point where they were 'coming through the wire', things were really serious. But even then, a massed assault could often be beaten back if an AC-47 could position itself in a pylon turn above the enemy and begin hosing down the area with its side-mounted machine-guns. 'Spooky' or 'Puff the Magic Dragon', the AC-47 fought effectively during the nocturnal hours, when 'Charlie' was at his best. No outpost was ever overrun, by night or day, when an AC-47 was on the scene.

On 8 March 1966 the 14th Air Commando Wing was organized at Nha Trang to manage and control the diverse Air Commando squadrons and detachments located in South-East Asia.

The next day, 9 March, the battle at A Shau demonstrated how air support could – and could not – help the fighting man on the

ground. The Special Forces camp at A Shau in South Vietnam was attacked by an estimated 4,000 North Vietnamese regulars. At first A–1E Skyraiders and other fighter-bombers were able to help the besieged friendlies to hold off the onslaught. But bad weather closed in and reduced available air support. A few Skyraider pilots were able to get in and out, but with overwhelming numbers the enemy was able to force evacuation of the camp on the evening of the second day.

During the day Major Bernard F. Fisher of the 1st Air Commando Squadron saw another Skyraider belly-in on the camp's wreckage-strewn airstrip. A Shau was under heavy fire at that moment and the airstrip itself appeared virtually unusable. Fisher believed a rescue was possible. He landed his A–1E Skyraider on the airstrip. The downed pilot came running and dived into the cockpit headfirst while Fisher poured on the coals and made a daring take-off. Major Fisher was later awarded the Medal of Honor, the first Air Force recipient of this war.

The Skyraider was ideal for the 'Sandy' role, directing rescue forces to pick up airmen downed by enemy fire. On a typical rescue flight, two to four A–1E Skyraiders worked under controllers in an airborne command post – a Grumman HU–16B Albatross in 1964–65, an HC–130P Hercules from 1966. A two-plane Skyraider flight escorted rescue helicopters to the crash site. A second Skyraider flight at the rescue area determined the condition of the downed aircrew, its location, and the disposition of enemy defenses with relation to terrain. This A–1E flight leader decided whether conditions would enable him to engage enemy guns and bring in rescue forces.

Forward air controllers (FACs) also were part of a search and rescue task force and often were first on the scene – able to feel out enemy defenses while the Skyraiders were en route.

Some of the most dramatic rescues took place deep inside North Vietnam. But rescues in South Vietnam were as important and could be equally perilous. In early 1966 a mass effort to save a C–123B Provider crew down in the Central Highlands pitted an O–1 FAC, A–1E Sandy aircraft and other fighter-bombers against a heavily armed, firmly entrenched Viet Cong force well hidden by triple-canopy foliage. While Skyraiders flew cover, a rescue helicopter dropped two pararescue jumpers (PJs) who assisted the injured survivors until all could be hoisted up and flown out.

At times the rescue mission involved exotic armaments. By 1966 riot control munitions were approved for use during rescues. The A–1E Sandy aircraft could carry an encyclopedic assortment of ordnance anyway. The controversial weapons included CBU–19A/B (cluster bomb unit) and CBU–30A anti-personnel area denial bombs, which were essentially

The North American F–100 Super Sabre was the heavy-duty bomb carrier of the war in the south. F–100s flew more sorties in the South-East Asia conflict than any other aircraft type. This F–100D (56–3197) belongs to the 416th Tactical Fighter Squadron, part of the 37th Tactical Fighter Wing, at Phu Cat. (USAF)

tear gas bombs, as well as the BLU–52A/B (bomb live unit) weapon concocted by mixing bulk tear gas with the ingredients of the BLU–1C fire bomb.

On 14 March 1966 the latest of a number of new airfields opened at Phan Rang. Like Tuy Hoa to be opened later in the year, Phan Rang is best remembered for F–100 Super Sabre operations. The two squadrons of B–57 Canberras in the country, the 8th and 13th, were also assigned to the Super Sabre wing and made the move to Phan Rang later in the year.

The F–100 Super Sabre had been transformed, in effect, into airborne artillery for the support of friendly ground troops. F–100s hauled bombs from home bases to locations on the map where there were 'troops in contact' – that is, a battle going on – and followed guidance from FACs, who marked the enemy with smoke rockets.

The missions were predictable, unglamorous: brief, take-off, cruise to target area, find the FAC, drop on his smoke, strafe, climb out, cruise home, land, debrief. The next day, more of the same. But once in a while there was an empty billet when an F–100 pilot lost a disagreement with enemy guns on the ground.

An unrelenting demand for close air support resulted in the deployment to Vietnam of additional F–100 squadrons and to the formation in-country of new tactical fighter wings. Two of the earliest F–100 wings were the 3rd and 35th, at Bien Hoa and Phan Rang respectively.

Home-based at England AFB, Louisiana, the 3rd TFW moved to Bien Hoa at the end of 1965 and eventually had four squadrons, the 90th, 416th, 510th and 531st TFS. The 416th TFS was actually shuffled around, moving from Tan Son Nhut to Bien Hoa to Phu Cat in 1966. Pilots of the 3rd TFW completed more than 13,000 sorties in their first six months in the combat zone.

The 35th TFW was activated in April 1966 at Da Nang and moved in October to Phan Rang. Its squadrons were the 532nd, 613th, 614th, and 615th TFS plus a detachment of the 612th.

Pilots of the open-throated, supersonic F–100 were not paid to be poets but once in a while a man came close. Major Donald W. Kilgus:

'I think the most impressive thing I ever saw was going down to the Delta. Mekong Delta rice paddies, fully flooded, early morning, high humidity. You dropped a 750lb [340kg] bomb that would hit in that rice paddy and the first thing you saw, in addition to the geyser of water coming up, was a doughnut-shaped cloud of moisture

This is the team which protected Navy carriers at sea from the enemy air threat – Grumman E–2A Hawkeye airborne early warning aircraft and McDonnell F–4B Phantom II fighter-interceptor. As it turned out, the Vietnamese communists never threatened the carriers on 'Yankee' and 'Dixie' Stations, but the Navy had to be ready. (USN)

By late 1966 C–130 Hercules transports had carried more tonnage in South Vietnam than C–123 Providers, CV–2 Caribous and C–47 Skytrains combined. The first aircraft type to be camouflaged, the 'Herk' was usually in-country on a rotating or shuttle basis rather than being assigned permanently. This C–130E Hercules belongs to the 776th Troop Carrier Squadron. (VIA JERRY GEER)

condensation from the shock wave of the bomb going off. And you'd watch and it looked like piranhas coming to the surface – and that would be the shrapnel, falling in the water, for as much as a mile to a mile and a half from the point of impact. And the first time you saw that, you thought, "Jesus Christ, we're dropping *that* close to friendly troops." So it made you very aware of what the weapon's effects were.'

Army Helicopters

While some US Army officers were questioning the continuing build-up of US troops in South Vietnam and questioning whether it had a clear purpose, most of these men believed in early 1966 that the war was being won, that it was only a matter of time until American firepower would prevail. In battlefield terms, they were almost certainly right – the Viet Cong and NVA were no match for an airmobile assault force – but they had forgotten whose country it was. In later years, at great cost, it would be demonstrated that winning the battle did not mean winning the war.

One of Army aviation's most effective tools was the helicopter gunship. One version in 1966 was the UH–1C version of the familiar Huey. Standard armament systems for the UH–1C included the M21 package with one forward-firing 7.62mm XM134 minigun and an XM158 seven-tube 2.75in FFAR (folding-fin aircraft rocket) launcher mounted externally on each side of the fuselage.

Another package used to arm the UH–1C was the XM16 in which four 7.62mm M60 machine-guns replaced the miniguns. Yet another was the all-rocket XM3 package made up of two 24-tube FFAR launchers. In addition, the UH–1C was fitted – often as a result of field modifications – with all manner of armament. Examples were the chin-mounted 40mm grenade-launcher and M24A1 20mm cannon pods. The Huey could also carry a smoke generator. Unfortunately the burden of a heavy armament load degraded the type's performance, so that UH–1C gunships had difficulty keeping up with the UH–1B 'slick' troop transport helicopters. It was clear that in due course a dedicated gunship would be needed.

In March 1966 the US Army ordered the Bell AH–1G Cobra into production and Cobras began arriving in Vietnam later in the year. Lightweight two-seaters, Cobras could carry an impressive load with a 7.62mm minigun in the nose turret, up to 52 FFAR rockets in four pods and a grenade-launcher without any sacrifice in performance. The AH–1G Cobra built up an impressive combat record and helped reduce transport helicopter losses by providing fire suppression during troop insertions.

So extensively used were Army Cobras that in the course of the Vietnam conflict, 173 were lost to hostile action and 109 to operational causes.

Starting on 13 May 1966, the 53rd Aviation Detachment (Field Evaluation) began operating four ACH–47A Chinook armed helicopter gunships at Vung Tau. Here the 228th Aviation Battalion and the 147th Aviation Company had successfully operated the CH–47A Chinook cargo-hauler for a year. The ACH–47A was something else, however. Nicknamed 'Guns A Go-go', it was armed with machine-guns, cannon, rockets and grenade-launchers.

Making a gunship out of such a big helicopter seemed, on the surface, a good idea. It was not. Three of the four ACH–47As were lost, with loss of life, one in a bizarre and tragic accident when a mounting pin on a 20mm cannon separated during a firing run, causing the gun to elevate and obliterate the forward rotors. All the crew were killed.

Marine Skyhawks

Marine A–4 Skyhawk pilot Dorsie Page insists that a forward air controller who called in Skyhawks to bomb Viet Cong as they attacked American positions, found himself in trouble because the A–4s had to roll into their 'break' over the Bob Hope show, the roar of their jet engines upsetting the entertainer's program. Snake and Nape (Snakeye fin-retarded bombs and napalm) were the standard Marine medicine for the Viet Cong, but the conditions under which the men worked were a challenge 24 hours a day.

In March 1966 the US Army ordered the Bell AH–1G Cobra gunship into production and it began to reach the battlefield before year's end. This shark-toothed Cobra belongs to Troop D, 3rd Squadron, 4th Cavalry, 25th Infantry Division. (US ARMY)

Chu Lai, the rough Marine airfield on the peninsula of the same name, had welcomed the 'Tomcats' of VMA–311, the first Skyhawk squadron to arrive in the country, brought in by B. M. Greely and a few good men.

Chu Lai had a runway like a piano board, as pilot Con Silard described it. The airfield was on an area of sand and laterite and was paved with metal stripping known as SATS (short airfield for tactical support). Its first runway, 70ft wide and 8,000ft long, was adequate for the Skyhawk but offered no margin for luxury. The second, crosswind, runway, 4,000ft in length, required Skyhawks to use JATO (jet assisted take-off) and hurl themselves aloft amid billowing clouds gushing back from the JATO bottles. A likeness of an aircraft-carrier deck, complete with wire-arrested landing apparatus and an LSO (landing signal officer) on 24-hour duty, helped to compensate for the airfield's inadequacies. 'But landing there was hairy,' Page remembered. 'There were usually no runway lights because there wasn't enough electricity.'

It was also difficult keeping track of who was doing what to whom in this war. Over Laos at a time when the administration said Americans were not fighting in Laos, Page was hit by a small-caliber bullet which passed horizontally through his cockpit and through both his legs just above the knees. Bleeding profusely, he managed to land at Chu Lai to be told that tomorrow's Skyhawk operations would take place over South Vietnam. 'I had five different ROE cards,' said Page, referring to the white flash-cards which told pilots the rules of engagement, 'one for each situation we might get into. There were so many rules and restrictions, no pilot could remember them all.'

Page recalls that squadron mate Pete Kruger displayed his view of military authority by naming his dog Major. A captain himself, Kruger, where appropriate, would put off a caller with the news that he was 'busy with Major right now'. Kruger went on to fly more than 500 combat missions in A–4 Skyhawks and O–1C Bird Dog observation aircraft.

There was one Marine air group (MAG–11) at Da Nang but no fewer than three (MAG–12, –13 and –36) at Chu Lai, where Marines were packed together in what Page called 'sandy, scary tents, all metal with sand underpinning'. In addition to three squadrons of A–4 Skyhawks (24 aircraft per squadron of which 18 or 19 were operational at a time), Chu Lai was home to Marine F–8 Crusaders and, after Christmas 1966, the A–6A Intruders of the 'Hawks' of VMA(AW)–533.

The Marine Corps has always taken pride in its aviation arm, which exists to provide direct support to the combat Marine on the ground. Men like Page, Kruger and Bill Egen, the skipper of the 'Green Knights' of VMA–121, took pride in being able to bring their Skyhawks down to treetop level in a hail of enemy fire to deliver Snake and Nape within a few hundred yards of Marines in direct contact with the enemy. It was widely acknowledged that Marine Skyhawk, Crusader and Phantom pilots were especially good at this difficult job of delivering ordnance down with precision right in front of friendly troops. The Skyhawk in particular was regarded as highly effective – a maneuverable, heavily armed and very survivable aircraft for the close-support mission.

On 1 April 1966 the 2nd Air Division in Saigon was discontinued and the USAF command in South Vietnam became the Seventh Air Force, activated at Tan Son Nhut.

General William C. Westmoreland and Premier Nguyen Cao Ky are among personalities on stage during a show by Bob Hope to entertain US troops in South Vietnam. Hope has taken his troupe to every battle zone since the Second World War to uplift the spirits of American soldiers at war. (US ARMY)

On 6 April agreement was belatedly reached on an issue that had provoked strong sentiment on both sides, the dispute between the Army and Air Force over the CV–2 Caribou aircraft. There were now no fewer than 88 Caribous in the country and the Army had stated its intention to acquire no fewer than 120 CV–7 Buffalo aircraft from the same manufacturer, de Havilland of Canada.

The chiefs of staff inked in an agreement which turned the entire Caribou fleet over to the USAF. The Army received virtually nothing in exchange, other than a meaningless concession on the right to operate helicopters in the supply role. Effective at year's end, the Caribou, now designated C–7A, continued flying throughout the country but with Air Force pilots at the controls.

The US Navy had its own helicopter pilots in South Vietnam and they were flying under the most unusual circumstances. Squadron HC–1 was flying short-boomed UH–1B Huey helicopter gunships in support of Army and Navy riverine forces in the Mekong Delta. In due course the squadron became the 'Seawolves' of HAL–3 with as many as thirty-three Hueys.

Although the Viet Cong and their North Vietnamese supporters were never able to mount a serious threat against US aircraft-carriers operating off the coast, the Navy suffered casualties nonetheless. On 26 October 1966 as two sailors were stowing parachute flares in a storage locker aboard the USS *Oriskany* (CVA–34), a massive fire erupted. Ordnance was touched off by the inferno and flames spread to the hangar deck below and into several living quarters. Flames engulfed the fantail and spread below decks, igniting bombs and ammunition. Through heroic efforts the fire was brought under control, but damage to aircraft and ship was severe. At final count, 134 were dead, 62 injured.

On the larger carriers the A–6A Intruder all-weather attack aircraft continued to fly combat missions and to progress toward being fully operational – despite teething troubles with its DIANE electronics system. By late 1966 the 'Tigers' of VA–65, commanded by Commander Robert C. Mandeville, were in the battle zone aboard the USS *Constellation* (CVA–64). *Time* magazine interviewed Mandeville and looked at DIANE, which it called 'a spaghetti bowl of instruments that combines . . . radars, an inertial navigation unit, and a small computer' and pointed out that the A–6A Intruder really proved itself when the north-west monsoon brought the 1966 version of its annual drenching rains and gale force winds. While Phantoms and Skyhawks were grounded, Mandeville's squadron flew 40 per cent of the missions logged by all the squadrons aboard the three carriers off the Vietnamese coast.

The American soldier. Airpower could transport him, cover him, extract him. But it was the man on the ground who mattered and everything else boiled down to how this man performed when the situation got tight.

To most, Private Bruce Finney of the First Cavalry Division is no more or less than a weary, combat-savvy RTO (radio-telephone operator) pausing for breath during Operation 'Thayer' 50 miles north-west of Qui Nhon on 29 October 1966. The 38-pound (17kg) radio added to the trooper's burden but his real ordeal came in keeping pace with the platoon leader, having the head set ready for the lieutenant's use under fire, and thrashing through the communications screw-ups which seemed to be endemic. Finney is not just tired, he is under stress.

What looks like a dome protruding above Finney's pack is actually an entrenching tool sticking up from the grassy paddy dike behind him. The canister behind his back is a smoke grenade. Two frag grenades hang from the kit at his web belt. Tucked into his burlap helmet liner is a clear plastic bottle of mosquito repellant, descented because of the Viet Cong's skill at sniffing out Americans. The repellant does not help much and 'Charlie' can smell Americans anyway: they consume too much protein and smell like butter.

Finney's M–16 assault rifle is an early model with metal clip, later replaced by plastic, and an open flash suppressor which tends to snag on grass, branches, anything that gets in the way. Early M–16s had a tendency to jam in combat.

This RTO's bulky PRC–25 radio is not the infantry model but was pulled from a vehicle – witness its chrome handle and the amplifier speaker aimed to his right. The whip antenna is an essential nuisance which also catches against foliage and branches. It is a UHF radio supposedly free of static, but the RTO will hear static anyway and the squelch button will not help much. Over his right shoulder Finney carries a plastic bag to keep the head set dry.

In a moment, Bruce Finney will pick himself up and continue humping through the field, shadowing his lieutenant. He has a heavy load. Finney is not just bushed. He is burdened. (US ARMY)

Airlift

In addition to the USAF C–123s, Army CV–2s and VNAF C–47s, the airlift mission inside South Vietnam was being increasingly taken on by the Lockheed C–130 Hercules. Although assigned on a rotating basis rather than bedded down permanently in South Vietnam, the Hercules force had risen to 44 C–130A, C–130B and C–130E aircraft by 1 November 1966.

Hercules aircrews felt that operating conditions in Vietnam were unsafe. Professionals, accustomed to regimented methods, they sometimes viewed C–47 and C–123 pilots as 'cowboys' who took undue risk. Hazardous taxying conditions were everywhere, not only at the overcrowded larger airfields but at forward sites where taxi strips were used by vehicles, helicopters, and sometimes water buffalo. Ramp delays were

The Fairchild C–123B Provider ranged from one end of South Vietnam to the other hauling people and supplies – and sometimes it got into trouble. This camouflaged C–123B is being extricated from a muddy ravine by a bulldozer after a crash-landing at a Special Forces camp. (USAF)

Soon after the former Military Air Transport Service acquired its new name Military Airlift Command (MAC), it began flying into Saigon with the Lockheed C–141A StarLifter, the USAF's first all-jet cargo transport. Sadly C–141A crews also drew the duty of bringing home the dead. This natural-metal StarLifter (65–0266), seen in November 1966, belonged to the 436th Military Airlift Wing. (RONALD W. HARRISON)

For Americans the war was far from home and required supply lines thousands of miles long. Airlift made it possible to support the troops in the field. A Douglas C–133A Cargomaster of the 436th Military Airlift Wing delivers equipment to South-East Asia. (USAF)

endemic, communications were poor, and cargo offloading facilities ranged from poor to non-existent.

In time things improved. Nevertheless, Defense Secretary McNamara supported recommendations that the C–130s continue to 'shuttle' in and out of South Vietnam for 15- or 30-day stays rather than be based permanently in the country.

By late 1966 C–130s had hauled more tonnage in Vietnam than C–123s, CV–2s and C–47s combined. With the growing role of the C–130, up to twelve squadrons were providing aircrews and aircraft to the combat zone at a time. Maintenance on the older C–130A models continued to be a nagging problem, but eventually dramatic efficiencies were achieved in Hercules operations.

The job never got easier and more than one C–130 pilot sucked in his breath and stiffened with apprehension while setting down a cargo-laden aircraft at a tiny outpost where Viet Cong mortar shells could fall at any time. As 'people-movers' the C–130s complemented Army helicopters in giving the infantryman a high degree of mobility – usually an advantage over the Viet Cong.

On 15 November 1966 Tuy Hoa opened. It was the first and only air base in Vietnam designed and constructed under USAF supervision. The base was built by a contractor under the 'turnkey' concept, under which PACAF received a complete ready-to-use facility.

As another of the seemingly endless years of American involvement in South Vietnam drew to a close, more and more Americans were wondering if it would ever be over. At Tan Son Nhut where he was a loadmaster on an Air Force cargo aircraft, Staff Sergeant Vernon L. Sewell was talking about his experiences to one of the newer men.

'You know,' Sewell said, 'I first came in here in 1962 when I was on a C–124 Globemaster. In those days every once in a while we would carry out a coffin with an American flag draped around it.

'I started coming back in 1964 when I was on a C–133. One day, the crew made a big deal out of the fact that we were taking out two coffins wrapped with American flags. Then on one of our flights it was three.

'Now I'm stationed in country and we're getting this new cargo plane, the C–141, coming in here from outside. Now we fill an entire airplane with coffins covered by American flags. An entire airplane! You want to know something? I'd like to know if this war is ever going to end.'

On 31 October 1966 US troop strength in South Vietnam was 385,000.

1967
STAYING THE COURSE

An official history makes 1967 sound like a year of retrenchment: 'Although the enemy failed to win any major battles in 1967, he demonstrated a willingness to accept the situation and continue to attack, harass, and terrorize. He was not beaten, and the war would continue until one side or the other grew tired and opted to quit.'

This was prophetic, for back at home many Americans were turning against the war. 'Out, now!' was the succinct but sharp outcry of the anti-war protester. Later in the year some of these protesters laid siege to the Pentagon itself, inserting flowers into the gun muzzles of troops called up to keep order. There was less and less order in American society and it was becoming harder to put on a uniform and go to war, knowing that the country was deeply divided.

President Johnson, in his State of the Union speech on 10 January 1967, spoke of the need for resolve. 'Our adversary still believes,' he said prophetically, 'that he can go on fighting longer than we can. I say to you that our pressures must be sustained . . . until [the enemy] realizes that the war he started is costing more than he can ever gain'. There was also a lot of talk about staying the course. Both those who supported the US commitment in Vietnam and those who opposed it readily acknowledged that the war was lasting far longer than they had expected.

Lieutenant General William W. (Spike) Momyer, who had replaced Major General Joseph Moore as the top airman in South Vietnam – working for Westmoreland as commander, Seventh Air Force – was not ready to concede that anybody was thinking about getting tired or quitting and was certainly not going to do anything the protesters would like. Momyer was keenly aware that while the war over North Vietnam was receiving plenty of attention – Phantoms from Colonel Robin Olds' 8th TFW 'Wolfpack' shot down seven MiG–21s on 2 January 1967 – it was the fight in the south that had to be won, and airpower was the key to winning.

Momyer was deeply concerned about command and control. The question 'who's in charge?' occupied a significant portion of his official writing. The arrangement whereby targets were chosen, almost always requiring decisions in Hawaii and Washington, was so cumbersome that the Viet Cong literally had time to escape before fighter-bombers or B–52s could arrive. After discussions with Westmoreland, in 1967 Momyer obtained greater control over B–52 planning and targeting than he had enjoyed earlier.

Momyer worked hard for early introduction of the AC–130 Hercules gunship (see later). He stressed the importance of paying more attention to the southward flow of supplies and armaments from North Vietnam to Viet Cong fighters in the south.

The Hughes OH–6A Cayuse, called the 'Loach' by pilots, became the principal US Army observation helicopter after its debut in South Vietnam on 15 February 1967. The 'bubble' or 'egg' where the flight crew sat offered superb visibility and made the helicopter very survivable. No fewer than 635 OH–6As were lost to anti-aircraft and small-arms fire. (US ARMY)

Momyer obtained 'single manager' authority over Navy and Marine tactical aircraft in South Vietnam and embarked on an effort to make certain close air support was planned and coordinated effectively.

Momyer was a veteran fighter pilot who had been an ace in the Second World War. He was rigorous about detail. As one of his officers described it, 'He was one of the few senior officers who kept a personal, handwritten diary. Every day after the work was finished he would have a 15–30 minute review with his deputy [Major General Gordon M. Graham], while he wrote notes in his horrible handwriting in his old-fashioned, ledger-type diary. He had been doing this for his entire service career and had a two-drawer safe full of these books.' A sergeant trained as a court reporter helped the Seventh Air Force chief to keep his notes.

Caribou Change

One decision gratified Momyer as the US continued to solidify and expand its presence in South Vietnam. On 1 January 1967 the USAF's 483rd Troop Carrier Wing at Cam Ranh Bay took over all CV–2 Caribou operations, transferred from the Army. Ninety-seven Caribous in South Vietnam changed owners overnight and changed designation from CV–2 to C–7A. The Air Force expanded the C–7A Caribou squadron at Vung Tau, which was primarily an Army base.

The air base at Phu Cat became operational on 29 May 1967, providing a home for the F–100D Super Sabres of the 37th Tactical Fighter Wing. Its initial unit was the much-moved 416th TFS, soon joined by the 355th and later the 612th. When a number of Air National Guard (ANG) F–100 units were activated, the 174th TFS of the Iowa ANG joined the wing with its 22 F–100s. At one point this huge fighter wing had between 80 and 110 F–100s, including 15 to 18 F–100F 'Misty FAC' aircraft – two-seat Super Sabres which flew the forward air controller mission at low level and high speed.

In addition to the 3rd, 35th and 37th wings, the huge F–100 Super Sabre force in South-East Asia (some 490 aircraft) included the 31st TFW at Tuy Hoa from mid-1967 onwards. The 31st Wing included the 308th

Douglas A–4 Skyhawk (foreground) was the US Navy's standard light attack aircraft at the outset of the war, while the Vought F–8 Crusader (background) was the principal fighter. Seen aboard the USS *Hancock* (CVA–19) in early 1967, these warplanes fought in North and South Vietnam and in the unannounced conflict in Laos. Flying from a carrier was dangerous and as many aircraft were lost in 'operational incidents' as in combat. (STOKES TOMLIN)

The EA–6A electronic warfare version of the A–6 Intruder was introduced to the combat zone by Marine Corps squadron VMCJ–2, the 'Playboys' (shown), which operated briefly at Da Nang before being replaced by VMCJ–1. This two-seat electronic warfare aircraft proved to be a 'force multiplier' for US air assets in South-East Asia. (USMC)

and 309th TFS and quickly gained the 188th TFS of the New Mexico ANG (the 'Enchilada Air Force') and the 136th TFS of the New York ANG ('Rocky's Raiders'). The air guardsmen operated the F–100C model.

Air traffic was plentiful at an F–100 base which was likely to be very busy. In 1967 Robert R. Rodwell of the British magazine *Flight International*, reporting from Vietnam, called the F–100 base at Bien Hoa the world's busiest airport. Rodwell's numbers showed that an F–100 landed or took off once every 42 seconds.

Tuy Hoa, on the coast and referred to by writer Dave Anderton as 'The Atlantic City of the South China Sea', was even busier than Bien Hoa for a time. Fuel for the base was piped overland from Vung Ro Bay, some 12 to 15 miles (20–25km). The Viet Cong blew up the pipeline occasionally, and the F–100s dropped bombs on them occasionally. Most F–100 missions continued to be in a 'troops in contact' environment, where the Super Sabre pilots were directly supporting the infantrymen in combat.

In the air war much attention was focused up north where Operation 'Bolo', Robin Olds' fighter sweep, shot down seven MiG–21s. The EC–121D Constellation airborne warning and control aircraft which supported the fight up north moved from crowded Tan Son Nhut on 21 February 1967, and relocated first to Ubon, then Udorn in Thailand. It was at about this time that the Thai Prime Minister announced what everyone knew, that US planes based in his country were bombing targets in North Vietnam. The agreement permitting this did not cover operations in South Vietnam, so US aircraft in Thailand rarely flew in the south. The out-country war and the in-country war remained clearly segregated from each other.

On 22 February the 173rd Airborne Brigade started Operation 'Junction City' with the only American parachute assault of the entire war. This was the latest American effort to track down and destroy the enemy's brains and heart, the so-called Central Office for South Vietnam (COSVN). At least one student of Viet Cong activity uttered skepticism that COSVN existed at all, but it scarcely mattered. This huge operation pitted Americans against the Cong and that was what US commanders wanted.

Supported by F–100 Super Sabres and some strikes by naval air, 'Junction City' operations broadened and by early March a major set-piece battle was building. The Army had a fire support base in the Michelin rubber plantation some 20 miles (32km) north-east of Tay Ninh. On 21 March six enemy battalions (2,500 men) hit the base and the defenders called for air support. An O–1 Bird Dog soon appeared overhead and began directing F–100s from Bien Hoa and F–4s from Camh Ranh Bay in laying Snake and Nape on the VC. Both air bases were but a few miles from the fire support base and soon the fighter-bombers were making the round trip, reloading, and making the trip again. By late morning more than 85 jet fighter-bombers were laying bombs and 20mm cannon fire on the enemy troops.

'Junction City' continued. Like many of the mass troop operations which received American geographical names to obscure their real whereabouts, this major battle in the plantation, followed by a prolonged series of lesser battles, made important use of close air support. F–100s and F–4s flew more than 5,000 sorties in support of 'Junction City' and in the end both Viet Cong and NVA units were defeated and pushed back into their Cambodian sanctuary. Without air support, the result would have been very different.

Observation Helos

The US Army in the field had long since found that its Bell OH–13 Sioux and Hiller OH–23 Raven observation helicopters were too old and too difficult to maintain. For the interim, the Bell UH–1A and UH–1B Huey

The Martin SP–5B Marlin was the only US Navy flying-boat in service at the time of the Vietnam War. SP–5Bs from VP–40 and other patrol squadrons flew 'Market Time' sorties searching for people and supplies being moved south by the enemy along the 1,000-mile (1,610km) Vietnamese coastline. Marlins were retired from service in 1967. (USN)

Every air base, large or small, had its boom town outside the gate with beer, bars and bar girls. The Quan Tan-Thanh 'Far West Bar' outside Kontum in the Central Highlands seems to have been a more modest watering-hole than many. While footslogging grunts were stuck with the war on a 24-hour basis, pilots could fly into danger, survive, and spend the evening over a cold San Miguel beer with entertainment readily at hand. (STOKES TOMLIN)

performed the observation function, but by 1966 the Army was beginning to field the Bell OH–58A Kiowa and Hughes OH–6A Cayuse. The latter had been the winner of the 1960 Light Observation Helicopter competition and was highly regarded by Army officers.

Fred Newman arrived in Vietnam shortly after the 15 February 1967 combat debut of the 'Loach', the soldier's term for the OH–6A, from the term LOH or light observation helicopter. Newman put his experience on paper in a private diary:

'I hold my helicopter, low, in a light drizzle while my observer in the right seat tells me that the Viet Cong are bunched up in a small gully to our right. This is my job. I'm a Hughes OH–6A Cayuse pilot with the 1st Cavalry Regiment. "Raise it fifty!" I snap. This tells our artillery guys to adjust their fire.

'"That's it," my co-pilot/observer confirms. Rounds impact in the gully, chewing up wet earth and forcing black-garbed VC soldiers back into the trees.

'Just at that instant I spot more Viet Cong. They come running in the open 100 yards to our left. Hunched in my pilot's seat in the Loach – that's what we call the OH–6A – I marvel, as always, at the wrap-around view from the "egg", our flight crew compartment, which gives us spectacular visibility in all directions with only a tiny blind spot to the rear.

'The new people are shooting at us. I see their red muzzle flashes in the rain. I pull the OH–6 up and out, tracers spending themselves beneath us. This chopper has power! We're okay.' Newman continues:

'On a typical mission, we spring off with a full load of fuel and go into a hover above friendly troops moving to stake out new positions. If they're attacked, we scuttle up to a good altitude to direct artillery fire against the Cong.

'My hooch mate didn't dance fast enough one day when "Victor Charlie" bracketed him with a 12.7mm machine-gun. He took hits which made a horrendous, crunching sound, ripped up some hydraulics, and sent metal fragments whipping around inside the cockpit. He managed to auto-rotate to a "controlled crash" landing and it was then that we realized the OH–6 is extremely survivable. If you look at the Loach, it's basically an "egg" with a tail boom. When you crash, the tail boom crumples and the egg just detaches. The crew often can walk out, suck in a deep breath, and continue living.'

In Newman's period, a typical Air Cavalry troop was equipped with seven to nine OH–6s, an aero rifle platoon with nine attack helicopters. On an Air Cavalry sortie the OH–6 could be armed with the XM–27 system comprising a 7.62mm M–134 minigun with 2,000 rounds. Installation of this system meant some sacrifice in performance and degraded the Cayuse's ability to carry from one to three passengers in the space behind the two pilots.

'Our usual tactic in the Air Cavalry was to operate in a White Team of two Loaches, the "high guy" keeping watch while the "low guy" prowled the combat area and trolled for enemy fire. Supporting the movement of our troops on the ground, we used various navigation techniques to keep constant tabs on their whereabouts and to advise them on movements. When we hit a sudden, heavy concentration of Viet Cong we called in a Red Team of attack helicopters from the aero weapons platoon to hose down the bad guys and a Blue Team of Hueys from the aero rifle platoon to insert our troops at a key node where our ground-pounders would be most effective.

'We were scouts and observers, remember, and it was *not* the Army's intent to pit us head-to-head against highly mobile Viet Cong maneuver units bristling with heavy firepower. Still, there were times when we blasted away at "Charlie". And once in a while we could lean out and shoot at him with an M14 or M16 rifle.'

Aussie Arrival

A new ally joined the air war in South Vietnam in April 1967 when the Canberra bombers of No 2 Squadron, Royal Australian Air Force, deployed to Phan Rang. The 'Aussie' squadron came under the operational control of Seventh Air Force in Saigon.

A major airlift undertaken over 9–14 April moved the entire 196th Light Infantry Brigade from Tay Ninh to Chu Lai. A total of 351 C–130 sorties did the job.

As part of the continuing effort to build up South Vietnam's own forces, on 17 April the eighteen USAF F–5 Freedom Fighters at Bien Hoa were transferred to the VNAF's 522nd Fighter Squadron. The VNAF was also to receive Cessna A–37 Dragonfly attack aircraft.

On 25 April the familiar C–123 transport reached South Vietnam in a new and improved form when the first of the jet-assisted C–123K Provider assault transports arrived at Tan Son Nhut.

Another new aircraft type in 1967 was the twin-boom Cessna O–2B PSYOPS (psychological operations) aircraft, which was bedded down at Nha Trang. Used for leaflet drops, the O–2Bs were the first versions of the militarized Cessna Skymaster to arrive in the country. The O–2Bs which arrived in May were quickly followed by the O–2A on 2 June 1967, which was intended to replace the familiar single-engined O–1 Bird Dog and make the forward air controller (FAC) job a little safer. The first O–2A aircraft went to Binh Thuy.

The USS *Intrepid* (CVA–11) arrived on the line on 21 June 1967, bringing a new category of aircraft-carrier into the conflict. The aging *Intrepid*, normally a small anti-submarine carrier operating with S–2 Tracker and SH–3 Sea King aircraft, had been given three squadrons of A–4C Skyhawks. Squadrons VA–15, VA–34 and VSF–1 (the last-named being an anti-submarine fighter squadron!) were on board. Nicknamed 'Valions', 'Blue Blasters' and 'War Eagles', these Skyhawks flew against targets in North and South Vietnam in just the same manner as did attack aircraft from other carriers.

On 26 July the USAF's 3rd TFW at Bien Hoa AB received its first A–37A Dragonfly aircraft. The attack version was considerably heavier than the T–37B trainer from which it was developed. Americans were to fly the A–37 while the aircraft was also being readied for the VNAF.

Three days later, on 29 July, sailors operating off the Vietnamese coast experienced the Navy's second major aircraft-carrier fire of the war. The USS *Forrestal* (CVA–59), traditionally assigned to the Atlantic Fleet but now taking her fair turn on a Pacific combat cruise, was en route to 'Yankee Station' when tragedy struck.

Aircraft had been spotted on *Forrestal*'s deck, armed and fueled, and were in final preparation to start up for the second launch of the day. As an auxiliary power unit was backed into position to start an F–4 Phantom, its hot exhaust blew directly on the Phantom's Zuni rocket pod. A Zuni, ignited by the starter's exhaust heat, streaked across the busy flight deck and slammed into a loaded A–4 Skyhawk, which burst into flames. The fire engulfed the fantail and spread quickly below decks, touching off bombs and ammunition.

In a booming barrage of noise, aircraft and ordnance exploded. Men were blown overboard. Some were trapped in searing flames and choking smoke below decks.

Nearby units came to assist in fighting the fire and caring for the injured. Above deck, the fire was controlled and extinguished within an hour. But in the subterranean depths of the giant carrier, the blaze persisted for twelve hours.

There were impressive acts of heroism by ship and air wing personnel who contained the fire and rescued many potential victims. Bombs and rockets had to be pulled off the loaded and burning aircraft and heaved into the sea. Blisteringly hot 250lb and 500lb (113kg and 227kg) bombs were carried or rolled to the deck edge to be thrown over the side. 134 men were killed and 62 injured. Twenty-one aircraft were totally destroyed with another 43 damaged. *Forrestal* had to leave the war zone and head home for repairs, estimated at $70 million.

On 8 September the USAF began operating the Sikorsky HH–53B Jolly Green helicopter, an enlarged and farther-reaching outgrowth of the HH–3E Jolly Green Giant. The HH–53 was a big step forward. Air rescue squadrons had previously had to make do with the Kaman HH–43B Huskie, alias 'Pedro', which was a fine machine for local airfield fire-fighting and rescue but which had never been intended for combat rescues under fire, and with the HH–3E Jolly Green Giant, which had been very successful rescuing downed airmen but existed only in limited numbers. An earlier variant of the new helicopter, the CH–53A, had been in service with the Marine Corps in South Vietnam. The HH–53B, soon to be joined by the HH–53C, was to become the principal USAF tool of air rescue behind enemy lines, north and south.

The US Navy continued to rely on the Sikorsky SH–3A Sea King, and later the SH–3G variant, operating from the decks of a variety of ships, and the Kaman UH–2A/B Sea Sprite, soon joined by the HH–3H, operating from destroyers in the Gulf of Tonkin. Throughout the war helicopter pilots and crews who went into harm's way to rescue their buddies rarely received the praise they earned.

Sergeant Duane D. Hackney was awarded the Air Force Medal in ceremonies on 9 September 1967 for rescuing a downed pilot

The Vought A–7A Corsair II was taken into combat by the 'Argonauts' of VA–147, under Commander James Hill, on 4 December 1967. Inspired by the manufacturer's Crusader but actually a wholly new aircraft, the A–7 began to replace the A–4 Skyhawk in the light attack role. Aircraft 153242 is seen following a combat cruise at NAS Lemoore, California, on 11 October 1969. (DUANE KASULKA)

Among the F–100 Super Sabre pilots who flew vast numbers of sorties were activated members of the Air National Guard. Here Captain Angelo Perfetti of the 110th Tactical Fighter Squadron, Missouri Air National Guard, and his wing man leave the 352nd TFS operations building for an F–100 mission. (USAF)

A McDonnell F–4 Phantom takes off on a combat mission from a carrier deck off the Vietnamese coast. Navy fast jet pilots, like those in the Air Force, faced a difficult challenge when asked to come in close to support friendly troops on the ground. Forward air controllers often found it easier to direct slower-moving Skyraiders than fast jets. (USN)

in South Vietnam. Hackney was a parajumper or PJ, one of those intrepid young men who went on rescue aircraft.

Gunship

The AC–130A Hercules (54-1626) developed under the Gunship II program was deployed to South Vietnam for an operational test of the concept. The aircraft arrived on 15 September and was soon flying missions into Laos. An entire war was taking place in Laos and it was virtually unnoticed by press, public and congressional critics, even those who found fault with what was going on in South Vietnam.

Also in September, the American preoccupation with numbers reared its ugly

For a time it was the 'Helicopter War', then it got too big. But helicopters like this UH–1D Huey of the US Army's Champagne Flight, 1st Aviation Battalion, were still the key to mobility and enabled US ground troops to move around in a way that was impossible for the Viet Cong. (BELL)

head once again when the USAF decided that the one millionth combat sortie was flown in September 1967. The number of Air Force aircraft deployed to South-East Asia reached 1,500 in October and total aircraft losses passed the 1,000 mark that same month.

On 29 October the North Vietnamese Army unleashed two regiments, the 272nd and 273rd, against the isolated town and Special Forces camp at Loc Ninh, north of Saigon near the Cambodian border. The NVA were expected to quickly overrun the camp. But once a battle unfolded, General Westmoreland oversaw the use of Army helicopters to bring reinforcements. A week-long battle ensued, fought at times with artillery, at times in pointblank firefights with rifles. It was here that a young Army lieutenant, under pressure, uttered one of those memorable lines which are remembered long after details are forgotten: 'We had to destroy the village in order to save it.'

Vertical envelopment – the use of helicopters to position troops – held the town and blocked escape routes. More than two thousand NVA were killed. To quote historian Jim Mesko, 'Loc Ninh became a charnel house for the two NVA regiments.' Exploiting the mobility afforded by the helicopter, the US field commander had been able to concentrate six US infantry battalions and their supporting artillery within a few days, in a location where no US regular troops existed when the battle began. Loc Ninh was a victory not for the NVA but for the Americans.

The first USAF member to accumulate 6,000 flying hours in a helicopter was Major Kyron V. Hall, a Sikorsky CH–3C Jolly Green pilot of the 20th Helicopter Squadron based at Nha Trang. The record was reached in November.

Another intrepid helicopter pilot was Captain Gerald O. Young. Launched on a rescue mission on 9 November, Captain Young's HH–3E Jolly Green was part of a rescue armada which included another HH–3E, a C–130 Hercules flare ship, and three US Army helicopter gunships. This force was headed toward jungles south-east of Khe Sanh where a US-South Vietnamese reconnaissance team was on the verge of being overwhelmed by NVA troops. The NVA had already shot down two helicopters attempting to rescue the besieged survivors.

Ahead of Captain Young, an HH–3E landed in low cloud and poor visibility and took heavy fire while rescuing three survivors. The lead HH–3E was so badly damaged that it seemed unlikely to return safely to home base at Da Nang. Young could have escorted his sister ship to safety but chose, instead, to attempt to rescue two Americans and several South Vietnamese who remained on the ground.

Young made a perilous landing and with the help of his pararescue jumpers – the fearless PJs – took the friendly ground troops on board. The HH–3E took hits from the deadly accurate fire of the North Vietnamese.

With the friendlies aboard, Young applied full power for take-off as enemy riflemen appeared in the open. They raked the HH–3E with small-arms fire and rifle-launched grenades. Suddenly the right engine sparked and exploded and the blast flipped the HH–3E on its back and sent it cascading down the hill in flames.

Young hung upside-down in the cockpit, his clothing on fire. Frantically he beat out the flames and struggled free, but he had suffered second and third degree burns on one-quarter of his body.

This was only the beginning of an incredible saga. Young snuffed out flames engulfing one of the survivors. A–1E Sandys arrived overhead in the late afternoon and plotted out an effort to mount another rescue attempt at first light the following morning.

At daybreak, when the A–1E Sandys reappeared, Captain Young, after nursing

A crew chief, standing in the 'crow's nest' of the aircraft, tells the pilot of a US Army CV–2 Caribou the way is clear to taxi and take off. Army personnel were training Air Force crews in the operation and maintenance of the Caribou in late 1966 so that the aircraft, redesignated C–7A, could be turned over to the USAF on 1 January 1967. (USAF)

the survivor with burn injuries all night, stuck his head out of hiding and shot a signal flare, trying to warn the Sandys that the North Vietnamese would probably use him as bait for a flak trap. But the North Vietnamese seemed to have melted into the jungle. The A–1Es brought in several Army and VNAF helicopters which picked up five survivors and hauled them out.

Abruptly, when it seemed that a rescue of Captain Young might prove possible, more North Vietnamese troops appeared. Young hid the wounded man and struck out on his own, trying to lure the NVA away from the survivor.

His scheme worked. The NVA pursued him. Dazed and nearly in shock, he hid frequently to treat his burns. As the day drew on, he found himself leading the NVA in circles through an open region of high elephant grass. He made a decision not to use his beeper radio to communicate with rescue aircraft – still seeking to prevent drawing his comrades into a flak trap. While he continued drawing the NVA away from the original rescue site, helicopters set down there and picked up one survivor and the bodies of those who had been killed.

Seventeen hours after his crash and 6 miles (more than 9km) from the crash site, Captain Young finally slipped free of his pursuers and was able to signal a friendly helicopter. His ordeal was over.

During 1967 a number of airmen received the Medal of Honor, the highest American award 'for conspicuous gallantry and intrepidity at the risk of life above and beyond the call of duty'. Two were prisoners of war who resisted the enemy, F–100 Super Sabre pilot Colonel George E. (Bud) Day and F–4D Phantom back-seater Captain Lance P. Sijan. Three were decorated for heroic action up north, attacking enemy missile sites: A–4C Skyhawk pilot Lieutenant Commander Michael J. Estocin and F–105F Thunderchief pilots Captain Merlyn H. Dethlefsen and Major Leo K. Thorsness. Still another was an intrepid forward air controller and O–1 Bird Dog pilot, Captain Hilliard A. Wilbanks.

Finally, the Medal of Honor went to heroic HH–3E rescue pilot Captain Gerald O. Young. Numerous participants in his rescue operation agreed that the award was deserved.

Ho Chi Minh Trail

An increasingly important part of the war which knew no boundaries was the effort to cut off infiltration into South Vietnam, as well as the movement of North Vietnamese troops into Laos. On 15 November 1967 the US Navy moved nine OP–2E Neptune maritime patrol aircraft up to Nakhon Phanom, Thailand, to take part in 'Mud River', a program to seed the infiltration route – the Ho Chi Minh Trail, Americans called it – with sensors capable of detecting enemy vehicles.

The effort against the Ho Chi Minh Trail also occupied a squadron of EC–121R Constellations at Korat, which relayed signals from the sensors to ground stations as well as strike, helicopter and observation aircraft based at Nakhon Phanom. It quickly became clear that the effort to halt North Vietnamese infiltration was hindered by a number of technical problems with the sensors, delivery systems, and support facilities. The program employed modern technology against an enemy who was capable of moving his supplies using nothing more modern than sheer manpower.

Land-Based Navair

Although the US Navy's carrier forces received plenty of press and public attention, much of it because of their combat missions over North Vietnam, less publicity accompanied the work of land-based naval aviation units. From very early in the conflict, patrol squadrons flew out of Cam Ranh Bay, Da Nang, and other bases. These

An F–4D Phantom in flight with fuel and bombs. Most of the USAF's Phantoms were stationed in Thailand and flew 'out-country war' missions over North Vietnam. The Phantom was also a familiar sight in South Vietnam and often came to the aid of US or ARVN troops when they needed help. (TONY MARSHALL)

The Lockheed F–104C Starfighter was in the Vietnam conflict for two short tours of duty but was generally regarded as not the right aircraft for this war. These camouflaged F–104Cs were at Udorn, Thailand, in 1967–68. (USAF)

flights were aimed at stemming infiltration of personnel and supplies down 1,000 miles (1,610km) of Vietnamese coastline and down rivers. P–2 Neptunes, P–5 Marlins, and later P–3 Orions were used. Each of these aircraft could mount a mission which might last for hours: they were well armed and had the endurance to handle the grueling hours of search punctuated by fast action when the enemy was found.

The Marlin, or SP–5B, was the last American flying-boat to serve in combat. A distinctive and imposing sight, the SP–5B operated with a detachment from VP–40 based at Sangley Point in the Philippines, and flying from Cam Ranh Bay. SP–5B Marlins were supported by the seaplane tender USS *Currituck* (AV–7). The vessel provided food, fuel and supplies to the Marlin crews while they operated from Vietnamese waters and flew continuous 8- to 9-hour anti-infiltration patrols. The effort was part of the Navy's larger battle against infiltration known by the program name 'Market Time'.

The SP–5B Marlin served intermittently from 1965 to 1967. In the latter year the last of these graceful big 'boats was pulled out of the combat zone. The final operational flight of a Navy seaplane came on 6 November 1967 when an SP–5B from VP–40 flew its last mission after returning to the US.

Another area of naval aviation (and Marine aviation) which never received the attention it deserved was the night and adverse-weather flying performed by the A–6 Intruder. A second Marine Corps A–6A Intruder squadron was deployed to Vietnam when VMA(AW)-533's 'Hawks' set up shop at Chu Lai. The EA–6A Intruder electronic warfare aircraft was also coming into service with the Marine Corps and squadron VMCJ–2 operated briefly at Da Nang before being replaced by VMCJ–1.

Another Navy Intruder squadron, the 'Boomers' of VA–165, entered combat in December 1967 from the decks of the USS *Ranger* (CVA– 61). The Intruder's complex array of electronic 'black boxes' was taking a long time to get ironed out and fully functional, but by the end of 1967 it was well on the way.

On 4 December the Vought A–7A Corsair II light attack aircraft was introduced into combat by the 'Argonauts' of VA–147 commanded by Commander James Hill.

Combat deployment of Hill's squadron had been announced the previous month by Vice Admiral Thomas F. Connolly, Deputy Chief of Naval Operations (Air). On their first strike, Hill's pilots used 5in (127mm) Zuni rockets to assault bridge and highway targets in the narrow neck of North Vietnam just above the 17th Parallel. In north and south, the A–7 was to be a participant for the remainder of the war.

An official wrap-up for 1967 showed that enemy forces launched sixteen attacks against air bases in 1967. Eighty-one aircraft were destroyed or damaged in these attacks and nearly 400 casualties inflicted.

Whatever else they could do, Americans could keep numbers. Somehow they knew that USAF aircraft flew 878,771 combat sorties in 1967, a 69 per cent increase over 1966. Of the total, B–52s mounted 9,686 'Arc Light' sorties. Munitions expended totaled 681,700 tons, or 87 per cent more than in 1966. It was apparent that the US had now dropped more bombs in Vietnam than it had during the whole of the Second World War. Unfortunately some took the numbers to mean that the war was being won. In fact, by the end of 1967 the Viet Cong controlled more territory than they had at any previous time – without having ever won a major battle. Political control of the Viet Cong was now firmly in the hands of the North Vietnamese. To the extent that the insurgency in the south had ever possessed a native character of its own, it now belonged to Hanoi.

1968
TET, HUE, KHE SANH

On 14 January 1968, scarcely half a year after a catastrophic fire aboard *Forrestal*, tragedy struck again while the USS *Enterprise* (CVAN–65) was working up off the coast of Hawaii in preparation for a combat cruise to South-East Asia. As if unearthly forces were at work, unseen, there was an eerie repeat of an almost impossible circumstance: for the second time, a Zuni rocket ignited by an auxiliary power unit exploded and created a monstrous fire. The conflagration took 28 lives and cost $50 million damage to the nuclear-powered carrier.

North Vietnamese forces equivalent to four divisions closed their snare on the US Marine Corps base at Khe Sanh in northern South Vietnam on 21 January 1968. The NVA cut the base off from all land transport and communications. For four months, only aircraft could support the base and bring in supplies. Crews of C–123s and C–130s made daring landings at Khe Sanh while under fire from mortars and artillery surrounding the base. To many it seemed as if the North Vietnamese wanted to turn Khe Sanh into a latter-day Dien Bien Phu, inflicting on the Americans the same kind of dramatic defeat they had handed the French in 1954.

On 29 January a 36-hour cease-fire for the Tet lunar new year began with many South Vietnamese troops going home on leave. Two days later, Viet Cong and North Vietnamese forces in the south launched an offensive all over South Vietnam. Viet Cong local insurgents and North Vietnamese regulars attacked every important city, provincial capital, and military installation in South Vietnam. In Saigon, Viet Cong blasted holes in the palace and US embassy walls and entered the courtyards.

The six-story chancery building that loomed over much of central Saigon had symbolized the US presence and had not been thought to be vulnerable. Americans felt so secure in the embassy that they had only a few Marines on guard. A sapper squad of nineteen Viet Cong, having blasted their way into the courtyards, was all set to storm the building itself. But their leaders had been gunned down by the guards and their assault lost momentum. With Military Police arriving to help the Marines, a six-hour battle ended with bodies everywhere, some American but mostly VC.

The effect on Americans, including those back home who watched the war on their television sets, was stunning. The sudden eruption of massive, close-quarters fighting in the cities was reported by the media as a stunning defeat for Saigon's forces and for the American purpose of securing the independence of the South Vietnam regime. TV viewers watched the fiercest fighting of the war in Pleiku, Nha Trang, Da Nang, Qui Nhon, and especially the ancient imperial city of Hue, which was overwhelmed and overrun.

A USAF history, looking back at Tet with the benefit of hindsight, presented one view: 'The Communist Tet offensive shattered the feeling of confidence felt by many in the administration and altered the conduct of the war. Although the Tet offensive and the subsequent attempt to seize Khe Sanh were colossal military failures, many national leaders came to believe that the enemy had been badly underestimated. Growing financial and domestic difficulties made the [Johnson] administration unwilling to increase its commitment or risk a wider war by relieving the long-enforced restraints on the use of US power.'

Korean Woes

Tet troubles in Vietnam coincided with trouble in Korea: on 21 January 1968 thirty-one North Korean commandos infiltrated through the lines on a mission to assassinate the South Korean president and were

The McDonnell RF-4C Phantom operated from Tan Son Nhut airfield and handled nearly all tactical reconnaissance in South Vietnam from 1968 onwards. The reconnaissance RF-4Cs of the 460th Tactical Reconnaissance Wing often operated at very low level within range of Viet Cong ground fire. An RF-4C crash killed Major General Robert Worley, ending combat missions by general officers. (USAF)

Wearing gas masks, apparently as protection against their own side's riot control agents, Marines of the 2nd Battalion, 5th Marines, head toward bitter house-to-house fighting in the old imperial capital of Hue on 6 February 1968. For Americans the fighting in Hue was perhaps the most intense of the entire war. (USMC)

detected and engaged in Seoul only a short distance from his residence. Gunfire throughout the city made it seem as if another war had already begun.

Then came North Korea's 23 January 1968 seizure of the US spy ship *Pueblo* (AGER–2). Americans in Seoul woke up on the morning of 24 January to read that *Enterprise* was coming to their rescue. In fact, *Enterprise* was still licking her wounds from the tragic fire and the USS *Ranger* (CVA–61) had to be diverted from South-East Asian waters to head north for Korea. The possibility loomed large that the US – under pressure to honor its defense commitment to allies – might find itself fighting two land wars in Asia. On 25 January President Johnson responded to the *Pueblo* crisis by ordering a limited call-up of Reserve forces, including some Naval Air Reserve squadrons and fourteen Air National Guard and eight Air Force Reserve squadrons.

The Tet offensive led to the attack on the old imperial city of Hue by Viet Cong and North Vietnamese regulars, who fought South Vietnamese troops and American Marines in savage house-to-house combat. As an incidental aside to the bitter fighting, the North Vietnamese at Hue destroyed four O–1 Bird Dog and four O–2 observation aircraft on the ground.

The communist attack on Hue began in pre-dawn darkness on 31 January. At first American soldiers in the MACV Compound in the New City were able to fight off a battalion-sized NVA assault. In the Old City, however, the elite ARVN Hac Do ('Black Panther') company was overwhelmed. Several battalions of NVA occupied the Old City and took up blocking positions north and south of Hue. Those hold-outs in portions of the old capital not yet under NVA control were cut off from the outside world.

A grim, gray overcast hung over Hue, making it difficult to get air support into the area. Major Denis J. (Deej) Kiehly, a Marine Corps F–8E Crusader pilot, sneaked in under the crud and engaged in a ferocious battle with NVA troops on the ground, including a sniper in a citadel tower who was almost as high as Kiehly's own altitude. With little room to maneuver, in poor light and poor visibility, Kiehly handled his supersonic Crusader so that he was in a one-on-one, head-on engagement with the sniper. A burst of 20mm cannon fire blew away sniper, tower, and an NVA supporting cast.

The 1st and 5th US Marines attempted to enter Hue, ran into fierce NVA resistance in bitter house-to-house fighting, and failed. On 1 February a second effort was made to counter-attack the Old City with increased Marine strength. For a time the weather improved slightly, enabling F–8E Crusaders and A–4 Skyhawks to support the men on the ground. West of the city, the 3rd Brigade, First Air Cavalry halted three new NVA regiments moving to reinforce Hue.

It is almost impossible to describe the ferocity of the fighting at Hue. Many years later, film director Stanley Kubrick attempted to recreate it in 'Full Metal Jacket'. The fighting was especially savage for the American Marines – who upheld an honored tradition going back almost to their country's founding. The conventional wisdom has made Khe Sanh the classic battle of the war, but the fighting in Hue was on a larger scale, at closer quarters.

The Marines' job was made more difficult because of an official hesitance to use heavy weapons (or B–52 bombing) in the ancient capital. Marines made effective use of Ontos, a tracked vehicle mounting batteries of six 106mm recoilless rifles, but most of the fighting was with grenades and rifles at point-blank range.

Supporting fire from naval warships was allowed and by 7 February the tide of the battle for Hue had turned against the communists. The New City was swept clean of NVA by 9 February, but it took until 22

February for Marines and ARVN troops to retake the Old City's ancient Citadel. Air cover played an increasing role as the weather improved. In the fight for Hue, 5,191 naval rounds, 18,091 land artillery rounds and 290,877lb (131,938kg) of aerial ordnance were expended.

Brigadier General Foster Lahue, the veteran of the Second World War and Korea who commanded Marines at Hue, called the fighting 'among the worst in our history', meaning American history.

VNAF Role

Another aspect of the Tet offensive and the events which followed was the effect of the fighting on the VNAF. According to the National Air and Space Museum's Robert C. Mikesh, when Tet began the VNAF had available just 69 A–1 Skyraiders at Bien Hoa, Binh Thuy, Da Nang and Nha Trang, plus F–5 Freedom Fighters at Bien Hoa. Mikesh tells us that these aircraft flew 215 sorties, H–34 helicopters a further 215, reconnaissance aircraft 196 and cargo planes 158 during the hectic final days of January.

During February the number of combat missions increased and the VNAF bombed and strafed Viet Cong forces throughout the country. The helicopter fleet hauled ARVN troops, supplied them, and conducted medical air evacuation missions. During Tet, the VNAF lost seventeen aircraft; ten on the ground and seven in the air, the latter figure including five A–1s, one C–47 and one U–17 (a high-wing Cessna 180 derivative).

Although there had been enormous problems getting personnel back to their units during the confusion of Tet, the VNAF had contributed substantially to the fighting during this period. Many believed that the VNAF was now showing maturity as a settled and able fighting force. Others noted that new pilots did not seem to have quite the same courage as some of the older hands. The VNAF seemed to have some men who were excellent and others who were at the other end of the spectrum.

Because of the Tet Offensive and the heavy fighting at Hue, B–52 Stratofortress bombing sorties were increased in number and frequency. Although the B–52F had been the first model employed, B–52D Stratofortresses with the 'Big Belly' modification enabling them to carry up to 108 bombs (as shown here) became the principal heavy bombers of the conflict. (USAF)

B–52 Missions

On 1 February 1968, in response to the Tet offensive, the number of B–52 sorties authorized for South-East Asia was increased from 800 to 1,200 monthly. On 15 February the figure was increased to 1,800.

B–52F aircraft configured for the strategic nuclear role began these heavy bomber operations. In December 1965 Strategic Air Command had begun the 'Big Belly' modification program to increase the capacity of the B–52D to carry 500lb (227kg) bombs from 27 to 84 or 750-pounders (384kg) from 27 to 42 internally. In addition, the modified B–52D could carry 24 500lb (227kg) or 750lb (384kg) bombs externally – a total of 108 of the former. At about this time, crews began referring to their aircraft as the 'Buff', an acronym for – in polite language – big ugly fat fellow. The name has stuck.

Although B–52s were used primarily against targets in South Vietnam, they bombed approaches to the Mu Gia Pass in North Vietnam, beginning on 12 April 1966. That month the 'Big Belly' B–52D replaced the B–52F in flying the long, tedious combat missions from Guam. In April 1967 'Buffs' began operating from U-Tapao, Thailand, as well as Guam, completing missions from the closer location without in-flight refueling. On 13 September 1967 the 'Big Belly' program was completed with modification of the final B–52D to the 108-bomb configuration.

The 1968 B–52 bombings in support of the siege of Khe Sanh became the largest such campaign so far. Although there was to be a halt in the bombing of North Vietnam later in the year, on 1 November 1968, this did not affect 'Arc Light' operations in the south.

As the siege of Khe Sanh drew a smaller and tighter circle around the Marines at the base, on 8 March 1968 General Momyer, the Seventh Air Force chief in Saigon, was named as single manager for air operations in the Khe Sanh area, despite vigorous objections by the Marines.

Probably no airmen had more courage than those who landed at Khe Sanh to drop off supplies and to pick up wounded. The C–130 Hercules had been designed for LAPES (low-altitude parachute extraction system) which in theory enabled the aircraft to get rid of its payload without its wheels touching the ground. But men were bleeding amid the mortar barrages which walked all over the Khe Sanh base and those men had to be gotten out. Although the runway was pock-marked with shell holes and the mortar and artillery rounds were still coming in, the C–123s and C–130s landed.

In all, there were 273 landings by C–130 Hercules, 179 by C–123 Providers, and eight by C–7 Caribous. 496 parachute drops were made by C–130s, 105 by C–123s, and 57 LAPES extractions from C–130s. The cargo aircraft delivered 12,400 tons of materiel to the besieged base. Hill positions around the airfield were supplied by CH–46 Sea Knight helicopters.

Air Support

General Westmoreland had asked for and gotten a contingency plan, code-named 'Niagara', to provide air support to the Khe Sanh bastion.

The first phase of the operation, 'Niagara I', consisted of building up a comprehensive intelligence picture of the enemy, identifying targets, and earmarking the forces needed to destroy them. 'Niagara II' was the total commitment of these forces as soon as the enemy took the offensive. As early as 21 January, at the outset of the most intense part of the Khe Sanh seige, 'Niagara II' was triggered.

In the first 24 hours, over 600 tactical air strikes were carried out by Air Force, Navy and Marine squadrons. B–52 Stratofortress strikes (see later) devastated those enemy bunkers, trenches and tunnel networks that had been identified in advance. In due course AC–47 gunships joined the fight and kept the pressure on the North Vietnamese. By the end of the Khe Sanh siege in April, 24,000 tactical and 2,700 B–52 strikes had been carried out. Incredibly, despite the bad weather and enemy gunfire, the only tactical aircraft lost were one A–4 Skyhawk, one F–4 Phantom, and seventeen Marine helicopters.

Operation 'Pegasus' was the name given to the First Cavalry effort to relieve the Marine garrison at Khe Sanh. By 5 April 1968, a partial reopening of the land route to the Khe

The Fairchild C–123 Provider supplied Khe Sanh and other American outposts, often under fire. It was not unusual to have only pierced steel planking for a runway. C–123K 55–4509 (WE) of the 19th Tactical Airlift Squadron was later turned over to the VNAF. (CHARLES ZEMPLE)

Sanh combat base was accomplished when the First Cavalry broke through NVA forces.

While the Air Force had some very brave men at the controls of its aircraft, it suffered no lack of other men who contributed only to the compiling of nonsensical statistics. Operation 'Niagara', conducted from 22 January to 31 March 1968 in support of Khe Sanh, including 24,016 sorties. In an airlift effort surpassed only by the Berlin Airlift, tactical transports made 447 landings and 576 airdrops, delivering 12,430 tons of supplies.

It should be mentioned that the US Marine Corps contributed much to the air support of its own people on the ground and that the role of the Marine helicopter has been largely overlooked. Following the 'Shu Fly' UH–34D helicopters earlier in the decade, Marines deployed squadron VMO–2 equipped with UH–1E Hueys, all-aluminium versions of the Army's UH–1C. The Hueys were used as both 'slicks' (troop carriers) and gunships. Some were fitted with a TAT 101 twin 7.62mm gun turret.

Like the Army, the Marines wanted a helicopter designed from the outset as a gunship – the AH–1G Cobra would not arrive until 1969, the AH–1J Sea Cobra until June 1971. Meanwhile, UH–1Es of various Marine observation squadrons continued to fly as armed helicopters. In addition, they were used to provide liaison, forward air control, and medical evacuation missions. Finally, there was search and rescue (SAR), which found brave helicopter crews pitting themselves against the enemy on the ground at point-blank range and fighting to save fellow combatants. SAR missions produced some incredible acts of heroism and two Marines on such missions – Captain Stephen W. Pless on 19 August 1967 and PFC Raymond M. Clausen on 30 January 1970 – received the Medal of Honor for their courage.

Bombs and Talks

As part of President Johnson's search for a settlement with Hanoi, bombing of North Vietnam above 20° North was halted on 1 April 1968 and the bomb line was moved down to the 19th Parallel on 4 April. Johnson called upon North Vietnam to act in good faith and de-escalate. Instead, Hanoi viewed the gesture as a sign of weakening US resolve and used the bombing halt for restoration and reconstruction, to reinforce air defenses and to move more materiel and troops to the south.

Robert McNamara, who was forever to be linked to the enormous build-up of American forces, was replaced as Secretary of Defense on April 1 by Clark M. Clifford. Soon thereafter, General Creighton W. Abrams was named to replace General Westmoreland as Commander, MACV. Clifford was an old-time Washington lawyer and savvy insider who had worked quietly for several administrations. Abrams was a tough former armor officer who was widely respected inside the Army. The pair were heirs to a situation they had had no role in creating. Both were well aware that it was election year again and that the war was issue number one to the voters.

The North Vietnamese must have wondered why the Americans fought so fiercely. With their own society in upheaval, with half their own population demonstrating and rioting to oppose the war, why did Americans risk their lives, day after day. Was it, as General MacArthur had suggested, because of duty, honor, country? Did they really believe that the inefficient, corrupt Saigon regime was bringing the world a new brand of democracy?

The truth was that the Americans fought with valor because they owed it to each other. Captain Don Crenna, who flew an F–4 Phantom in night missions against the Ho Chi Minh Trail, put it more crudely than most. 'I don't care shit for democracy or patriotism,' admitted Crenna. 'But when one

The Huey remained the most numerous helicopter in Vietnam and the most familiar sight on American TV screens. The UH–1D Huey model, shown here, had a longer fuselage than the earlier UH–1B and various internal improvements. (US ARMY)

of my own guys is down out there, I'm going to risk everything to rescue him. And because so many of my friends have been killed or wounded, when I have a chance to get even, I will. Why do we fly into a hail of gunfire to bring our bombs to the NVA? Because we want to bomb the shit out of the bastards who waxed our pals, that's why.'

Marine Corps Cobra helicopter pilot Con Silard: 'I've seen guys do some incredibly dangerous things. Imagine a helicopter guy setting down in the middle of the enemy, at night, in the fog, with bullets whining all around him, just to pick up a buddy. Why does he do it? It has nothing to do with whether he believes in the war or not. He does it because all of us will go to hell and back to help each other.'

The troops in Vietnam read about peace talks in their *Stars and Stripes*, but few expected the negotiations to have much effect on their lives. After a 34-day impasse over location, preliminary peace talks opened in Paris on 10 May 1968. The communist side almost immediately made a tactical mistake by allowing itself to be seen quibbling over the size and shape of the negotiating table instead of showing interest in working towards peace.

In May attention shifted to the Special Forces camp at Kham Duc, which became increasingly difficult to hold under pressure from the Viet Cong and was not, in any event, of much value. From 12 to 14 May C–130 Hercules extracted personnel from Kham Duc, including the US 2nd Battalion, 1st Infantry and ARVN troops.

Abrams succeeded Westmoreland as the US field commander in Saigon on 10 June 1968.

After the lavish expenditure of munitions and supplies in support of the besieged Marines, the combat base at Khe Sanh was dismantled and abandoned on 23 June. President Johnson had hailed the defense of the base as a decisive victory, but the success was overshadowed by the pessimism generated by the Tet offensive. The base had outlived its usefulness and there was no reason to keep it any longer.

Enter the Bronco

Another new aircraft type joined the fighting in South Vietnam when the twin-turboprop OV–10A Bronco arrived at Bien Hoa in late July and was assembled at the air base. The first OV–10As thrown into the forward air control (FAC) operation were assigned to the USAF's 504th Tactical Air Support Group, the same outfit that had lost four O–1s and four O–2s during the fighting in Hue.

The UH–1 Huey helicopter was most widely used by the US Army to move troops to and from combat zones (right), but the other services used the helicopter as well. UH–1F warming up in the rain at Ban Me Thuyet (below) is similar to the Air Force aircraft in which Lieutenant James P. Fleming won the Medal of Honor. (BELL/JOE VIVIANO)

A USAF OV–10 Bronco is assembled at Bien Hoa air base, South Vietnam, in August 1968. In size, the twin-boomed OV–10 lay between small unarmed liaison aircraft like the O–1 Bird Dog and fully fledged fighter-bombers like the A–1 Skyraider. The OV–10 could fly armed forward air control missions, assist in rescues, and escort river and road convoys. With short take-off and landing (STOL) characteristics, the OV–10 could operate from rough, unpaved airfields. (USAF)

War at Home

1968 was to be the year when domestic events would intrude again and again into Americans' perception of the Vietnam War. Few Americans were untouched by a presidential campaign which saw the wounding of Governor George Wallace, the murder of Martin Luther King, and – above all – the death of Robert F. Kennedy in Los Angeles after the senator had won the California primary and assured himself a claim to the White House. 1968 was the year rioting and violent death inflicted itself on the American body politic. By the time police went berserk in Chicago at the democratic convention which nominated Vice President Hubert Humphrey, it was only one more example of the continuing tumult. By mid-summer it was probably true to say that more Americans opposed the war in Vietnam than supported it.

Presidents Johnson and Thieu met in Honolulu for two days, 19 and 20 July 1968, to discuss the war. Johnson called rumors of a major US policy change 'absolute tommyrot and fiction', an almost certain sign that the rumors were true. The presidential meeting had been preceded by the visit to Saigon in early July of Defense Secretary Clark Clifford, who also denied that anything new was impending. By now the world had heard Johnson's dramatic announcement on 31 March that he would not seek a further term in office – a virtual admission that the war was now so unpopular that he could not be re-elected – and the race for the White House was boiling down to a contest between Humphrey and Richard M. Nixon.

In an incident which was to end combat flying by flag-rank officers, Major General Robert F. Worley, vice commander of the Seventh Air Force in Saigon, was killed along with his back-seater, Major Robert F. Brodman, when their RF–4C Phantom was hit by enemy fire in the DMZ area and Worley's attempt to bring the aircraft home ended in a fiery crash. This happened on 23 July 1968.

The longstanding, on-again, off-again deployment of a detachment of F–102A interceptors to Bien Hoa ended on 25 September and the delta-winged fighters were removed from South Vietnam for the last time.

The bombing of most of North Vietnam, halted on 1 October 1968, was replaced on 1 November by a prohibition against US combat sorties anywhere in the north. Reconnaissance missions continued and revealed that the enemy was moving rapidly to repair bridges and roads, strengthen anti-aircraft defenses, and improve airfields. Truck movements of supplies to the south increased fourfold.

To return to the Martin RB–57E Canberras of the 'Patricia Lynn' reconnaissance program which had been in South Vietnam since May 1963, this unit suffered its second casualty on 25 October 1968 when aircraft 55–4264 was hit by ground fire in the left engine. Captain J. J. Johnson and Major Phil Walker ejected safely. The dull black Canberra, sinister in its appearance, augered down and exploded in the jungle. In due course a replacement was assigned to keep the complement of RB–57Es at five.

With their call-sign changed to 'Moon River', the RB–57Es began gathering intelligence with a system called Compass Eagle. The RB–57E was equipped with an infra-red scanner and an in-flight display screen which showed, in real-time, what was happening in the darkness below. The RB–57E could prowl the Saigon River at night, detect sampans being used by the enemy to move supplies, and call in artillery fire, gunships, or PBR patrol boats to despatch the enemy. Throughout the war there were difficulties in communication between those who gathered intelligence and those who used it, but this sidelight to the RB–57E story was apparently a successful one.

President Johnson had suffered the humiliation of having to abandon any thought of re-election in 1968. Now he had to suffer a devastating loss by his party. In a country rapidly being torn asunder by violence in the streets, much of it directed against US participation in the war, Nixon defeated Humphrey in the 5 November 1968 presidential election. Nixon had gotten into office in part by announcing that he had a plan to end the war, but he had not said what the plan was.

Medal Mission

An official US Air Force history tells the story of a remarkable combat mission:

'Just before noon on 26 November 1968, a transport helicopter inserted a Special Forces team into hostile territory in the western highlands of South Vietnam. The UH–1F Huey chopper was manned by Lieutenant James P. Fleming, aircraft commander; Major Paul E. McClellan, co-pilot; and the gunners, Staff Sergeant Fred J. Cook and Sergeant Paul R. Johnson.

'Four hours later the reconnaissance team made contact with the enemy. Their leader, Lieutenant Randolph C. Harrison, sent out a radio call for gunship fire support, but the Green Berets quickly realized that they were hopelessly outnumbered and called again for immediate evacuation.

'Overhead, an Air Force FAC responded to the urgent request. He found the six men pinned down along a river bank and under intense fire from heavy machine-guns and automatic weapons.

'The FAC, Major Charles E. Anonsen, spotted a clearing in the jungle 100 yards from the Green Berets and a second, much smaller, clearing within 25 yards. He doubted whether a chopper could land in the second clearing, but the question was academic because the beleaguered Americans were trapped in the dense undergrowth and unable to move toward either one.

'Meanwhile, a flight of three transport and two gunship helicopters had also heard the call. The five choppers were en route to a refueling stop but quickly changed course and headed for the river bank. Lieutenant Fleming flew the second transport bird.

'Major Anonsen briefed the arriving helicopters and asked the Green Berets to pop a smoke grenade. The red smoke filtering up through the foliage pinpointed the position of the friendly soldiers.

'The jungle on three sides of the Americans came alive as the two gunships sent a stream of fire slanting earthward and the enemy instantly answered back. The airborne gunners strained to spot the hostile machine-guns as Major Leonard Gonzales and Captain David Miller wheeled their UH–1s above the river.

'The gunship crews located the guns 200 yards south of the Green Berets and ripped the positions with high-explosive rockets, destroying two of the heavy weapons. But the North Vietnamese had also found the range and laced Captain Miller's aircraft with machine-gun fire.

'Despite a rapid loss of oil pressure, Miller's crippled craft made two more firing passes before being riddled by a second accurate burst. Dave Miller knew he was done as he pulled up and headed north-east. As the bird lost power, he steered it to a safe landing in a clearing across the river, performing what Major Anonsen would later call "a beautiful auto-rotation."

'Now the first transport helicopter commanded by Major Dale L. Eppinger swung into action. While the stricken gunship settled into the emergency landing, Eppinger maneuvered his UH–1 to follow closely behind. He touched down alongside the downed bird and instantly Captain Miller and his crew climbed aboard. Low on fuel, the transport bird wheeled away to the forward base at Duc Co.

'Within minutes, Miller's abandoned chopper was ripped by enemy fire and destroyed. A second helicopter was forced to depart because of low fuel and only the FAC, one gunship, and one transport bird remained.

'The FAC radioed the Green Berets to move to the small clearing while Lieutenant Fleming descended toward the river. Major Gonzales forces the enemy gunners to keep their heads down and he made multiple passes with guns blazing to cover Jim Fleming's approach.

'At treetop height, Jim realized that the clearing was too small and overgrown for a landing, and he headed instead for the nearby riverbank. Perhaps he could hover just above the shoreline with his landing skids bumping the bank and his tail boom extended out over the water. That's exactly what Jim did, performing a feat of unbelievable flying skill as his crew searched frantically for the recon team.

'They were nowhere in sight and the team's radioman could barely be heard above the chatter of the hostile guns. Finally, the message came through. The team could not make it to the pickup point.

'Fleming's bird was an inviting target as he backed out over the river through a hail of bullets. His gunners, Sergeants Cook and Johnson, answered back, raking the concealed emplacements with M60 machine-gun fire. Major Gonzales said later. "It was a sheer miracle that he wasn't shot down on the take-off."

'Gonzales was nearly out of ammunition, and both he and Jim Fleming were critically low on fuel. If the rescue force withdrew, the American soldiers were doomed. With their

Vice President Hubert H. Humphrey – seen at Chu Lai with Westmoreland and Marine Lieutenant General Robert E. Cushman, Jr. – campaigned against Richard M. Nixon in the presidential election contest of 1968. A police riot at Humphrey's Chicago nominating convention and Nixon's claim of a plan to end the war defeated Humphrey at the polls. (USMC)

Martin RB–57E Canberra 55–4264 was lost in combat on 25 October 1968. Both crew members ejected safely. This and other RB–57Es of the 'Patricia Lynn' program used a system called Compass Eagle to provide real-time, infra-red tracking of Viet Cong supply vessels on the rivers near Saigon. The RB–57E could then call in friendly forces in the form of artillery, gunships, or the PBR Mark II patrol vessel shown here, to intercept and engage the enemy supply vessels. (USAF/USN)

backs to the river, the Green Berets hastily ringed their position with Claymore mines and hoped for a miracle.

'Overhead Jim prepared for one last-ditch attempt. He recalls, "The first time we went in I wasn't really conscious of the danger. You know, it was what we had been trained to do. And so we did it. But then I guess it all got to me. Watching Miller getting shot down, the heaviest hostile fire I'd ever seen . . . Frankly, I was scared to death!"

'Nevertheless, Jim let down to the river for the second time, dropping below the bank to partially shield the UH–1 from the deadly barrage. But this time the North Vietnamese knew precisely where he was headed and concentrated their fire on the pickup point, strafing the chopper from all sides.

'By now, the six Special Forces men had been under siege for an hour, and the enemy began to move in for the kill. Jim witnessed a grisly scene as the North Vietnamese reached the string of mines and one enemy soldier was blown into the air. The Green Berets killed three attackers who advanced to within ten yards of the landing zone, then turned their backs on death and desperately dashed for the helicopter.

'In the hovering UH–1, Sergeant Cook fired at the advancing foe while Sergeant Johnson tried in vain to clear a jammed gun. As the team reached the rope ladder, Cook continued firing with one hand, while pulling the soldiers aboard with the other. "Sergeant Cook is about 5 feet 7 and weighs not much more than 120 pounds," Jim Fleming said later. "But those Special Forces boys, some of whom were 200 pounds or more, said that Cook literally lifted them into the helicopter with one hand!"

'Jim struggled to hold his craft steady while it rocked and bounced as the Green Berets climbed aboard. Sergeant Johnson helped Cook drag the last man in as the ship backed out from the bank and sped downriver, the rope ladder dragging in the water.

'Overhead, Major Gonzales, who had been supporting Lieutenant Fleming throughout, ran out of ammunition at the very moment that the team climbed to safety. He had strafed within five yards of the friendly soldiers to screen them from the enemy.

'It was only as the two choppers whirled eastward to Duc Co with fuel tanks nearly dry that Jim Fleming and Paul McClellan noticed the bullet holes in the windshield. Neither could remember being hit and neither cared to dwell on the fact that they had missed death by inches.'

This quote from an official history by Major Donald K. Schneider covers one of four Medals of Honor won by USAF fliers in 1968. Captain Lance O. Sijan, an F–4 Phantom pilot, received the Medal posthumously for his conduct as a prisoner of war during the period ending 22 January 1968. Lieutenant Colonel Joe M. Jackson received the Medal for landing a C–123 Provider at a besieged camp to rescue Americans on 12 May 1968. Lieutenant Colonel William A. Jones III received the Medal for an A–1 Skyraider mission over North Vietnam on 1 September 1968.

As the year drew to a close, in a deployment called 'Combat Hornet', the first of the newly modified AC–119G gunships

1968 was the last year the Convair F–102A Delta Dagger stood guard in South Vietnam, waiting for enemy aircraft to intercept. This view, taken in Korea where tensions were also high, shows F–102As in flight with Northrop F–5A Freedom Fighters. (USAF)

At Chu Lai, a Marine Corps ordnanceman loads the 20mm cannon on an A–4E Skyhawk belonging to Marine Aircraft Group 12 (MAG–12). The Marines supplied much of the air support to their own men at Khe Sanh and other locations. (USMC)

arrived at Nha Trang on 22 December. Deployment of the AC–119G had been delayed due to the overweight condition of the airframes after modification. In yet another deployment, dubbed 'Combat Cougar'. EC–47Q Sentinel Eagle aircraft arrived in South Vietnam in December 1968. Essentially an electronic snooper version of the venerable 'Gooney Bird', the EC–47Q carried radio and electronics receiver gear and a crew of specialists.

Viet Cong Losses

At the Paris peace talks the Viet Cong, or the National Liberation Front as they called themselves, were represented separately from the North Vietnamese. Their political arm was now called the PRG, the Peoples Revolutionary Government. The irony was supreme. For many years, while the US had insisted that the Viet Cong was a powerless puppet of the north, the communist insurgency in the south had actually been led by southerners. At the very time that the separateness of the Viet Cong was being recognized in Paris, it had ceased to exist. The American view of the situation had become self-fulfilling: now the Viet Cong

Towards the end of 1968 the cannon-armed version of the Phantom, the F–4E, came to South-East Asia with the 469th Tactical Fighter Squadron. Shark's teeth were painted on the Phantoms by Captain Stephen R. Stephen, here with his aircraft. The F–4Es arrived at Korat, Thailand, just as the bombing halt over North Vietnam took effect – and were used over Laos and South Vietnam. (STEPHEN R. STEPHEN)

were completely controlled by Hanoi.

The best Viet Cong units had led the Tet assault and had been more than decimated; 38,794 men had been killed, 6,991 captured. Their hope of sparking off a widespread popular uprising had failed completely and after some initial faltering most of the populace rallied to the Saigon government. Nor did the ARVN collapse – the South Vietnamese Army and Police emerged from Tet more confident and stronger than before.

According to Harold T. Nelson, a former State Department official who was in South Vietnam at the time, 1968 was the year the Viet Cong was effectively wiped out as a viable fighting force. Tet, and smaller offensives in May and August, led to battles which created the highest number of casualties yet among indigenous communist forces in the south. 'Their recruiting base was being wiped out in these battles,' says Nelson. 'The Viet Cong were being wiped out faster than they could create new fighters.'

'Some of the tactics in 1968, where VC units were sent off to be slaughtered,' Nelson explains, 'were intentional on the part of the north. The North Vietnamese never wanted the communists in the south to control the insurgency. The way to do it, of course, was to kill off the southerners who contributed to any differences between the Viet Cong and the North Vietnamese.'

The ARVN's own recruiting effort was more successful than it had been. There really were more people who supported the Saigon regime, for all its faults. The South Vietnamese Army was able to form new divisions and increase its size at the very time the Viet Cong were suffering most.

The number-keepers concluded at the end of 1968 that 392 USAF aircraft had been lost in South-East Asia, no fewer than 257 of these to ground fire. Of the total, 304 were combat losses, 88 operational. The cost of the aircraft lost was $441 million. Ground attacks on air bases in South Vietnam had resulted in 35 aircraft being destroyed. Up north, surface-to-air missiles (SAMs) and MiG fighters had claimed only twelve USAF aircraft as compared with 40 the previous year, which reflected the halt in bombing of North Vietnam.

More numbers: Air Force air munitions expended in 1968 totaled 1,092,200 tons, a 60 per cent increase over 1967 expenditures. The USAF flew 1,034,839 combat sorties, 20,568 of which were B–52 'Arc Light' strikes.

At the end of 1968 – Richard Nixon having been chosen by the voters in November – American troop strength in South Vietnam was near its peak at 536,100.

Carrier-based US Navy aircraft continued to carry an enormous share of the burden over North and South Vietnam. A Grumman KA–6D Intruder refuels a Vought A–7 Corsair high above one of the Pacific Fleet's aircraft-carriers. (LTV)

1969 YEAR OF TRANSITION

Richard M. Nixon took office as president on 20 January 1969, in part because he had promised a way out of the deepening quagmire in Vietnam. An early step by Nixon was to name Henry Cabot Lodge – his vice presidential running mate in 1960 and a former ambassador to Saigon – as senior American negotiator at the Paris peace talks. Henry Kissinger was named as the new national security advisor.

Before he revealed his plan to end the Vietnam war, Nixon asked for a review of the South Vietnamese forces – telescoping his intent to shift much of the burden of the war to Saigon's own troops.

The hard-working Vietnamese Air Force (VNAF) was now becoming a jet force. Very effective in Vietnamese hands, perhaps in part due to its simplicity, was the Cessna A–37 Dragonfly, derived from the T–37 basic trainer. By early 1969 no fewer than 54 A–37s were in action with three VNAF squadrons, as will be noted later. An ambitious program was under way in the US to train Vietnamese pilots on this aircraft.

The A–37 really was simple, but it was also a tough, potent fighting machine. The pilot sat beneath a high round clamshell cockpit. Although the aircraft had been conceived as a two-seater, it was almost always flown by one man. This had some disadvantages. It was hard to roll in on a target from the right, for example, for visibility was less effective on

By 1969 the Cessna A–37 Dragonfly was an important contributor to the war effort. In August 1967 about ten had arrived at Bien Hoa and Pleiku for evaluation by the USAF's 604th Fighter Squadron under project 'Combat Dragon'. American A–37s (below) were quickly joined by Vietnamese-flown A–37s of the VNAF 524th Fighter Squadron at Nha Trang. One of the early American A–37 pilots was Lieutenant Cort Durocher (right), who graduated from the US Air Force Academy in 1968 and went to war almost immediately. (USAF/DUROCHER)

the side located away from the pilot. But the 14,500lb (6,577kg) A–37 could carry a formidable load of napalm or HE (high-explosive) bombs and was fast enough to be relatively immune to Viet Cong ground fire. It was no Phantom, but it was just what the Vietnamese needed.

First deliveries were of the A–37A model, which was a rebuild of the T–37 trainer. Soon afterwards came the sturdier A–37B, a new-build aircraft.

VNAF Maintenance

A young and energetic officer, Nguyen Cao Nguyen, had the thankless job of being the Vietnamese Air Force's chief of maintenance. Nguyen began work with the 83rd Special Group, Premier Nguyen Cao Ky's outfit, equipped with A–1H Skyraiders and C–47 transports. The C–47s were used to drop special operations troops – often, it was widely rumored, inside North Vietnam.

'Maintenance never received the resources it needed,' says Nguyen. 'Almost everything else seemed to come first.'

Nguyen remembers an occasion when Ky visited a base under fire from the Viet Cong. Ky's wife Mai was present. 'A very average pilot' was how Nguyen described the well-known air marshal and premier. 'He climbs in, he doesn't know where the starter is.' But Ky was also a man of unquestioned bravery. When the mortar rounds started to come in, 'he refused to hide from the incoming fire'.

According to Nguyen, the VNAF had considerable difficulty keeping the Cessna A–37 and Northrop F–5 in the air. These types had been chosen precisely because they were simple and easily maintained, and their American providers had gone to some length to set up an effective supply line for needed parts and equipment. 'Somehow we always had everything but what we wanted.'

There were some leadership problems, says Nguyen, because Ky purposely appointed officers who were better known for their loyalties than their strengths. The A–37, he opines, may have been cost-effective but was not an improvement over the A–1 Skyraider.

The hand-over of twenty A–37A Dragonflies to the VNAF's 524th Fighter Squadron at Nha Trang was accomplished with considerable ceremony on 19 April 1969. Major Dang Duy Lac, squadron commander, praised the aircraft. Less fanfare attended the equipping of the 526th and 528th Squadrons with the same aircraft.

Another VNAF 'first' occurred with the conversion to turbo-powered Bell UH–1H Huey helicopters in mid-1969. Three VNAF squadrons had converted from H–34s to UH–1Hs by the end of the year.

'We were receiving equipment very rapidly,' says Nguyen. 'Some of us worked very hard to integrate it into our forces. We were not always sure we succeeded.'

The US was increasingly carrying out bombing operations in Laos while denying that they were going on. Virtually all the aircraft which had been flying from Thailand against North Vietnam prior to the bombing halt up north were now directed towards Laos. This meant no increase in the number of warplanes available for the war in South Vietnam. A US House of Representatives Armed Services Committee report stated that, since the 1 November 1968 bombing halt, the enormous increase in North Vietnamese logistics operations toward Laos and the DMZ were of such volume that it appeared that they were establishing a massive logistics system as a foundation for future expanded operations. The report concluded that if peace talks failed, the bombing halt would have provided the North with a new lease on life and the war would drag on.

The ageing, chugging A–1 Skyraider was beginning to be less visible than jets like the F–5 and A–37, but the venerable 'Spad' continued to be important – not just with the VNAF but with American units as well. In South Vietnam, as it had done up north before the bombing halt, the A–1 continued to be best known as the warplane which covered the scene when a friendly pilot was down.

A 15 February 1969 combat rescue mission was one of the few discussed in public where CBU–19 tear gas bombs were employed. It began when an F–4 Phantom was hit by gunfire and went down in the NVA-dominated A Shau Valley near the Laos-South Vietnam border. The attempt to rescue the F–4 pilot was marred when North Vietnamese gunners shot down and killed the rescue commander in his A–1 Skyraider.

A North American F–100D Super Sabre drops napalm over a Viet Cong concentration 21 miles (34km) east of Ban Me Thuot. Beneath the high jungle canopy are Viet Cong guerrillas, now controlled by Hanoi, moving relentlessly through a conflict with no front lines and no rear areas. (USAF)

There appeared to be no way that a new rescue commander could authorize rescue helicopters to move in when NVA gunfire was so heavy. The effort to rescue the F–4 pilot might have to be abandoned.

A decision was made to attempt a rescue using riot control munitions. A–1 Skyraiders belonging to the 8th Special Operations Squadron at Pleiku were loaded up with CBU–19 ordnance and proceeded to the trouble spot in the A Shau Valley. Running a gauntlet of 37mm and 57mm anti-aircraft fire, the Skyraiders made a straight and level run covering a mile (1.6km) at the dizzyingly low altitude of 300 feet (less than 100m), dispensing the bombs on NVA anti-aircraft gun positions. An HH–3E Jolly Green helicopter, its crew wearing gas masks, was ready and moved in while North Vietnamese gun crews retched, coughed, and choked. The helicopter pick-up brought the F–4 pilot out of harm's way.

Typical of US Navy carrier pilots who faced death during a seeming lull in the war was Tom Scheber, A–4E Skyhawk flier of the 'Roadrunners' of VA–144. In August 1969 during the period when bombing over North Vietnam was temporarily halted, Tom began flying combat missions over the south from the USS *Bon Homme Richard* (CVA–31). His Skyhawk was the only carrier-based aircraft without folding wings as well as the only type which required a ladder – not popular among maintenance men. (COURTESY COMMANDER SCHEBER)

A Vought F–8J Crusader taxies on the flight deck of the USS *Bon Homme Richard* (CVA–31) off the coast of South Vietnam. The Crusader was primarily an air-to-air fighter and most models were not even equipped to carry bombs, but they were often able to strafe communist troops when no other help was available. Fortunately the enemy never sent MiGs into the south to instigate an air-to-air war there. (USN)

Navy Operations

Navy land-based aircraft continued to fly unpublicized missions which often crossed borders as they sought to block the north-south flow of weapons and supplies. The US Navy's use of the Lockheed P–2 Neptune patrol bomber was not limited to any single geographical sector.

VO–67, the only 'observation' squadron in the Navy for many years, had operated the OP–2E variant of the Neptune against the Ho Chi Minh Trail, flying from Nakton Phanom, Thailand, in unique jungle-green camouflage during 1967–68. VAH–21, a heavy attack squadron at Cam Ranh Bay, flew heavily instrumented AP–2H Neptunes with the TRIM (Trails and Roads Interdiction, Multi-Sensor) electro-optical system in bomb missions against the Trail in 1968–69. More traditional patrol squadrons such as VP–1 operated SP–2H Neptunes in 'Market Time' operations against enemy coastal and river traffic.

The aircraft-carrier remained a high-tension, high-risk place to work while the carrier-based pilot continued to plunge ahead with perhaps the most dangerous occupation of all. Apart from the undeclared and unadmitted war in Laos, the bombing of North Vietnam remained off-limits, so naval air power was used to a greater extent in the south.

Aircraft which had been in service at the beginning of the conflict, such as the A–4

The 'Sidewinders' of VA–86 operating from the USS *Lexington* (CVA–62) introduced the A–7C version of the Corsair II and later flew the A–7E (shown). The C model had only minor internal improvements, but the E introduced a new and more powerful engine. Bombload shown was entirely practical on relatively short-range combat missions. (USN)

A USAF HH–53C Super Jolly Green Giant belonging to the 40th Aerospace Rescue and Recovery Service moves up to take on air refueling from a Lockheed HC–130P Hercules during a combat rescue operation in South-East Asia. The awkward-looking, off-center refueling probe of the HH–53C gives it a capability to remain in the air for hours during rescue attempts. (USAF)

Skyhawk, F–4 Phantom and F–8 Crusader, continued to serve valiantly. Introduction of the Grumman E–2 Hawkeye airborne early warning aircraft had bolstered the Fleet's capabilities. Aircraft which had been introduced only after the outset of the fighting, such as the A–6 Intruder and A–7 Corsair II, were making rapid progress towards getting the kinks worked out.

Lieutenant Ben Short communicated some of the flavor of A–7 Corsair II missions in a personal log. 'We lost one pilot during the first line period by USS *Independence* [CVA–62], Randy Ford. He was out on an early morning flight and suddenly ejected. While on the ground he never said [over his beeper radio] what happened. We surmise he was captured just about sun-up. I launched just before dawn, and talked to him a couple of times. We learned many years later that he died, shortly after he was taken prisoner.'

There was the continuing problem with bomb fuses, which caused bombs to explode the instant the pilot pressed the pickle button. 'The skipper [of squadron VA–86] was out on a night mission in South Vietnam with an Air Force F–4 leading on a LORAN drop [a high-altitude, instrumented bomb release]. The skipper used electrical and mechanical fusing for a straight and level drop from 16,000ft [4,877m] and one of the electric fuses went off at the end of safe separation time. It blew the skipper's aircraft and the F–4 out of the sky almost instantly. One of the other A–7s was so badly holed he ran out of gas over the gulf heading for Da Nang. Only the third A–7 survived. We picked up the skipper [who had ejected safely] the next morning and also got the pilot out of the Gulf. The two F–4 [crew members] were captured.'

Beginning in April, Project 'Misty Bronco' was a test to evaluate the effectiveness of armed OV–10A Broncos providing an immediate Air Force strike presence just as readily available to ground troops as their own artillery. This meant arming Broncos with rockets and gun pods, and enhancing communication between air and ground. The concept of using the OV–10A as a kind of flying artillery piece was deemed successful and the arming of all OV–10As was authorized on 10 June 1969.

With the war itself readjusting to a new administration in Washington and the entire breadth of North Vietnam off-limits to US warplanes, 1969 was apparently the year of the 'little guy in the little airplane', to quote Captain Verne Saxon – as thousands of men struggled to keep the fight going amidst confusion of purpose and flagging morale.

Saxon, with the 19th Tactical Air Support Squadron and flying his O–1 Bird Dog from a detachment near Pleiku, never hesitated in his determination to do his job and get his part of the war taken care of. When a proposal was lofted to rename the forward air controller (FAC) and make him a forward air guide, Saxon and his buddies shouted up a storm in protest over the acronym likely to result from the change. They continued, however, to fly their small, frail-looking O–1s in harm's way.

On a typical mission, Saxon would slip a flak vest over his flight coveralls, stash the nearly useless parachute in the back seat, and take the O–1 off for a 1- to 3-hour mission pinpointing enemy troops and guiding in fighter-bombers.

'At one point I got into a personal disagreement with some Viet Cong in black pajamas who had laid siege to an ARVN fire base and would neither attack nor go away. When fighters were not immediately available, I went down in my O–1 and zapped some smoke rockets at them, hoping somehow that the small, lightweight projectiles would do "Victor Charlie" some harm. I got some muzzle flashes – in daylight, it's usually hard to see them shooting at you – and I actually saw one of my rockets scatter some of them!'

They were shooting at Saxon and he had nothing with which to shoot back. After some time, he was given a flight of F–100 Super Sabres and was able to direct them to accurate bombing passes on the enemy.

A FAC's most rewarding experience was often his direct communication with Army troops on the ground. These men might be mere specks to the pilot of a fast-moving jet fighter, but in an O–1 Bird Dog they became very personal. 'I never forgot that we were helping out the footsoldier on the ground. No matter what the politicians might think the war was for, we always got satisfaction out of knowing we were helping our own guys.'

Perhaps the littlest guy of all was the PJ, or pararescue jumper, who flew as a crew member on a rescue helicopter and put forward a variety of special operations skill to save downed airmen.

On 18 February 1969 Sergeant Michael E. Fish, a PJ from Detachment 11, 38th Aerospace Rescue and Recovery Squadron, responded to the crash of a US Army UH–1 Huey in a hostile area approximately 25 miles (40km) south-west of Tuy Hoa. Five men were reported trapped inside the Huey wreckage.

A Kaman HH–43 Huskie, or 'Pedro', helicopter reached the scene and lowered Fish and a firefighter to the ground. Despite sporadic enemy fire, three of the trapped survivors were quickly freed and hoisted aboard the HH–43. Another survivor and a deceased soldier were extracted by another Army Huey. Still, one injured man remained trapped inside the downed helicopter.

Due to ensuing darkness, Fish's own rescue helicopter was forced to depart. Enemy forces attempted to infiltrate Fish's position. Fish and friendly troops fired back and the enemy were repelled. Early on the morning of 19 February, still under sporadic fire, the rescue HH–43 returned. Fish freed the trapped survivor and finally all were evacuated from the area. 'The hardest part of it all for me,' said Fish, 'was appearing later on the TV program "This Is Your Life" and being treated like a celebrity.'

In another dramatic rescue effort later in the year, two HH–3E Jolly Green helicopters

Lockheed AP–2E Neptune (BuNo 131531) 'Crazy Cat' is perhaps the most unusual of all Neptunes, having been used by the US Army's 1st Radio Research Company at Cam Ranh Bay for air-to-ground relay of radio transmissions, apparently from clandestine agent networks in South Vietnam. In operational use the aircraft was festooned with aerials which had been removed by the time this picture was taken after the aircraft's return to the USA in mid-1969. (DUANE A. KASULKA)

assigned to the 37th ARRS were scrambled from Quang Tri to rescue two downed F–100 aircrewmen. One of the HH–3Es arrived at the scene and lowered Technical Sergeant Donald G. Smith to the ground.

Gunfire came pouring through the jungle from NVA troops. It was apparent that the enemy had used the downed F–100 fliers as bait. Smith found one of the survivors and secured him to the HH–3E's hoist. But NVA bullets spattered into the helicopter and rendered the hoist inoperative.

The HH–3E flight engineer was forced to cut the cable. Smith and his survivor fell back into the jungle. This first HH–3E was then forced down, but its crew was rescued by another Jolly Green. The day began to unfold slowly with the NVA shooting at everything in sight and Smith – although injured – caring for survivors, directing air assaults against the enemy, and repelling NVA probes with M–16 rifle fire.

After four more attempts by HH–3Es, Smith and one survivor were successfully rescued. The other F–100 flier was picked up by yet another HH–3E. Smith, like Fish, was later awarded the Air Force Cross for valor – second in importance only to the Medal of Honor.

Thieu Travels

Saigon's President Thieu visited Korea from 27 May to 3 June, his first trip to an ally which put two divisions totaling nearly 50,000 troops on the ground in South Vietnam. Presidents Nixon and Thieu met at Midway Island on 8 June. General Abrams was present. The withdrawal of 25,000 US servicemen from Vietnam was ordered, the first really significant attempt to wind down the war and turn it over to the South Vietnamese. The US actually withdrew the 25,000 men by late August, a remarkable reversal of the established trend of increase after increase.

President Nixon for all his talk of ending the war, had not officially committed himself to a total withdrawal. He felt that the pace at which South Vietnam could take over the bulk of its defense was dependent upon balancing domestic opinion against both communist activity and South Vietnamese capabilities. Nixon had inherited the Paris peace talks and, with them, had also acquired their frustrating lack of concrete negotiation and progress. Negotiator Henry Cabot Lodge and his able assistant Ambassador William J. Porter were talking to the communists and TV footage showed them arriving and departing from meetings, but very little of substance was actually being talked about and even less was being revealed publicly.

Nevertheless, the mere talk of 'getting out' had a devastating effect on the morale of American soldiers in South Vietnam. Many were draftees. Most had been willing enough to take risks and fight as long as they saw a purpose, but the news of withdrawal seemed to undermine any sense of purpose. Sagging morale led to the first reports of men using drugs, of racial tensions, and of 'fragging' – killing your own officers with weapons intended for use on the enemy.

The collapse of morale probably had the smallest impact on pilots and aircrew, who were more likely to be volunteers and professionals. Still, even among Air Force and Navy support people, evidence of low spirits was everywhere. The rate of AWOLs (absences without leave) went up 20.3 per cent from 1967 to 1969. A few Americans simply deserted, – some of them proceeding to Sweden for refuge.

In September 1969 US Army Lieutenant William Calley was charged with war crimes in the previous year's My Lai massacre. The incident in which American troops shot innocent civilians was concealed until reporter Ronald Ridenhour dug up details, closely followed by Seymour Hersch. Excluding My Lai, 241 war crimes allegations were made against American troops between 1965 and 1972. Many, obviously, lacked a basis in fact. But the belief has remained that at least some Americans killed civilians, among them Calley who was later convicted of murdering at least 22 innocents. This was perhaps the worst reflection of flagging American morale.

Viet Cong Attacks

Unburdened with morale problems, the Viet Cong launched country-wide attacks on installations and population centers in mid-May. Meanwhile, the National Liberation Front offered a ten-point peace proposal at

With F–4 Phantoms taxying in the background, a C–7A Caribou lands on the main runway at the huge Cam Ranh Bay air base. Caribous had a limited load capacity but could carry around 6,000lb (2,721kg) or seventeen fully equipped combat troops and could land at places inaccessible to the C–123 and C–130. (USAF)

Secretary of Defense Melvin Laird (foreground) was a savvy ex-businessman who had a major role in shaping withdrawal policy for new President Richard M. Nixon (left). Accompanied by General Earle G. Wheeler, Laird and Nixon make a tour of the Pentagon shortly after the new administration took office. In July 1969 the new chief executive was to enunciate the Nixon Doctrine calling for Asian allies, including South Vietnam, to provide the manpower for their defense. (USAF)

the stagnated talks in Paris. The offer came on 8 May 1969, virtually a year after the talks had opened on 10 May 1968.

In June the ban on bombing North Vietnam was lifted long enough to permit retaliation for the shooting down of a US reconnaissance aircraft. Retaliatory strikes of this kind were to occur from time to time. Later, Defense Secretary Melvin Laird would give them a name by coining one of the unforgettable terms of the war – the 'limited duration, protective reaction air strike'.

As another token step in winding down the war, the number of authorized B–52 sorties was reduced on 15 July 1969 to a rate of 1,600 per month, a reduction of 200. The rate was further reduced to 1,400 in October.

As an aside, it is perhaps worth mentioning that at the very time the Vietnam war was on 'hold' and anti-war protests were continuing throughout the US, men went to the moon. On 21 July 1969 astronaut Neil Armstrong – a former Korean War fighter pilot – stepped out of the Apollo 11 lunar excursion module and made his 'one giant leap for mankind'. It was a far more dramatic achievement in the middle of a long war than any that had been accomplished in peacetime. If one student of history is right, long after the Vietnam War and the social turmoil of the period is forgotten, that first lunar landing may remain one of the most significant events ever to occur.

Nixon Doctrine

One of the most important pronouncements of the war came from President Nixon on 25 July 1969 during a visit to Guam. Known at first as the Guam Doctrine and later as the Nixon Doctrine, the policy shift held that the US would look to its Asian allies to provide the bulk of the manpower in their own defense and would support them with outside aid. In short, US servicemen would not be expected to do the bleeding and dying in Asian wars. The diplomatic language said, in plain English, that Nixon was going to withdraw Americans from South Vietnam in response to domestic opposition and that Saigon was going to have to defend itself, with US-supplied weapons.

The Guam Doctrine also had significance elsewhere – one of the two US infantry divisions long garrisoned in Korea would be withdrawn – but to most people the new policy meant something called 'Vietnamization'. The war would be 'Vietnamized'. Critics argued that this was exactly what the Viet Cong had been trying to do all along.

On 15 August Defense Secretary Melvin Laird issued a statement formalizing the Nixon Doctrine by assigning new missions to US troops – in effect, reducing their combat role and turning more of the ground fighting over to Saigon's troops.

The initial increment of the American withdrawal, known as Operation 'Keystone Eagle', was completed on 29 August. President Nixon was now able to show the American public that 25,000 young men had been pulled out and brought home. This was only a token to anti-war protesters and really satisfied no one, but the policy was continued. On 16 September Nixon ordered the second round of withdrawals, involving 35,000 troops by mid-December. The second round was known as 'Operation Keystone Cardinal'. On 15 December the President announced the withdrawal of 50,000 more troops from South-East Asia by 15 April 1970.

As part of withdrawal and consolidation, Air Force operations at Nha Trang were terminated, the 14th Special Operations Wing moving to Phan Rang.

As part of Vietnamization, the newly designated and activated VNAF 8th and 90th Attack Squadrons at Bien Hoa were fully equipped with the improved A–37B by the end of December, adding to the strength of VNAF fighter squadrons already described. Earlier models of the A–37 in Vietnam were also slated for replacement by A–37Bs. Plans existed to increase the size of the VNAF by no fewer than 1,100 additional aircraft.

Looking at its achievements in 1969, the USAF's history for the period pointed out: 'The improvement and modernization program for the VNAF, formalized in 1968, was greatly expanded and stepped up in 1969. The ultimate goal was for the VNAF to be self-sufficient in all areas and capable of handling the combined VC–NCA threat. The VNAF was to be doubled in size by 1972, with more modern and effective aircraft. Seventh Air Force was directed to place as much emphasis on training the VNAF as on conducting combat operations.'

Ho Chi Minh Dies

While an argument raged as to whether the war was being won – whether, indeed, the Saigon government was winning the 'hearts and minds' of its people – on 4 September 1969 North Vietnam announced the death of Ho Chi Minh at age 79. The charismatic Hanoi leader who had devoted a lifetime to ridding his land of foreign occupiers left the reins of leadership in the hands of party head Le Duan and Prime Minister Pham Van Dong. In name only, there was still a separate Viet Cong leadership in the south – but in fact, 'Victor Charlie' now took his marching orders from Ho's northerners.

Because it was such a difficult war to evaluate – did greater numbers of enemy dead mean that the war was being won, or that the enemy had more troops? – symbols were important, and Saigon's Thieu and Ky were never able to muster the popular appeal that Ho had enjoyed. The struggle for the will of the people was serious – the Americans even had department of State officers humping around in the boondocks, lugging M–16 rifles and preaching civic action – but in the absence of visible military success it was hard to claim that moral success was being achieved. It was not true, as a Green Beret lieutenant asserted, that 'if you grab 'em by the balls, their hearts and minds will follow'. Even while being taken over by Hanoi and being whipped on the battlefield. 'Victor Charlie' was gaining popularity.

In October 1969 the Canberra bomber absented itself from the war scene. The 8th Tactical Bomber Squadron deactivated and its B–57s were ferried to the continental US for storage.

Marine Corps pilots and back-seaters flew the F–4 Phantom in South-East Asia from 1965 to 1974, with some squadrons converting from the F–4B to F–4J model mid-way through in 1969. F–4J Phantom (153785) of the 'Red Devils' of VMFA–232 is typical of Phantoms flown in combat by Marines as the war approached the 1970s. (R. W. HARRISON)

On 20 September 1969 an F–4D Phantom of the 366th Tactical Fighter Wing at Da Nang collided in mid-air with an Air Vietnam DC–4 approximately two miles north of the air base. The DC–4 crashed, killing 75 people on board and two on the ground. The Phantom landed safely only after its back-seater ejected.

The F–4 Phantom, already well established for its role in the out-country fighting, was becoming increasingly important within South Vietnam and was soon to be almost as visible as the ubiquitous F–100 Super Sabre.

The USAF was flying Phantoms from Da Nang (366th TFW) and Cam Ranh Bay (12th TFW) and the Marine Corps was flying them from Chu Lai. On a close support mission the F–4 could carry eight 750lb (340kg) bombs or napalm tanks, or a variety of rockets and rocket projectiles. The extra crewman in the back seat gave the F–4 an extra pair of eyes and ears, an extra opinion, and sometimes the edge over the battlefield which enabled the pilot to overcome the disadvantages of a fast jet and achieve accuracy while bombing. Working with a forward air controller, a flight of four F–4 Phantoms could bring a truly devastating amount of ordnance into the fray – and frequently there were times when friendly troops were not too close and precision delivery was not necessary.

Forward air controllers began to receive the Cessna O–2, an off-the-shelf purchase of the civil Model 335 Skymaster. The twin-engined, twin-boom O–2 had greater endurance and a little more speed than the more familiar O–1 Bird Dog but remained essentially unarmed, carrying only smoke rockets to mark targets for fighter-bombers. (USAF)

The Phantom was also expensive, sophisticated, and difficult to maintain. It did not like the wet gloom which often hung over Vietnam at low level. Its afterburning J–79 engines infuriated crews with their long, black exhaust plumes which made an inviting target for Viet Cong gunners. Men who flew the Phantom respected the aircraft and consciously sought to avoid mistakes.

USAF
97624

8
WT
-2.32
3785

The Marines, who were always asked to do more with less, were flying some of the oldest F-4B Phantoms at the time the Navy had already introduced, and was rapidly shifting to, the improved F-4J model. Neither had a gun. Marine pilots bolted on cannon pods and used the Phantom to strafe the enemy – wondering why such a superb aircraft had been built without guns.

Fixed-wing Gunships

In that turning-point year of 1969, when a new president was on record as planning to end the war, combat operations over North Vietnam – outside the scope of this narrative – were now limited to reconnaissance missions.

The total bombing halt which had gone into effect on 1 November 1968 could not have been more awkwardly timed from the standpoint of military men. The F-4E Phantom, the new model armed with an internal 20mm cannon, had arrived in Thailand, piloted by men who were psyched up for missions against MiGs. The General Dynamics F-111A variable-geometry wing fighter-bomber had arrived in Thailand as well, making a temporary deployment which was widely regarded as unsuccessful, although it would return. Even the battleship *New Jersey* (BB-62) was refurbished and put to sea on a Vietnam combat cruise, to employ its mighty guns against targets well inland from the shoreline. F-4E, F-111A, and *New Jersey* were armed to the teeth for a vigorous war against North Vietnam – but it was not happening.

Important to the war on the ground in South Vietnam – described by American soldier Sid Reeder as a 'stinking, lousy, gut-wrenching point-blank slugfest' – was the progress being made with the USAF's fixed-wing gunships. The employment of sideways-firing guns on an aircraft making a pylon turn at low level over 'Charlie' and the NVA, begun dramatically with the AC-47 'Gooney Bird', had now extended to an entire family of gunships.

Eerie names from the spirit world identified these aeroplanes: 'Spooky' was the twin-engined AC-47, also known as 'Puff the Magic Dragon', now used regularly to relieve besieged friendly outposts, especially at night. 'Spectre' was the name assigned to the AC-130 gunship – bigger, heavier, with four engines, long range, and greater loiter time – and now being refined and enhanced under an improvement program known as 'Surprise Package'.

'Shadow' was the AC-119G Flying Boxcar and 'Stinger' the jet-augmented AC-119K version. (The K model was equipped with two General Electric J-85 turbojets which increased its ability to evade enemy gunfire.) In due course it was planned that AC-47 and AC-119 gunships would be flown not merely by the USAF but by the VNAF as well.

Flying in a gunship was not exactly like airline travel. At low altitude, the aircraft could buck and tremble in turbulence. There was the confusing and disorientating effect of flares and muzzle flashes.

On 24 February 1969 an AC-47 with the call-sign 'Spooky 71' flying from Bien Hoa, engaged Viet Cong guerrillas at night near the air base. As was typical, the AC-47 was carrying Mark 24 flares, 3ft (almost 1m) in length, weighing 27lb (12kg). Abruptly, due to an incredible mishap in which an NVA 82mm mortar shell struck the right wing and exploded in the wing frame, the AC-47 was shaken and set on fire.

At least two men were badly wounded, one drenched in blood. Airman John L. Levitow, the loadmaster, thought one of the plane's own guns had exploded. He quickly discovered that a live Mark 24 flare, fully armed, was rolling around on the AC-47's floor!

The flare, white-hot, bounced around near ammunition cans which contained over 19,000 rounds of ammunition. In seconds the AC-47 would be blown to bits! The aircraft was in a 30-degree bank, the men inside struggling for balance.

The flare could 'go' at any instant. Already wounded, losing blood, numb, and struggling as the plane banked, Levitow threw himself on the flare and painfully dragged it towards the cargo door, leaving a trail of blood behind. With a superhuman effort, he heaved the flare out – and it exploded only instants after clearing 'Spooky 71's' tail.

The AC-47 had 3,500 bullet holes in it when the plane set down at Bien Hoa. Levitow, badly hurt, was rushed to hospital – and survived. He was the only individual to be awarded the Medal of Honor for action in a fixed-wing gunship. He had saved the lives of eight men aboard the AC-47 'Spooky'.

The gunships were vital. The early AC-130A Spectre, a sinister black armed version of the ubiquitous Hercules transport, was operating primarily in the out-country war, flying night missions to attack men, vehicles and supplies moving south over the infiltration route known as the Ho Chi Minh Trail. The trail – as has been pointed out, not really a trail at all but a spiderweb-like network of supply routes – began in North Vietnam and reached the south either by directly crossing the DMZ (demilitarized zone) or by swinging around to the west, poking through Laos, and then stabbing into South Vietnam to terminate in the A Shau Valley or farther south around Kontum.

From the beginning, American leaders had been almost derelict in underestimating the task of choking off the supply flow. Particularly in early days, many of the supplies flowing south were being carried by the communist foot soldier who might or might not have a bicycle. A single man might travel many miles to deliver a single artillery shell – hardly an easy target to interdict, even when extant in thousands. By 1969, however, supplies were coming down the Ho Chi Minh Trail in trucks and their numbers were going up exponentially. 'It gets bumper-to-bumper like the Los Angeles freeway,' said one of the early AC-130 pilots. Even then, at night, over hostile terrain, cutting off the supplies was no easy task.

AC-130A Spectre crews worked in collaboration with pairs of F-4 Phantoms flown by men who had expertise in night operations. Equipped with FLIR (forward-looking infra-red) and other 'black box' magic, the AC-130A would employ intelligence, sensors, and guidance from an airborne command post to locate and attack supply convoys. If enemy anti-aircraft guns engaged the gunship, the Phantoms would suppress the AA gunfire.

An informal history of the 14th Special Operations Wing described a 7 April 1969 gunship mission by an AC-130A, equipped with FLIR, which went perfectly:

'The AC-130, labeled "Schlitz" for the night mission, took off at 1905 [hours] and the crew went through the usual pre-strike checks of sensor equipment, pilot's gunsight, and fire-control system. (A central traffic circle in downtown Ubon, easily seen by sensor operators and the pilot, was used for the checks.) Equipment in order, the gunship flew to the fragged area of routes 23 and 917 in central Laos. In the face of light anti-aircraft fire the aircraft sighted, attacked, and destroyed two vehicles within the first thirty minutes.

'The ABCCC [airborne battlefield command and control center, a non-gunship C-130] next diverted "Schlitz" to interdict vehicles spotted on one of the most heavily defended areas of Laos – route 911, just south of Mu Gia Pass. The route segment pushed north-west to south-east through rolling jungle country with karsts soaring

2,000ft [608m] above the road its entire length. Many rivers and creeks bisected the route, slowing traffic. Utilizing the NOC [night observation device] and FLIR, the gunship crew sighted 23 trucks. All were struck, the 27 secondary explosions and twelve secondary fires destroying 23 trucks. Even more remarkable, the job was done amid an estimated 900-round barrage of enemy 37mm fire. "Schlitz's" work for the night totaled 25 vehicles detected and 25 destroyed.'

The war in Laos also lies outside this narrative – but the potency of USAF gunships must be described in order to illustrate their role, as well, in South Vietnam.

The 'Surprise Package' improvements to the AC–130A Spectre were intended to give the gunship greater stand-off range to improve its capacity for survival and better night-targeting equipment. Two of the AC–130A's four 20mm Gatling-type guns were to be replaced with 40mm Bofors cannon. A variety of improved sensors were to be installed. FLIR, low-light-level television, a Black Crow AN/ASD–5 direction-finding radar, and a digital fire-control computer were among improvements on the AC–130 'Surprise Package' aircraft, which reached South-East Asia by year's end.

As for the AC–119G Shadow which was more important within South Vietnam, it had four GAU–2B/A 7.62mm machine-guns, 50,000 rounds of ammunition for day operations (35,000 rounds and 60 flares for night), and ceramic armor protection for a crew of six to eight. The AC–119G Shadow began operational sorties and its combat evaluation in January 1969 and the USAF's 71st Special Operations Squadron under Lieutenant Colonel James E. Pyle was up to strength by 11 March.

As part of the deployment code-named 'Coronet Hornet', the first six examples of the jet-augmented AC–119K Stinger belonging to the 18th Special Operations Squadron under Lieutenant Colonel Ernest E. Johnson arrived at Phan Rang. With two AC–119 squadrons in South Vietnam, the USAF inactivated its two AC–47 squadrons and scattered the AC–47 machines among Laotian and South Vietnamese units. Meanwhile the AC–119G unit became the 17th Special Operations Squadron.

These black, twin-boomed gunship versions of the Fairchild Flying Boxcar had had a variety of developmental problems stateside and were later getting into the war than had been planned. A typical ground-support mission by the gunship occurred on 7 June 1969 when enemy forces tried to overrun Fire Base Crook, a 25th Infantry Division outpost in Tay Ninh Province. Fighters and both AC–47 and AC–119G gunships were called in to help the fire base's defenders. While fighters delivered high-explosive and napalm, the gunships roved over the area using flares and miniguns. In a characteristic example of the oft-used and oft-deceiving body count, friendly forces later found 323 enemy dead. Prisoners told of being awed by the gunships.

The numbers count for 1969 held that Air Force aircraft losses for the year were 294, or 97 fewer than in 1968. The total number of USAF aircraft lost in South-East Asia was put at 1,783, valued at $2,254,948,000.

By the end of 1969 American troop strength in South Vietnam had dropped from the previous year's 536,100 to 474,000.

Fixed-wing gunships used in the South-East Asia conflict included the AC–47 Spooky, AC–130 Spectre, AC–119G Shadow and AC–119K Stinger. Several versions of the C–130 Hercules operated along the Ho Chi Minh Trail, interdicting the flow of supplies from the north. (USAF)

1970
VIETNAMIZATION

Americans at home drew some encouragement from the public commitment of the Nixon administration to bring about a withdrawal – through Vietnamization – and to end the US role in the war. Many were still not satisfied. Many wanted an immediate withdrawal, even if it meant taking no measures to help South Vietnam's prospects for survival. Many simply wanted the war to end, now, and their numbers were on the rise while those who supported the US role in the conflict grew fewer and fewer.

The objective of the Vietnamization program was progressively to transfer to Saigon's forces responsibility for all aspects of the war. Since the South Vietnamese armed forces had grown from a small force to nearly one million men, out of a population of only 17 million, an enormous strain was placed on the technical and administrative skills of the country's civilian and military leaders.

The effort included enhancing the VNAF's capabilities. Vietnamization efforts focused on in-country improvements to maintenance and logistical capabilities, and improved equipment. By the end of the year the VNAF was able to fly approximately 50 per cent of the in-country combat sorties and was successfully planning and conducting complex operations, including interdiction, close air support, and troop lift missions.

As yet another symbol of the 'drawing down' of the US presence, three US fighter squadrons at Cam Ranh Bay were inactivated on 31 March 1970, and the 12th Tactical Fighter Wing was moved to Phu Cat; the change released three squadrons of F–4C Phantoms which returned stateside.

Some plans to bolster Saigon's air arm did not work out successfully. The VNAF's brief experience with the B–57 Canberra bomber had been a failure, apparently because the B–57 was too sophisticated for the people charged with maintaining and flying it. The VNAF apparently acquired some C–7A Caribou transports, but no record exists of their being employed operationally, for reasons not clear. In the realm of the fixed-wing gunship, the 817th Attack Squadron at Nha Trang equipped with AC–47s was noticeably busy and useful. The 819th and 821st Attack Squadrons at Tan Son Nhut, equipped with the AC–119G Shadow and AC–119K Stinger respectively, never made a mark on the war and today there are no surviving photographs or documents from either unit.

More Withdrawals

On 21 April 1970 President Nixon announced that 150,000 more American

The crew of an Army OH–6A Cayuse – the 'Loach' – usually survived a mishap because the helicopter was extremely safe and sturdy. Still, broken 'Loaches' had to be fixed or retired. In Saigon on 22 April 1970 these OH–6A Cayuse helicopters await shipment to the continental US for salvage at an Army aviation maintenance depot. (US ARMY)

The Lockheed SP-2H Neptune received very little notice as it flew 'Market Time' patrol missions to detect, identify and intercept supplies being shipped by the enemy along the Vietnamese coast. This Neptune (BuNo 140964) flies over two Vietnamese junks which apparently are not under suspicion. (USN)

troops were to be withdrawn from Vietnam.

But if Nixon wanted to please opponents of the US role in the war, any chance he might have had disappeared with the decision that came next. US and ARVN forces launched massive ground operations into Cambodia on 30 April, intending to eliminate enemy forces and supplies in safe-havens on the far side of the border. It was a massive military operation in a war where fewer and fewer such operations were taking place – and it crossed a border.

In the bland manner of official histories, a document from the period notes that 'joint US and South Vietnamese operations into Cambodia were launched after Prince Sihanouk was ousted as chief of state by General Lon Nol'.

'For five years,' the document continued, sanctuaries in Cambodia had afforded the enemy a safe haven and a massive supply storehouse, all secure from US air attack'. The Cambodian invasion ended that and meant that the US was now conducting some kind of combat operations, including air operations, in four countries – Laos, Cambodia, and North and South Vietnam. Even after the 'incursion' (the administration's word) ended, US air strikes in Cambodia continued under the program name 'Freedom Deal'.

The heaviest military operations were carried out by ARVN troops in the Parrot's Beak and by the First Cavalry Division in the Fishhook, both being protuberances on the map of the Cambodian frontier. US Army helicopter gunships were sent against formations of Viet Cong and NVA who had been caught exposed, supposedly safe in their sanctuaries. Fighter-bombers, B-52s and fixed-wing gunships supported ARVN and American ground troops.

Like Tet, this was another campaign where perception was more important than reality. The Cambodian incursion was a success in that it led to the capture of enemy food and supplies and millions of rounds of ammunition. The ability of the enemy to hide in his Cambodian sanctuary was snatched away from him. But in another way the Cambodian incursion was a colossal failure.

The Cambodian invasion was the last straw for an American public increasingly convinced that the US effort in Vietnam was misguided, if not downright wrong. In the US, a horrible blunder by inexperienced Ohio National Guardsmen with M-1 Garand rifles and live ammunition resulted in the fatal shooting of protesting college students at Kent State University. The slaughter of citizens doing nothing more than exercising their right of speech triggered off a new round of demonstrations – some of them fully fledged riots – against the war, against the move into Cambodia, and against Nixon. To Americans who knew nothing of Asia, the word Vietnam became a symbol of divisions on their own domestic scene and which were wrenching their country apart.

The US Congress, of course, had a democratic majority and was anything but a rubber stamp for the White House. Reflecting domestic opposition to the war, Congress passed the Cooper-Church Amendment, making it illegal to insert American troops into Laos or Cambodia after 30 June. In due course there would be additional legislative constraints against the use of American troops in South Vietnam itself.

In later years the North Vietnamese would willingly admit that they had done everything in their power to encourage domestic dissent by Americans back home. But the truth was, they had almost no influence. No communist conspiracy lay behind the waving of signs, the chanting, the singing, the unfurling of protest banners in the streets. Opposition to the war was a genuine popular sentiment, growing now to the point where *most* Americans opposed the war. Those who still supported the commitment, and who sneered at the demonstrators, had forgotten that their own society was rooted in majority rule.

This was to have devastating consequences for an American citizen army which since 1940 had been made up of draftees typical of the population at large. Its final consequence, after the war's end, was to be an end to the draft and the creation of

On 6 April 1970 a Douglas A–1J Skyraider belonging to the 1st Special Operations Squadron taxies out for a mission at Da Nang. The Skyraider is perhaps best remembered for its role in leading rescues of downed airmen. Inherited from the Navy by Air Force pilots, it was also an exceedingly accurate close-support aircraft able to take punishment and dish it out. (USAF)

America's first professional army – no longer typical of the populace it served, living separately and apart from the rest of the American people. One related effect: in later years, working-age American men were to rise to senior levels in business, industry, and government without ever having been exposed to military issues and without understanding them.

While protests went on about Cambodia, the US armed forces were being weakened by racial disputes and drug problems. The Army which had beaten the North Vietnamese regular in 1965 was described in 1970 as being incapable of fighting its way out of a paper bag. This was an exaggeration, for many dedicated warriors remained.

It was not uncommon for black and white soldiers to reinforce the very segregation that many had fought against earlier in the 1960s, gathering at segregated places of amusement in off-duty hours. In the tacky, tinsel boom towns which grew up around American bases, blacks and whites each had their own bars, their own beer halls, their own women. One fighter wing commander at Da Nang was more concerned about racial tensions among his enlisted troops – there were several incidents of knife fights, and one death – than about the very real prospect of the Viet Cong mortaring his F–4 Phantoms.

The American armed forces, which had always had superb leadership and still included many dedicated and courageous people, were coming apart at the seams. In Saigon or any populated Vietnamese location, marijuana and heroin were readily available to anyone who wanted them. Dope-smoking became so common and so widespread, particularly among ground combat soldiers, that commanders sometimes had no choice but to look the other way. The local heroin in particular was extremely powerful and, of course, addictive. The Army instituted urine tests, but these helped only to identify some careless offenders.

There were still men of incomparable courage in American uniform, and in general the Air Force and Navy were less affected by these problems than the Army and Marine Corps, but things were falling apart. Everyone knew the war was winding down and nobody wanted to be the last American to die in Vietnam.

Spraying Ends

A controversial program came to an end when herbicide operations by UK–123K Provider aircraft of the 12th Special Operations Squadron at Bien Hoa ended on 14 May 1970. Stocks of herbicide White were exhausted and restrictions on the use of herbicide Orange prevented further use. Spraying of Agent White, itself not controversial, was resumed at a later date but Agent Orange was to be known, hereafter, only to those veterans whose health was harmed by the chemical.

The US pulled out of four air bases during 1970. Binh Thuy in the Delta area was turned over to the VNAF in March. Pleiku was handed over in June and Tuy Hoa in December. In July Air Force flying units were moved out of Vung Tau. During the year no fewer than six USAF combat wings were inactivated or transferred out of country. The Nixon administration periodically put out statements reminding the public that a withdrawal was under way.

VNAF F–5s

The Vietnamese Air Force continued to grow, probably at a greater rate than its personnel could handle. VNAF pilots flying the Northrop F–5 were getting better and better with their lightweight, nimble fighter-bomber. The F–5 was effective in close-support operations, including many flown in

US Marine Corps personnel pose at Da Nang with the weapons of war employed by Marine aviation in South Vietnam. In the background is a two-seat TA–4F Skyhawk and a C–117D 'Gooney Bird' of Headquarters and Maintenance Squadron 11. Closer is a F–4B Phantom of VMFA–115; a OV–10 Bronco of VMO–2, a A–4E Skyhawk of VMA–311, and a A–6A Intruder of VMA(AW)–225. Also seen are an MB–5 fire truck and P&H crane/wrecker. (USMC)

support of the Cambodian episode. The twin-engined configuration of the Northrop fighter greatly improved its prospects for survival when hit, while its supersonic speed reduced the chances of getting hit in the first place.

The F–5A and virtually identical F–5C used by the VNAF were extremely reliable but there were occasional problems. As had sometimes happened with the wingtanks of the F–4 Phantom, it was found that 750lb (340kg) napalm tanks sometimes failed to separate cleanly from the F–5's ordnance pylons. When the worst occurred, the napalm tanks bucked and hit the underside of the wing. The F–5 was also prone to trouble when its guns caused the windshield to cloud up during a firing run.

'Fixes' for some of these problems were found even before the VNAF's 552nd Fighter Squadron became the first unit fully operational with the F–5. Other problems, including over-wear on the brakes, were addressed when a much-used F–5A (aircraft 64-13317) was shipped back to the US and thoroughly analyzed by Northrop experts.

The integration of the F–5A/C into the VNAF was perhaps only slightly more troublesome than that of the A–37, yet for more than five years the 522nd remained the only F–5 squadron.

USAF Lieutenant George Swannman went for a flight in one of the few two-seat F–5B Freedom Fighters assigned to the VNAF, an aircraft which in performance was identical to the F–5A/C. Not solely a trainer, the combat-capable F–5B was carrying two 750lb (340kg) HE bombs. It was one of four F–5s being scrambled to attempt contact with Viet Cong troops spotted in the field only 14 miles (23km) from Bien Hoa air base (to which the VNAF F–5 squadron had moved from Tan Son Nhut in January 1968).

'My pilot was a young lieutenant who had been through the F–5 training syllabus in the US,' said Swannman. 'He was a spindly guy with glasses but inside that F–5, he became a tiger. Have you ever heard of a fighter pilot getting motion sickness? I almost did, in the back seat with that guy. The F–5 can handle something like six Gs fairly easily, and he wasn't reluctant to fling it around the sky.'

Swannman was impressed that the flight of four F–5 pilots went to the trouble to make their firing passes from different directions. Too often American and Vietnamese pilots alike had made it too easy for enemy gunners. 'These guys had it all orchestrated. To the observer, it must have looked as if F–5s were heading in all directions with no plan. In fact, they got back together very smoothly – just like a stunt team at an air show.'

Swannman's impression was that VNAF pilots were capable and willing to take risk. But for a period of time the VNAF had more F–5s than it had F–5 pilots. Later in the war, when additional squadrons of F–5As and later F–5Es came into being, this imbalance was exacerbated.

Enter the Galaxy

Introduction of a new aircraft type to the conflict occurred when the Military Airlift Command's first mission with the Lockheed C–5A Galaxy to Vietnam occurred on a 5 June 1970 trip to Cam Ranh Bay. A C–5 Air Transportable Loading Dock was placed in operation at Cam Ranh Bay on 10 August.

The first trans-Pacific helicopter flight was completed by two HH–53 helicopters of the 37th Aerospace Rescue and Recovery Squadron on 24 August 1970. The two aircraft were ferried from Eglin AFB, Florida, to Da Nang. Two HC–130N Hercules tankers accompanied the helicopters, providing thirteen aerial refuelings during the 9,000-mile flight.

In 1970 US Navy squadrons which had been operatng the A–7A and A–7B Corsair began to receive the newer A–7E model, which had a more powerful TF–41 turbofan engine. A–7E Corsair (156808) of the 'Maces' of VA–27 circles over a blue sea and the carrier USS *Enterprise* (CVAN–65). After suffering a devastating fire on her first combat cruise in 1968, *Enterprise* got through her 6 January–2 July 1969 combat cruise without a major mishap. The E model Corsair did not reach this particular carrier until its third combat cruise in 1971. (ROBERT F. DORR)

General Lucius D. Clay, Jr. took over Seventh Air Force on 1 September 1970. The chief airman in Saigon remained a four-star officer but his job was receiving less attention than it had a couple of years earlier. Clay's predecessor, General George S. Brown, had completed a tour of duty without making any mark on the conduct of the war.

In September 1970 the USAF completed the chore of replacing A–37A aircraft with the A–37B model. Twenty-three aircraft replacements had occurred, and the earlier machines were assigned to Reserve squadrons in the States.

Hercules Happenings

The little-known and wholly unpublicized men who flew C–130 Hercules airborne command posts underwent a minor change on 16 September 1970, as the USAF moved to consolidate its C–130 forces as a part of the draw-down of American troops. The eleven HC–130P Hercules aircraft belonging to the 39th Aerospace Rescue and Recovery Squadron were moved on that date from Tuy Hoa to Cam Ranh Bay.

This was a move of only 70 miles (113km) down the coast, but it was the only major move of a USAF unit in 1970. The change had little effect on the ability of the HC–130P fleet to serve as airborne command and control centers (ABCCCs) or to refuel other aircraft on combat rescue missions. The squadron continued to keep one aircraft on airborne alert and two more ready to be scrambled on short notice.

The 'vanilla' C–130 Hercules was now the backbone of the tactical airlift effort inside South Vietnam. Although it could not land at as many airfields as the C–7 Caribou or C–123 Provider, the Hercules nonetheless took its crews into tight spots. In one incident, knowing their aircraft would be destroyed if left overnight for engine repairs, a crew was forced to make a three-engine emergency take-off from Song Be at dusk, under small-arms fire from enemy troops within 300 yards. In another, a pilot was recommended for an award for making an emergency landing after sustaining mortar damage which pocked the fuselage with more than 100 holes.

In terms of tonnage carried, both inside South Vietnam and on the trans-Pacific supply route which brought men and machines to the war, the transport which made the greatest contribution was the Lockheed C–130 Hercules. C–130E Hercules (63–7839) of the 779th Tactical Airlift Squadron is seen at Elmendorf AFB, Alaska, en route from a supply run to Vietnam. (NORMAN TAYLOR)

All the while, C–130 crews carried the ammunition, gasoline, supplies, animals and people knowing that they were heavily burdened. In June 1970 296 men were available as C–130 crews for the three tactical airlift wings which had a minimum requirement for 400.

B–52 Operations

Although the number and frequency of B–52 Stratofortress missions had been drastically reduced with the slow-down of the war, the big bombers continued to operate from U-Tapao, Thailand, as well as very distant Anderson AFB, Guam. B–52s were also being used for bombing operations in Cambodia which were supposed to be secret. The Cambodian incursion brought them out into the open.

No B–52 had ever fallen to enemy fire – in South Vietnam, none ever did – but there were tragic instances when men and machines were lost. At U-Tapao a B–52 mishap occurred because of confusion between one pilot's airspeed indication and the other's. At near-rotation speed near the middle of the runway's length, the aircraft commander aborted and the B–52 hydroplaned into the grass with a full bombload.

Although the crew evacuated the Stratofortress safely, there was a communications mix-up which caused the pilot of a Kaman HH–43 rescue helicopter to understand that the gunner was still trapped inside the B–52. Passing over the burning bomber to drop fire-retardant, the HH–43 was engulfed by the final explosion and both men aboard were killed.

Operation 'Good Luck', launched in 1970, kept B–52s busy bombing targets on Laos, while the number of their missions over South Vietnam remained low. The charge continued to be made that B–52s were merely opening up long rows of craters in the jungle. Occasionally, friendly forces would move in and confirm that the big bombers had inflicted damage on the enemy. Most of the time any assessment of bomb damage relied on intelligence – and when the enemy moved silently and swiftly through the jungle, intelligence was never easy to acquire.

The 45th Tactical Reconnaissance Squadron ('Polka Dots'), which had first deployed its RF–101C Voodoos over Vietnam in 1961, departed Tan Son Nhut on 16 November 1970, ending the Voodoo chapter in South-East Asia.

The sleek, heavy, powerful RF–101C Voodoo had been one of the first American warplanes in combat. It had flown the fastest missions ever carried out in combat by any aircraft in any war – routinely carrying out its reconnaissance sorties at speeds up around 1,400mph (2,240km/h) or Mach 2.0 – much faster than the 'Thud' or Phantom flew under actual fighting conditions. At one point a Voodoo squadron had more planes than pilots, yet had kept up a daily schedule of two combat missions per aircraft daily. Most of these missions were up north and a disproportionate number of RF–101C pilots were languishing in the Hanoi Hilton while fruitless peace talks foundered.

It was never easy being a reconnaissance pilot. Major Kent Harbaugh arrived at Tan Son Nhut in early 1970 to join the 12th Tactical Reconnaissance Squadron, part of the 460th Wing, commanded by Colonel Lovic P. Hodnette and flying the RF–4C Phantom. He and his fellow pilots lived in two-story concrete block billets which, except for those belonging to MACV, were the only air-conditioned buildings available. Harbaugh and his fellow pilots were flying visual daylight reconnaissance and night missions with photo-flash cartridges over South Vietnam, Laos and Cambodia.

RF–4C Mission

It worked like this: for a daylight mission, an RF–4C pilot would go to the squadron four hours before scheduled take-off. The squadron's own truck would transport him

A US Navy UH–1B Huey helicopter gunship lifts off from the USS *Harnett County* (LST–821) anchored in the Mekong Delta of South Vietnam. Operation of Huey helicopters and OV–10 Bronco aircraft by the Navy in Vietnam marked an unusual episode in that service's history as Navy fliers sought to prevent the Viet Cong and NVA from disrupting friendly river traffic. (USN)

from his billet to the ready room. Each pilot had a small but distinctive scarf, not the flamboyant First World War type but only 1½ inches wide, used by the truck driver to identify the squadron; the scarf was removed before flight.

At the squadron, located on the Tan Son Nhut flight line in an old French colonial two-story concrete Operations Building, the pilot picked up the frag order giving groupings of targets and reconnaissance parameters wanted (scale, heading, etc) and was assigned to an individual RF–4C.

After a weather briefing, pilot and back-seater 'attacked the maps'. Recce pilots always had more experience flying and navigating than did fighter pilots. 'We had to. We went in alone.' The navigator did pre-mission paperwork while the pilot determined the IP (initial point) for his photo run.

Still preparing for the mission, the crew briefed together on emergency procedures, escape and evasion possibilities, radio frequencies, and other details related to survival. The crew then proceeded to the life support room, across the ramp closer to the aircraft, to suit up with G-suit, harness, and vest and arm themselves (Smith & Wesson .38). Their survival radio ('a kind of big Walkman') was hand-operated and gave two-way communication or could be used as a beacon for a rescue helicopter in the 'transmit only' mode. This was the same 'beeper' used by most crews in South-East Asia.

The crew walked to their aircraft. The RF–4Cs were in hangarettes. The navigator checked cameras, started up the inertial nav system. The pilot did the usual pre-flight.

On a typical mission the RF–4C might check infiltration on trails and rivers. This was one Phantom pilot who did not have to worry about seeing over his aeroplane's long nose: at medium altitude, the viewfinder showed what was obscured by the nose and told the pilot if it was being recorded on film. To hunt for infiltrators, the RF–4C's panoramic camera took pictures horizon-to-horizon.

It was hard to say which was worse, day take-offs ('lots of planes queued up to take off and had to be cleared by the tower on to the runway, knowing they could be targets for VC mortars the whole time') or night landings ('you come back and don't know who owns the runway; we know there can be VC in the area outside the runway; you can have a look with your landing lights but that also makes you a target').

Because the RF–4C Phantom played such a major role from 1965 until war's end, it is perhaps worth while to quote from a squadron report on a mission by Major Kent Harbaugh. The report is written in 'basic Air Force' and covers a mission when heroism was the order of the day:

'Yoyo 23'

'Mission 3401 was fragged as a visual photo-reconnaissance sortie to photograph troops in contact in the vicinity of Kampong Thom, Cambodia (a provincial capital), coordinates 1243/10455E.

'RF–4C aircraft s/n 65–0878, call-sign "Yoyo 23", departed Tan Son Nhut at 0620, 1 August 1970, for refueling with KC–135 tanker aircraft, call-signs "Chestnut 33" and 34 (offload from two tanker aircraft was required to satisfy 17,000 pounds [7,711kg] JP–4 fuel requirement). "Yoyo 23" made rendezvous with "Chestnut" 33/34 at 0745; fuel offload completed; then departed for target. Upon arrival in target area at approximately 0800, the pilot established a left-hand orbit holding pattern; 8,000 feet [2,428m] above MSL (main supply line]. 400 knots ground airspeed, at a point approximately 3–5 miles [5–8km] south-east of target. Orbit location was selected to avoid heavy rain showers in the target area while making contact with the forward air controller (FAC), "Rustic 06", an OV–10 aircraft.

'Holes in cloud coverage were present at the pre-target orbit locations. Meteorological conditions in target area were generally scattered to broken clouds at 3,000 feet [914m]; visibility 2–3 miles [3–7km] with restrictions caused by rain, smoke, and haze. "Rustic 06" briefed "Yoyo 23" that enemy troops were in the target area, that strike

Captain Kent Harbaugh, who was promoted to major days after this March 1970 portrait, flew the RF–4C Phantom with the 460th TRW at Tan Son Nhut on combat reconnaissance missions over South Vietnam, Laos, and Cambodia. (USAF)

aircraft in the same vicinity had received heavy ground fire from small arms and automatic weapons, and that "Yoyo 23" should expect the same threat. "Yoyo 23" began first photo run at approximately 0825 entering target from a south-south-easterly direction in a descending, accelerating attitude down to approximately 200–300 feet [60–85m], 500–550 knots IAS [indicated air speed]. Military rated thrust was used on both engines. Number one photo run was an approximately 2–3 mile [3–7km] strip, requiring a right 45-degree turn after crossing the target center. Upon completion of run number one, the pilot pulled up into a left climbing turn, then reversed to the right, altitude 5–6,000 feet [1,524–1,828m]; 350 knots IAS.

'Run number two, a similar strip run but in the opposite direction, was entered from a north-easterly direction. A descending flight path was flown down to approximately 500 feet [152m], 500 knots IAS, so as to enter the number two photo run of approximately 2–3 miles [3–7km] in length. At the approximate mid-point of the run, a 45-degree left turn was required. Turn was made in a descending attitude (approximately 5 degrees pitch down) to an estimated 400 feet [122m], 550 knots IAS. Fuel state estimated to be: empty centerline external tank; full internal and external wing tanks.

'Soon after rolling out level for the final portion of run number two, the pilot noted number two engine fire warning light illuminated on the instrument panel. No other sensation to indicate that the aircraft had sustained battle damage was experienced by either pilot or navigator. The pilot immediately retarded number two engine to idle position; number one engine thrust was maintained at military rating (afterburner not used); a right climbing [turn] was initiated and a check made to determine aircraft status.

'Front cockpit warning indicators, in addition to the number two engine fire warning light, were: a red warning light illumination in the landing gear handle, flashing red wheels, camera master operate light on, master caution light on, tail hook light on, left and right auxiliary door lights on, speed brake out position light on. Pilot experienced electrical trim inoperative which required holding hard left rudder to compensate for the yaw effect created by the asymmetrical engine thrust configuration.

'Pilot leveled off at 8,000 feet [2,438m] and was forced to enter a thunderstorm located directly in exit flight path as airspeed was insufficient to allow safe maneuvering of aircraft. Upon penetration of the thunderstorm, moderate to heavy rain was encount-

Just after a combat mission in which Major Kent Harbaugh made a remarkable 'save' of the aircraft, RF-4C Phantom 65-0878, alias 'Yoyo 23', belonging to the 12th Tactical Reconnaissance Squadron, rests in a hangarette at Tan Son Nhut. Although it is not apparent here, the aircraft is scorched and badly damaged. (USAF)

ered. Shortly thereafter the fire warning light went out. The pilot actuated the manual speed brake retract switch to insure that speed brakes were retracted.

'Shortly thereafter, the aircraft emerged from the thunderstorm activity and encountered other electrical problems. Pilot attempted to make air to ground communication, eventually making contact with tanker aircraft "Chestnut 34". "Stormy 04" [an F–4 Phantom "fast FAC" [forward air controller] was contacted and requested to join up for a visual inspection of the aircraft. Position was at this time approximately 150 miles [240km] west-north-west of Tan Son Nhut, altitude 9,000 feet [2,743m].

'Generator was off. All electrical indicators were inoperative.

'To determine status, pilot lit number one engine afterburner. Number one engine generator was determined to be operable. Number two engine thrust was accelerated from idle to 80 per cent. Engine instruments read normal. Then thrust was reduced to idle again.

'Radar pick-up was established 75/100 miles [120/160km] from Tan Son Nhut with a state of emergency declared. Pilot contacted squadron operations and advised that conditions were stabilized. He had no utility hydraulic pressure. Internal fuel tanks were full and external wing tanks were full if they had not sustained battle damage. 25L barrier erection was made [a reference to the aircraft carrier-style "wire" barrier] and BAK–13 barrier coordination effected. Radar vector to drop tank jettison area [was] requested.

'"Stormy 04" joined "Yoyo 23" [and] made visual inspection of the aircraft. No fire was observed. The right-hand side of the aircraft appeared scorched. The right-hand auxiliary air door was open and burned. Fluid was streaming from the lower fuselage area. When approximately 20–25 miles [32–40km] out from Tan Son Nhut, the aircraft lost remaining A.C. [aircraft] electrical power. Intercom and battery were available. Pilot extended ram air turbine (RAT) and maintained intermittent radio contact with "Stormy 04". Pilot was advised to jettison external fuel tanks which was accomplished. Manual release was used. Radio contact was intermittent. "Yoyo 23" assumed the wing position on "Stormy 04" and remained there throughout the [approach to the] traffic pattern.

'Approach was made to the field from a high base (4,500 feet) [1,372m], 280 knots IAS, 290-degree turn-in. Tail hook was dropped [and] confirmed to be down. When rolled out of final turn, landing gear was blown down with the emergency system. Checked down by "Stormy 04". Flaps down with emergency system.

'On final approach, "Yoyo 23" was advised by tower that a landing could not be made because barrier crews were [on the] runway. These instructions required the pilot to make two 360-degree turns before the runway was ready for a landing.

'The pilot elected to fly a higher than normal final approach airspeed. Approximately 80–85 per cent thrust on number two engine was used during final approach. Runway touch-down was made at 160 knots airspeed. Engagement was made with the BAK–13 barrier 1,000 feet [305m] from approach end of runway at 140 knots IAS. Aircraft gross weight was 37,000 pounds [16,782kg] with 7,000 pounds [3,175kg] of fuel aboard. The drag chute deployed normally. Engagement with the barrier was made in the center of the runway but the aircraft pulled left and halted forward movement approximately 25 feet [8m] from the edge of the runway. Engines were shut off immediately and navigator began preparing for emergency egress. The aircraft was snapped backward approximately 400 feet [122m], fishtailed 45 degrees left, passed through the runway centerline at an angle of 45 degrees right, then fishtailed 60 degrees left, stopping on the next oscillation. Emergency brakes were applied during the rollback but were inoperative. Emergency egress procedures were used by both crew members to exit the aircraft.'

Although the preceding report is written in the execrable style of English favored by the Pentagon's Air Staff, the intransitive verbs fail to conceal an act of almost incredible heroism by Major Kent Harbaugh – an act which saved an aircraft and certainly saved his back-seater's life. Harbaugh later

A US Marine Corps Vought F–8E Crusader lifts off from Chu Lai on a combat mission. As the 1960s ended, the Marines began doing most of their fighter work in South Vietnam with the F–4 Phantom; but many of the Corps' fighter pilots, especially those who relished the single-seat, single-engine design, retained their fondness for the Crusader. (USMC)

wrote to the 366th TFW at Da Nang to praise Captain Thomas A. Brooks and Lieutenant John D. Holmquist, the crew of 'Stormy 04', who contributed to the 'save'.

Because all pilots of the Phantom, including Harbaugh, praise the aircraft lavishly, Harbaugh (now an active-duty colonel and until recently US Air Attache in England) was asked if he could find something 'wrong' with the RF-4C. He was reluctant to do so because of his obvious appreciation for the aircraft but managed to cite the fact that its exhaust smoked, the air-conditioning did not work well ('the water separator doesn't work') and there was poor forward visibility when landing in heavy rain. Harbaugh also noted that his wing, the 460th TRW, had the oldest RF-4Cs in inventory.

The RF-4C was to continue its role as a key reconnaissance aircraft until the end of US participation in the conflict.

Son Tay Raid

In the 'out-country war,' on 21 November 1970 a daring attempt was made to rescue US prisoners of war from a camp at Son Tay, 20 miles (32km) west of Hanoi. The Son Tay raiders were not stationed in South-East Asia; the force had been assembled in secret in the US and came to bases in Thailand only at the last minute to mount the raid. The mission was flawlessly executed, but no prisoners were found.

Only one aircraft was shot down during the Son Tay raid, an F-105F Thunderchief whose two-man crew ejected safely and were rescued. The F-105F pilot, Major Donald Kilgus, had been fighting the Vietnam war in one way or another for almost a decade. Denied a chance to go to war as an F-100 Super Sabre pilot in 1963, he shifted to the O-1 Bird Dog and flew a tour as a forward air controller. Later he returned for two tours of duty in the F-100, scoring a probable kill of a MiG-17 on a mission up north in 1965. Finally, he pioneered 'Wild Weasel' operations against enemy missile sites – another key part of the out-country war – and flew the F-105F and F-105G. Kilgus was typical of many who refused to give up and refused to sink into the morass that the American armed forces were becoming. Every time he

Scenes like this – a 'dust-off' medevac Huey helicopter picking up wounded American troops at the scene of a battle – became less frequent as the war descreased in intensity in 1970. South Vietnamese troops were participating in a higher percentage of ground combat actions as Americans withdrew, but the enemy too was lying low and the level of fighting stayed down throughout the year. (US ARMY)

Near Chu Lai, US Army M-551 armored reconnaissance vehicle and M-113 armored personnel carrier from the 23rd Infantry Division push on with the war, oblivious to Vietnamization and withdrawal. If airpower in South Vietnam was to be effective, it had to support the men who fought on their feet and in their tracks. As the number of American soldiers grew fewer, more and more air support missions meant covering the South Vietnamese. (US ARMY)

F–4E Phantoms of the 469th Tactical Fighter Squadron fly formation with KC–135 Stratotanker. 'We do the job with Es,' proclaimed a squadron slogan when the E model Phantom went into action just after the 1 November 1968 bombing halt over North Vietnam. In 1970 the shark-toothed Phantoms were still not flying up north, but their fighter missions in Laos and South Vietnam helped the allied war effort. (USAF)

got knocked down, he stood up and fought on.

For prisoners of war who had been held in North Vietnam for years and had gone more than two years without hearing American warplanes overhead, the Son Tay raid was not the glimmer of hope its planners expected. 'We learned about it months later,' said Major Ken Cordier, held in a Hanoi prison. 'It seemed a sign of desperation. If they would go to such lengths to try to get us out, it meant there was no hope of getting out any other way.'

The plight of the POWs inside North Vietnam has been mentioned only in passing thus far in this narrative of the fighting in the south. These men were sorely mistreated – tortured, isolated, denied medical treatment. In four groups, a total of twelve were released early by the North Vietnamese, all but one of these without permission of the POW commander, Colonel John Flynn. The premature releases were apparently intended to generate propaganda for Hanoi; instead, they drew attention to how badly the men were being treated. The eleven unauthorized releases are viewed with contempt by those who stayed – many of whom were prisoners for five, six, seven years – but the remaining 555 military and eight civilian prisoners resisted the North Vietnamese to the end. Many died in captivity, some from gross mistreatment, some when attempting to escape. Three men were awarded the Medal of Honor for their conduct as prisoners – Air Force F–100 'Misty FAC' pilot Colonel George (Bud) Day, Air Force F–4D Phantom pilot Captain Lance Sijan, and Navy A–4 Skyhawk pilot Captain James Bond Stockdale. Sijan's award was posthumous, for the young captain never came home from imprisonment by the North Vietnamese.

The POWs were to become increasingly important to any understanding of the war in the south, for Hanoi hoped – with grounds for optimism – that the US could be wearied down to the point where it would agree to a settlement with no condition other than the return of its prisoners.

C–130 Finale

The last C–130A mission in South Vietnam was flown by a 374th Tactical Airlift Wing aircraft on 27 December 1970. The A model Hercules, distinguished by its 'Roman nose' lacking a radome, was thereafter no longer included in Military Airlift Command operations.

Once again at year's end, numbers were put together – and again they looked impressive. Air Force combat sorties flown in South-East Asia in 1970 totaled 711,400, which represented a considerable reduction from the previous year (966,949). Nearly 30,000 sorties were flown in Cambodia. B–52 'Arc Light' sorties totaled 15,103, of which 1,292 were in Cambodia. Although the total number of sorties was less than in the previous year, PACAF had lost nineteen tactical squadrons with over 500 aircraft and 32,000 personnel, so the remaining units were heavily tasked.

The numbers-keepers reported that in 1970, 171 USAF aircraft were lost in South-East Asia, 127 in combat and 44 to operational causes. The total number of aircraft lost in South-East Asia was now put at 1,950, representing a cost of $2,500 million.

By 31 December 1971 the Vietnamese Air Force had 728 aircraft assigned and had over 700 formed aircrews, organized into 30 squadrons. The VNAF flew a total of 292,523 sorties in 1970. A total of 1,512 aircraft of all types had been delivered to the VNAF since the beginning of US aid, 415 of which had been lost to combat or operational causes.

The number on most Americans' minds, as always, was the size of the commitment. At year's end, just as Congress repealed the Gulf of Tonkin Resolution which had once given Lyndon Johnson broad powers, American military strength in South Vietnam was 335,800.

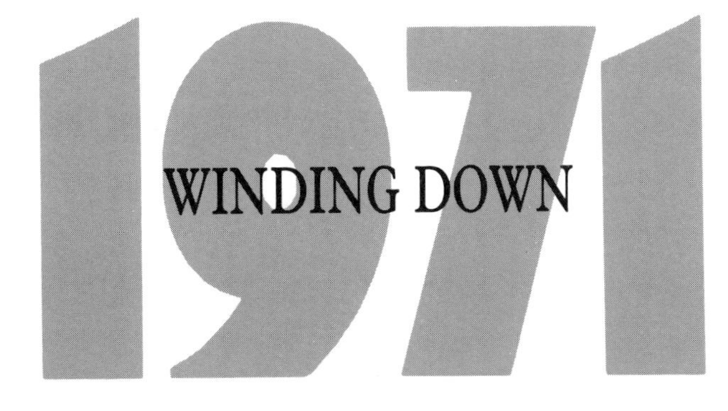

Even the Viet Cong and North Vietnamese behaved as if the war was winding down. Figures for combat actions for 1969, 1970 and 1971 show that the communist side was licking its wounds, avoiding large-scale operations which would involve high risk, and looking for solutions to the peace talks and other political machinations.

For all the blood shed on the battlefield by men of both sides, it was by no means certain that the future of South Vietnam would now be decided in battle. A few worried analysts were warning that North Vietnam still possessed reserve forces sufficient for a major offensive; but it was arguable that the issues were going to be resolved through some political process, not necessarily the publicly visible peace talks but *some* process.

For the North Vietnamese, the key was to whittle down American demands and arrive at a set of conditions under which the US was willing to withdraw. The communist leaders understood that, with opposition to the war so overwhelming at home, most Americans would be willing to leave in exchange for nothing more than the return of their prisoners of war. Any conclusion to the fighting would have to honor the appearance, at least, that South Vietnam was able to survive on its own – but Hanoi understood correctly that Washington had few chips for tough bargaining.

South Vietnam's embattled leaders, particularly President Thieu, could not help but fear that their interests would be abandoned by their American allies. Earlier in the year the American leadership had seemed determined to stay the course. Even now, leaders from President Nixon on down repeatedly said that they would never abandon Saigon. Such statements were becoming less and less credible.

To the opposition movement inside the US, the solution to the problem was expressed in two words, 'Out now!' It was becoming increasingly apparent that the Nixon administration was willing to get out – with the return of POWs and some cosmetic arrangement for a continuing regime in Saigon.

Caribou Pilot

Everyone was aware that the war was winding down in March 1971 when Lieutenant Larry Nilssen arrived at Cam Ranh Bay to begin flying the C–7A Caribou on short, risky, in-country airlift missions, a task which had been performed by Army aviators in earlier years.

Although the war was supposedly winding down, pilots of C–7A Caribou airlifters still flew perilous missions to remote outposts, often surrounded by the enemy. C–7A 61–2596 of the 536th Tactical Airlift Squadron, an aircraft which once belonged to the US Army, takes off from Cam Ranh Bay flown by a USAF crew. (USAF)

Most of the pilots were very young – like Nilssen, highly motivated new airmen who wanted to fly the F–4 or the B–52. Their job was perilous. It simply was no easy thing, flying strange cargoes over the Central Highlands in bad weather. 'People did this as a part of their job,' says Nilssen. 'There was not much of a fear of death. To navigate, you'd be looking at a map, and you'd find a road and river intersection. "Well," you'd say to the co-pilot, "if that's this road and this river, then our destination is up ahead. On the other hand, if that's *this* road and *this* river, we have the side of the mountain coming up at us."'

C–7A Caribou crews actually communicated by having a montagnard on the ground report whether he could hear the approaching Caribou's motors.

Lieutenant Nilssen was much aware that American armed forces were facing new problems as the war decreased in intensity. He saw numerous examples of drug overuse.

The C–7A pilot also saw 'crazy' people – but crazy in a constructive sense – willing to perform courageous acts. As for the war winding down, that was a strategic mind set, not a local issue: 'People knew that they had an airplane, a cargo, and a place to go. There was a job to do. Nothing else mattered.'

On alert at Cam Ranh with another C–7A driver named 'Combat' Kelly, Nilssen got word that Pleiku was under attack. Nilssen and Kelly with their crews and two C–7As flew ammunition into a besieged outpost near Pleiku with the enemy shooting at them.

The C–7A typically carried a payload of around 6,000lb (2,722kg), although not very far ('that's with no gas'), or seventeen fully loaded combat-equipped troops. The C–7A could go where other airlifters could not. As a rule of thumb, pilots were told that the Caribou could land in 1,000ft (305m), the C–123 Provider in 2,000ft (606m), the C–130 Hercules in 3,000ft (908m). Nilssen often hauled people and supplies into Ha Than, where the runway was just 970ft (439m) long. On one end of the runway was a stream and on the other a cliff, so there was no way to increase runway length. There were also trips up to montagnard redoubts in the Central Highlands – places like Dak To, which had been a scene of heavy fighting in the past – where runways were dust or mud, depending on the season.

Crew of the C–7A Caribou was three – pilot, co-pilot, and flight engineer/loadmaster. The trio often worked together to get out of a 'hot spot' as quickly as possible. 'The airplane obviously becomes a target once it lands. If they can hit it with a mortar, we lose an airplane. If they can hit while on the runway, they also tie up a runway.' The aircraft had rollers to unload cargo through its rear door and Nilssen often carried out what he called a speed offload. He untied the cargo, reversed propellers to start the aircraft going backwards, then when up to about 5mph (8km/h), he kicked the propellers forward. The untied cargo then rolled smartly and smoothly out the back. 'It works like a champ.' Nilssen had a flight engineer/loadmaster, Tom Agee, who *stood* on the cargo while it rolled out. Paradrops and LAPES (low altitude parachute extraction) were too exotic for the mission being carried out and were never used.

The CH–47 Chinook helicopter flown by the US Army and the Vietnamese Air Force could carry almost anything. Airlifting howitzers and other items of field equipment was a routine task. More important, the 'Hook' could salvage downed aircraft and return them for repair. Few helicopters were as powerful or as versatile. (US ARMY)

Even with the war petering out, there were still American soldiers at farflung outposts and the most popular cargo was mail or beer. C–7A Caribous did a lot of relocating people. They carried live animals, pigs and cows – and artillery shells.

Because things were winding down, Nilssen was at one time or another a member of various squadrons, including the 436th and 535th Tactical Airlift Squadrons. He and his companions were told that they would turn over 100 Caribous to the VNAF. At one time Nilssen was assigned a Vietnamese co-pilot. But the turnover apparently never happened and many C–7As were later relocated stateside.

Army Chinooks

As the American role in the war began to dwindle, not only men but significant items of equipment were removed from South Vietnam. One flying machine which belatedly reached Saigon's forces – despite a need for them in other areas where US forces were stationed – was the Vertol CH–47 Chinook helicopter, which had been on the battlefield since 1965. The VNAF received its first CH–47A Chinooks, making up the 237th Helicopter Squadron at Bien Hoa, on 30 September 1970, although the bulk of the transition occurred later. In due course there were four VNAF Chinook squadrons in the country's four military regions, the others being the 241st at Phu Cat, the 247th at Da Nang, and the 249th at Can Tho.

Nearly all US Army CH–47 operators came under the 1st Aviation Brigade, being organized into assault support helicopter companies, each with an authorized strength of sixteen aircraft. A few CH–47s belonged to organic field commands such as the First Cavalry and 101st Airborne Divisions.

CH–47A, B and C variants, in addition to the already described ACH–47A gunship, saw service in Vietnam. At the high point of the conflict, twenty-two American CH–47 units were in operation, carrying out the heavy-duty missions with which the twin-rotor helicopter was identified. The Chinook saved millions of dollars' worth of hardware by retrieving downed aircraft and transporting them to recovery depots, in what eventually became known as 'Pipestem' missions. In fact, CH–47s were credited with the recovery of no fewer than 11,500 disabled aircraft. CH–47s also hauled armed troops, ammunition, food and people.

In its role as a carrier of fuel supplies, or 'bladder bird', the CH–47 carried a 3,500lb (1,588kg), 500-gallon rubberized fuel cell. The CH–47 routinely hauled around howitzers, mortars and other field weapons of various sizes. A less-known use of the twin-rotor Chinook by the US Army was as a dispenser of tear gas on the rare instance when this riot control agent was employed against Viet Cong forces.

The US Army continued to make effective use of one fixed-wing aircraft the Air Force had not succeeded in taking away, the Grumman OV–1 Mohawk. Mohawks were employed to collect intelligence on the enemy's whereabouts and movements. Since the machine could virtually slide over the grass and look over the enemy's shoulder, the information was invaluable in planning B–52 strikes against the Ho Chi Minh Trail, naval artillery missions against coastal targets, and fighter-bomber missions.

The OV–1B Mohawks equipped with SLAR (sideways-looking airborne radar) did a good job of monitoring North Vietnamese activity along the DMZ, the inaccurately named Demilitarized Zone along the 17th Parallel. These missions brought the Mohawks within range of North Vietnam's SA–2 surface-to-air missiles (SAMs) which, by 1971, had been moved rather far to the southerly reaches of North Vietnam. Fortunately for the Army crews, a lock-on by SAM radar set off a signal on their own SLAR indicator. Still, at least one Mohawk is thought to have been downed by a SAM.

Designed with a kindly view towards the wrench jockey who had to keep it flying, the OV–1 Mohawk was relatively easy to maintain and repair, even when it operated from rough forward airfields. The US Army holds that the Mohawk had the highest sustained operational readiness rate of any Army aircraft that served in Vietnam, often producing an availability rate of better than 95 per cent.

The build-up of the Vietnamese Air Force (VNAF) continued in 1971, even though Saigon's air arm seemed actually to be receiving more aircraft than it could absorb. This VNAF Douglas A–1H Skyraider, seen in a hangarette at Tan Son Nhut, is typical of the aircraft received by the VNAF as the American withdrawal went on. (NORMAN TAYLOR)

Marine Cobras

The AH–1G Cobra gunship, employed with considerable success by the Army and Marine Corps, was neither as easy to maintain nor as amenable to rough airfields, but the Cobra was an effective weapons system and its contribution was undeniable.

Although the G model had been conceived for the Army, Marine Corps AH–1Gs had been in combat since early April 1969 when the first few joined squadron VMO–2 at Marble Mountain. After a three-month evaluation period, which solved some of the problems of bringing a new type into service, AH–1Gs began to replace UH–1E Huey gunships. The Cobra proved far superior to the UH–1E in the delivery of accurate, close-in fire support during helicopter assault operations. Furthermore, the gunships were able to free the Marines' hard-pressed UH–1E gunships to perform the light helicopter missions for which they had originally been intended.

In the American withdrawal from South Vietnam, the Marines, who had arrived in large numbers first, were also the first to leave. Although Marine units began their pull-out from Vietnam as early as August 1969, the leathernecks' AH–1G Cobras remained in service until well into 1971 and, indeed, served during Operation 'Lam Son 719', the incursion into Laos early that year (see later). On 26 May 1971 the Marine Corps' last squadron flying the G model Cobra, HML–167, ended its participation in combat and began its return to stateside duty.

A considerable amount of work was going on to improve the Cobra for both the Army and the Marine Corps. Included in these efforts was the development of the TOW (tube-launched, optically sighted, wire-guided) missile, intended primarily for anti-tank operations. In 1971 it was not yet apparent that there was much need for an anti-tank weapon in Vietnam, but a different era was coming.

C–123 Operations

Lieutenant Colonel Charles J. Zemple took command of the 19th Tactical Airlift Squadron, flying C–123K Providers from Tan Son Nhut, and almost immediately had orders to prepare to turn over the squadron's assets to the VNAF.

C–123Ks of the 19th TAS, known as 'Bookies' from an old call-sign, had been lugging cargo and fuel all over South Vietnam, the fuel being carried in 'bladder birds', or C–123Ks with portable bladder containers. Crew of the aircraft consisted of pilot, co-pilot, engineer, loadmaster, and sometimes a dog named Butch (part beagle) who flew with the 'Bookies' when he felt like it.

Zemple found the C–123K mission dull and boring but necessary. Briefings began at 6.00 a.m., with first launch at 7.00 a.m. and the last aircraft recovery was at 7.00 p.m. During the incursion into Cambodia the C–123Ks carried 'tons and tons' into Bu Dop, yet Zemple told others the work was 'dull', 'routine', and that his aircraft was a 'trash hauler'. Secretly he was very proud of the C–123K, which was exceedingly versatile.

He remembered that flying along the coast, the country was gorgeous. Especially the beaches at Vung Tau. It seemed a pity that the Viet Cong had damaged old French homes along the shoreline. Zemple also remembered the peculiar difficulties of hauling food up-country to the montagnards, often including pigs and cows.

The C–123K was well liked but not perfect. In the harsh Vietnam climate, flap hinges would break causing the flaps to fly up and make the aircraft asymmetrical. The 'fix' was achieved with glass beads which strengthened the hinges.

Unfortunately the 19th TAS suffered one major accident during Zemple's tenure. Fuel-laden C–123K aircraft 54-0650 experienced a collapsed nose gear oleo strut at Thein Ngon, a South Vietnamese-controlled forward operating location, on 19 March 1971 and was completely destroyed by the ensuing fire. All crew members escaped from the aircraft without injury.

Like so many other US units, the 19th wound down its own operations to prepare

The AH–1G Cobra gunship helicopter ended its combat service with the US Marine Corps in South Vietnam in 1971. The AH–1J Sea Cobra was still to follow and, indeed, variants of the Cobra have remained potent weapons long after the end of the Vietnam conflict. (USMC)

for the South Vietnamese to handle their own affairs. The last fragged mission flown by Americans used the call-sign 'Bookie 102' and terminated at Phan Rang on 30 April 1971. Ten of the squadron's C–123Ks were turned over to the VNAF 421st Transport Squadron and six transferred to other US units.

'Lam Son 719'

With a single exception, there was no major military operation in 1971 that was important to influence the course of the war. It was a war of dirty, small-unit actions. A vast number of American troops – and some South Vietnamese – were REMFs (a derogatory term for rear-area troopers), but the men who were in combat were in *constant* combat. In the Second World War or Korea, men fought for a day or a week, then went for a week or a month without being in action. In Vietnam combat soldiers were in combat every minute of every day and night. Often the logistics provided by cargo planes, the airmobility offered by helicopters and the cover provided by fighter-bombers made the difference to these soldiers. But few of their combat actions made the headlines.

The exception: Saigon's President Thieu announced on 8 February 1971 that South Vietnamese troops, supported by US aircraft and artillery, had crossed the border into Laos to cut the Ho Chi Minh Trail and interdict the flow of supplies from the north. Three ARVN divisions were involved in Operation 'Lam Son 719'. The ARVN forces around which the attack was planned were the 1st Infantry Division, the 1st Airborne Division, the Marine Division, the 1st Armored Brigade, and three Ranger battalions. Extensive US air support prevented the operation from turning into a disaster when ARVN forces found themselves over-extended and outnumbered, and were forced to conduct a fighting withdrawal from Laos. Again the public in the US became riled at the idea that the war was being expanded.

Like the Marine Corps AH–1G Cobra gunships which have already been cited, US Army helicopters played a major role in supporting 'Lam Son 719'. Army AH–1G Cobras were far more numerous and proved to be extremely rugged, capable of absorbing damage and inflicting it. The Sikorsky CH–54 Tarhe, or Skycrane, performed herculean cargo-moving tasks, often shifting heavy items of equipment such as tractors and bulldozers. The Boeing Vertol CH–47

An F–4J Phantom from the US Navy's squadron VF–114, the 'Aardvarks', swarms down on a Viet Cong target in 1971. Although the level of ground fighting remained relatively low in 1970–71, a Phantom crew was still confronted by the familiar proposition that the enemy had guns and was shooting. Air-to-ground work was always risky and even a single 7.62mm round from an AK–47 infantry rifle could wreak havoc inside the guts of such a complex aircraft. (US NAVY)

Not often mentioned in accounts of the air war in Vietnam is the Sikorsky CH–54 Tarhe, or Flying Crane, the versatile airlifter which carried almost any cargo – including a bulldozer when necessary – from one location to another. This CH–54 (67–18445) is carrying a square-shaped 'People Pod' from Vinh Long to Vung Tau. (US ARMY)

Chinook was another workhouse. More familiar Army UH–1H Huey helicopters performed vital service, too, but they proved relatively vulnerable to ground fire and large numbers were lost.

Not often mentioned in accounts of the air war in Vietnam, the CH–54 Tarhe was built around the concept that its cargo could be detachable and thereby easily loaded and unloaded; the CH–54 had more load-lifting capacity than most of the heavy helicopters. It had been in action since the earliest days with the First Cavalry Division in 1965.

One of the more unusual weapons of the war was the CH–54 equipped with a 10,000lb (4,535kg) bomb. The purpose was not bombardment, but rather the clearing of jungle foliage to creat helicopter LZs (landing zones). A similar operation was carried out by the Air Force dropping a bomb of the same size from a C–130 Hercules. The technique was not widely used and its cost-effectiveness is debatable.

Bringing much-needed war supplies into South Vietnam – and bringing out troops who were being withdrawn – placed heavy demands on Military Airlift Command's transport force. At the time the Lockheed C–5A Galaxy joined the aerial pipeline from the US to Vietnam, it was the world's largest operational aircraft. This example belongs to the 75th Military Airlift Squadron. (USAF)

Secretary of State William P. Rogers arrives at Tan Son Nhut for a visit to confer on Vietnamization with President Thieu (not shown) **and other leaders. Rogers was one of the key figures in the Nixon administration who planned the US withdrawal, but although he was the senior American foreign policy official – equivalent to a foreign minister in other countries – he was not as influential as the White House's Henry Kissinger.** (USAF)

More Withdrawal

President Nixon announced on 7 April 1971 that he intended to withdraw 100,000 more US troops from South Vietnam by 1 December. These incremental announcements were the President's way of making it clear that his administration had a plan, although further details of the planning process were not revealed. Nixon's first concern was the American soldier on the ground and he had not yet decided that all American airpower could be withdrawn from the war zone.

In June the last O–1 Bird Dog in USAF service was transferred to the VNAF. During their South-East Asia service, so the figures said, Air Force O–1s had flown 471,186 combat sorties and had suffered 119 losses. It is doubtful that any single aircraft type in history served with greater distinction. The Bird Dog had also been at war in Korea. To many it seemed timeless.

The last F–100D Super Sabre unit in South-East Asia, the 35th TFW at Phan Rang, ceased operations on 26 June 1971. The last F–100 left for the US on 30 July, ending a combat employment which had begun in 1964, encompassing 360,283 combat sorties and the loss of 243 aircraft. Employed over North Vietnam only in the very earliest days of the fighting up north, the F–100 is repeatedly said to have flown more combat sorties in the south than any other aircraft type.

Pentagon Paper

As often happened during this period of low-intensity conflict, what happened at home was more important than what transpired on the battlefield. On 13 June 1971 the *New York Times* began releasing the 'Pentagon Papers', a top-secret study of US involvement in the Vietnam war which had been originally prepared for Defense Secretary McNamara and was leaked to the press by Daniel Ellsberg. The 'Papers' contained dozens of previously highly classified documents which seemed to show that American officials had lied publicly about the 'how' and 'why' of US escalation of the war.

In August 1971 the USAF withdrew the last Martin RB–57E Canberra operating with the 'Patricia Lynn' reconnaissance program. The RB–57E was widely viewed as the most cost-efficient reconnaissance aircraft in the conflict. According to Canberra pilot Robert C. Mikesh, the RB–57E excelled in stability, maneuverability, versatility of equipment, long duration over target, and – not to be overlooked – crew ability.

While flying from Tan Son Nhut on missions in Laos, the small 'Patricia Lynn' detachment – never more than five aircraft – had been commended by MACV for providing 94 per cent of all battlefield intelligence. Apparently the few Canberras acquired more targets, day and night, than the two RF–4C Phantom and one RF–101C Voodoo squadrons of the 460th Tactical Reconnaissance Wing. It was said that with only four more RB–57Es, the 'Patricia Lynn' outfit could handle all day and night reconnaissance in-country for the entire war.

Even less sophisticated versions of the Canberra had proven too much for the VNAF, however, and consideration was never given to turning the sophisticated, sensitive RB–57Es over to Saigon's pilots. The 'Patricia Lynn' operation ended with one or more of its RB–57Es having reached the 8,000 flying hours mark.

This was still not the final episode of the Canberra in Vietnam. Apart from the Australian Canberra bombers flying from Phan Rang, there was a brief period ahead when the heavily instrumented B–57G version, known by the program name 'Tropic Moon', would return to the war.

The F–4D version of the Phantom, which had been in action since 1967, was optimized for Air Force operations and no longer had the internal systems of earlier models built for the Navy. An F–4D could carry eight 750lb (340kg) bombs or a variety of other ordnance loads. This Phantom is in clean condition without under-wing ordnance. (USAF)

Troop Draw-down

In September it was announced that US troop strength in South Vietnam would be down to 177,000 by the start of December. With a real withdrawal undeniably taking place, the numbers of men in the country became more important to TV audiences back home than the body counts and casualty totals which had so far been the center of attention. What was more important, massive amounts of equipment were being withdrawn or transferred.

On 8 September 1971 the final AC–119G Shadow gunship was transferred to the VNAF. As noted earlier, the VNAF's 819th Attack Squadron at Tan Son Nhut did not distinguish itself with these aircraft, nor did the 821st at a later time when it received the jet-augmented AC–119K Stinger.

The USAF's AC–130A Spectre and the improved AC–130 Surprise Package gunships gave way to still further improvements of this highly successful design. A program to convert C–130E Hercules aircraft to the Surprise Package configuration was well under way. In addition, tactics were being improved. The truck-killing record of fighters escorting the AC–130 had improved dramatically with the introduction of laser-guided bombs and the Pave Sword laser seeker pod employed by F–4 Phantoms. In the first combat test of this 'smart' weapon on 3 February 1971, F–4 Phantoms accompanying an AC–130A Spectre destroyed a 37mm gun position with a laser-guided bomb. The technology became fairly widespread as 1971 continued.

In 1971 Air Force Secretary Robert Seamans approved a program which would put eleven of the latest-model AC–130A aircraft, all modified to the Surprise Package configuration, into South-East Asia by 1 October 1971. In addition, six further improved AC–130E Spectres would be in the area by 1 January 1972 and eventual procurement would total twelve AC–130Es. The E model, under the Pave Aegis project, would include a 105mm howitzer in place of one of the two 40mm Bofors cannon.

Bronco

In 1971 the US Navy received OV–10 Bronco aircraft and commissioned a new kind of squadron, VAL–4 (Light Attack Squadron 4) which served alongside another new unit, HAL–3 (Helicopter Light Attack Squadron 3), flying UH–1B Hueys. These two Navy squadrons were charged with protecting river convoys traveling the Mekong from the South China Sea to the Saigon docks.

Carrier War

Nor should the Navy's carrier war be forgotten. There had been some reduction in the number and duration of aircraft-carrier line periods to put the seagoing Navy in synch with everybody else – but carrier action was continuing. Indeed, carrier aircraft helped to facilitate the withdrawal from land bases.

AO2 Richard Leach was an aviation ordnanceman aboard the carrier USS *Shangri-la* (CVA–38), an aging, wooden flight-decked ship which dated to the Second World War and was one of a number of carriers which repeatedly pulled combat cruises in the war zone. Leach worked in an ordnance shop with twenty men. Putting bullets, bombs and rockets aboard the Navy's warplanes was gruelling work. It was hard manual labor. 'Everything was loaded by hand.'

Leach remembers that early A–4 Skyhawks carried a mere sixty 20mm rounds per gun (not 250, as on some models). The ammunition came belted up. There were armor-piercing, HEI (high-explosive incendiary), and tracer rounds. Although loading its guns was no easy task, Leach considered the A–4 Skyhawk highly reliable, a simple aircraft which usually worked right. Occasionally there was the risk of a strut collapse.

Life aboard a carrier was a constant reminder of danger. Leach watched an A–4 skid wildly while attempting to land, miss the arresting wire, and come to a halt only after hitting a helicopter hard enough to send it careering off the flight deck and into the drink. On another occasion a malfunction on one of Leach's A–4 Skyhawks caused the aircraft to fire a cannon round into another *Shangri-la* aircraft.

Turning around an A–4 Skyhawk to enable the light attack aircraft to fly a new sortie in less than 1½ hours was a finely orchestrated event with everything organized: the bombs were located in the

No single aircraft type was more ubiquitous, more widely recognized, than the UH–1 Huey series of helicopters. With a war going on, there was not a lot of time for posed pictures, but this Huey gunship crew stood inspection for the camera with examples of the ordnance carried by the aircraft. Note the 57mm grenade-launcher in the nose of this UH–1. (US ARMY)

Deck crews on US aircraft-carriers in the South China Sea never got to see South Vietnam – when they had liberty, they spent it in Hong Kong or the Philippines – but they made an indispensable contribution to the fight. These armorers are moving 500lb (227kg) Snakeye fin-retarded bombs across the deck of the USS *Kitty Hawk* (CVA-63). (US NAVY)

bomb skid (the device used to move them around deck), the weapon/bomb elevators ready with items to be loaded from the magazine below decks, men and equipment lined up behind the ship's island. 'Everybody moved and moved fast.'

There was a cavity called the 'hell hole' inside the A-4 where 20mm cartridges had to be inserted and were difficult to load. To arm the guns pneumatically, you had to push an air compressor around the deck with a 100ft (30m) line.

As one of the last steps before a Skyhawk was catapulted off the ship, 'you always made damn sure that people knew how to pull safety pins from the bomb fuses. You'd pull the pins and hold them high in the air to show the pilot so he'd know'.

Deck personnel on carriers could be distinguished by the colors they wore. Red denoted ordnance men like Leach, green signified avionics personnel, and brown the

The Grumman C-2 Greyhound was the carrier on-board delivery (COD) aircraft which brought people, supplies and mail to US Navy aircraft-carriers. Supplanting the earlier C-1, this twin-engined turboprop was a real workhorse. Their numbers were few and these aircraft were frequently overtaxed. (US NAVY)

squadron line crew, including the plane captain. All these men belonged to the squadrons embarked on the ship. Purple indicated aviation bosun's mates and yellow signified aircraft directors, both members not of the squadrons but of the ship's company.

Fewer than 120 men among the 3,800 to 5,000 aboard a carrier like *Shangri-la* ever strapped into a fast jet and flew off to bomb the enemy. The contribution made by the others is difficult to quantify and easy to ignore. A few were lost at sea. They should not be forgotten.

The South Vietnamese soldier. Much depended on him. By 1971 the ARVN or Army of (South) Vietnam had some superb combat units and larger numbers of troops who were at least adequate. There was talk of leaving a US air presence in South Vietnam for as long as possible, perhaps until 1980, but the withdrawal of American ground troops was on a firm timetable and President Nixon did not intend to change it. (US ARMY)

F–4D Phantom (65–0589) of the 389th Tactical Fighter Squadron, carrying a bomb load on the centerline, taxies out at Phu Cat on 16 April 1971. Hardened aircraft shelters in background were built not out of fear of enemy air attack – which never happened – but out of healthy respect for the Viet Cong's ability to mount mortar attacks, even in areas controlled by friendly forces. (NORMAN TAYLOR)

VNAF Pilots

Staff Sergeant Daniel J. Henry was a USAF meteorologist assigned to Binh Thuy in the Mekong Delta region, a typical airfield location where the VNAF was struggling to absorb the training, expertise and equipment being foisted upon it with almost wasteful eagerness by the great American supply machine.

'I would sit there and watch Vietnamese fliers come and go on combat missions in the A–1 and A–37,' Henry remembers. 'The most experienced pilots had a resigned mood about them. Most had great confidence in their ability. They'd flown hundreds of missions, thousands of hours, and they knew every trick of survival in the book. But to them the war was endless, so they were resigned to the fact that no matter how good they were, they would die.'

Because young pilots were being recruited and trained with almost dizzying speed, Henry noticed that most were skittish, gun-shy, reluctant to make hard decisions, unwilling to commit to action where the situation was not crystal clear. 'With clear instructions, a clear target, and no ambiguities in the situation, the young VNAF pilot was tops. There was no question that these guys had bravery. But they weren't equipped for the unexpected. In warfare things are unpredictable. These guys would find themselves in the "fog of war", and they wouldn't know what to do next.'

This was the dilemma of Vietnamization. At the very time the American Army had its problems, the Vietnamese armed forces were peopled with an extreme mix of the very good and the very bad. Binh Thuy was a relatively small base and the Americans and Vietnamese there had excellent rapport – perhaps in part because there were very few Americans. 'We'd have a few beers in the old Quonset hooch that served as a club,' Henry remembers. 'There's a special bond between men at war and we enjoyed a real spirit of camaraderie. Sometimes we'd hoot and howl, like we were the oldest friends in the world. One night, surrounded by our Vietnamese pals over beer, cigarettes and rock music, an American buddy of mine pulled out a snapshot of his girlfriend, wearing a bathing suit and sunning on the beach. "Look what I've got to go home to!" he grinned. There was this sudden silence in the room. After a pause, we remembered that the Vietnamese in the conversation didn't have any place to go from here.'

Henry actually knew a Vietnamese so short he had to sit on a copy of the base directory to see out of his A–37. Another made a personal crusade of rousing up the maintenance troops, creating intra-squadron competitions to raise morale. One VNAF pilot dropped bombs by day and wrote poems at night. A senior officer wore a chequered scarf, boasted loudly, avoided the dangerous missions, and wrote himself up for awards. There were all kinds, but very few who were simply mediocre.

White House Warning

On 10 December 1971 President Nixon warned that North Vietnam would be bombed if it increased the level of fighting while US troops were being withdrawn from the south. Here again political forces were sometimes more important than military: Hanoi knew full well that Nixon wanted to find a way out of the war that could be seen as honorable and would probably accept any reasonable way out which included the return of the POWs. Nixon knew full well – his intelligence advisors frequently reminded him – that Hanoi had the potential to mount a combat offensive if it chose to do so. Nixon's 'warning' could be viewed as taking credit for the low level of conflict Hanoi had maintained for more than two years.

None of this was very convincing to President Thieu, Premier Ky, or the other leaders in the South Vietnamese capital who had a deep-rooted fear that their survival was not a part of the stakes. It did not help that the few allies who had joined the war effort were also withdrawing – the New Zealanders, the Australians, the Koreans. Hardly a day went by when some official in Washington did not proclaim that South Vietnam would soon be able to defend itself alone; but nobody really believed it, least of all South Vietnam's men in charge. The American soldier had defeated the North Vietnamese on the battlefield but his valor seemed almost irrelevant to the likely outcome.

The US presence ended at two more air bases during the year, Bien Hoa and Phu Cat being transferred to the VNAF in August and December respectively. To some extent these turnovers were symbolic. A few American aircraft continued to operate from both.

Although many Americans had been withdrawn by year's end, those who kept the numbers were not among them. USAF aircraft flew a total of 450,031 combat sorties and expended 642,900 tons of munitions in South-East Asia operations with a loss of 87 aircraft. Sorties included 87,052 attack sorties and 12,554 B–52 missions. KC–135 Stratotankers performed over 62,500 refuelings. Tactical airlift operations within South Vietnam moved 2,282,883 passengers and 283,556 tons of cargo. Eighty-seven USAF aircraft were lost during the year, 70 to combat causes.

The war was at its lowest ebb. Both sides were avoiding large-scale actions. If it kept winding down like this, the war would simply disappear. There had been no important fighting over North Vietnam since the 1968 bombing halt and no sign of any was in sight. In the south the level of conflict was the lowest since the early 1960s. The military solution – American success on the battlefield – remained irrelevant.

But history has a way of cheating politicians who seek to avoid any solution in war that does not rely upon the valor of men under arms. At that juncture in history, Americans whose job was to fly and fight sensed – they felt rather than knew – that they were going to have to return to the embattled region around Hanoi to settle things, finally, with the North Vietnamese. In the parched heat at Davis-Monthan AFB near Tucson, an American fighter wing commander walked in small circles, pondering his experience in three wars, pondering the enemy, counselling a young wife. She had sought him out. Her man, her F–4 Phantom front-seater, was training over the Arizona desert to do battle in the skies of North Vietnam. There was a bombing halt. There were negotiations. She had to know. Would her young captain find himself pitted against the heaviest defenses the world has ever known, against men in MiGs bent on killing him? Or would the bombing halt hold? Would the war wind further down?

Colonel Andrew Baird, not an eloquent man, did not believe that the politicians were going to settle it. After all these years, there was no way but the hard way. Baird said to Mary Ackerman:

'Maybe I'm wrong. Maybe our diplomats in Paris will wrap it up before I have to take these men back to Hanoi. But my sense of timing tells me that some of these men will bleed and die before we put this one away. It has always been so . . .'

There remained, after all, those forces being held in reserve by Hanoi. There remained the papers being written by intelligence analysts warning that an offensive was possible. For the Americans the final resort on the cutting edge of policy lay not at some conference table, not in some politician's rhetoric, but in the final battles that awaited them in a new and very different year.

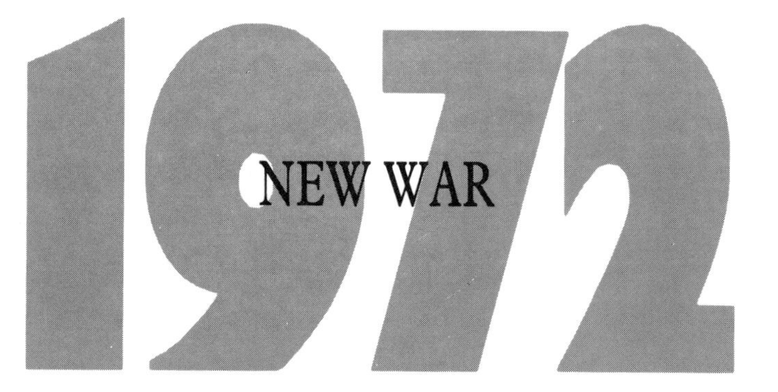

1972 NEW WAR

It was another election year in the United States. In South Vietnam it was a time when the conflict remained at a low level, both sides feeling each other out, avoiding any full-scale test of strength, staying away from large-scale battles.

Negotiations were under way – secret talks between Henry Kissinger and Le Duc Tho were to be the most important sessions of the year – and the stakes were little changed from the period 1970–72. The American decision to withdraw was irreversible. The survival of the Saigon regime did not seem to be assured. It was widely understood that the Americans were going to seek little more than the return of their prisoners of war. Perhaps, said some, there was no reason for Hanoi to fight. The talks would end it.

On 13 January 1972 President Nixon announced the withdrawal of some 70,000 American personnel, to reduce troop strength in South Vietnam to 69,000 by 1 May.

1972 was the year the lull ended and the North Vietnamese came down the pike in a full-scale Easter Invasion, using reserve troops, tanks, and missiles. But the enemy also persisted in his old tricks, including booby traps. Air Force personnel at Tan Son Nhut unearthed this soda can used to cover a grenade – a booby trap aimed at blowing apart an unsuspecting American or South Vietnamese soldier. (USAF/HERMAN J. KOKOJAN)

A USAF squadron which had been in South Vietnam longer than any other finally departed the country on 15 January 1972. The 19th TASS had been in the war so long that many could remember when Defense Secretary McNamara had said it would be withdrawn at the end of the war – in 1964! After nearly a decade with the O–1 Bird Dog and a few months with the OV–10 Bronco, the 19th TASS finally left Phan Rang and was relocated to Korea.

USAF personnel in South Vietnam were in the contradictory position of simultaneously conducting a fully fledged air campaign and carrying out reductions in force. The reductions were consistent with what the American public and its leaders wanted, but were undoubtedly viewed as a sign of weakness by Hanoi.

Obvious and ominous build-ups in North Vietnamese infiltration and logistic stockpiling were countered by an increase in air sorties, but reductions in the number of warplanes available, coupled with vastly improved enemy defenses, restricted these efforts.

Easter Invasion

On 30 March 1972 North Vietnam invaded the south. After more than two years of low-level activity by both sides, the Spring Offensive – or Easter Invasion – was the all-out assault which had been predicted by analysts, making use of forces Hanoi had long held in reserve.

The architect of the 1972 Spring Offensive, as far as US intelligence could tell, was General Vo Nguyen Giap of North Vietnam. Giap had been an early associate of Ho Chi Minh and had laid siege to the French at Dien Bien Phu. Unlike previous episodes, he now had the use of well-organized regular Army forces including tanks.

In fact, the invasion was backed up by a staggering array of weaponry which the communists had previously used not at all or only in limited numbers – T–34, T–54, and PT–76 tanks, SA–2 and SA–7 surface-to-air missiles (SAMs), the Soviet-made 130mm howitzer, and the AT–3 wire-guided anti-armor missile. About all the communists lacked was air cover. Their MiGs never joined the fray in the south, although the recent growth of the enemy air arm up north was a complicating factor. The weather also seemed to favor Hanoi. In the first days of the invasion, low ceilings, thick overcasts, and intermittent rain hampered efforts to provide air support.

The invasion was really three separate actions – straight across the DMZ, south then east toward Kontum in the central highlands, and farther south across the Cambodian border towards the border provinces immediately north and north-west of Saigon. It was a calibrated coordinated effort.

Because of the continuous withdrawals since the advent of the Nixon administration, the US fighter-bomber force in South Vietnam was but a shadow of its former size and strength. The US had only three F–4 Phantom and one A–37 Dragonfly squadrons in the country, just 76 aircraft in all.

Tactical Deployments

The invasion caused an instantaneous reaction aimed at bolstering tactical airpower in the war zone. Plans were immediately

A Sikorsky HH–53C Super Jolly Green helicopter approaches a stretcher-borne survivor at a landing zone. The HH–53B and C models carried out numerous combat rescues in all four South-East Asian countries. Communist ground troops often sought to lure the helicopters into their gunsights. (USAF)

carried out to reinforce US air strength in South Vietnam.

Perhaps the quickest action based on these plans occurred on 31 March when F–4D Phantoms of the 3rd Tactical Fighter Wing in Korea deployed to Da Nang and Ubon to augment existing fighter forces. On 3 April the USS *Kitty Hawk* (CVA–63) was the first of four additional carriers to join the two already on station off Vietnam.

In a reduction which had been planned long before the North Vietnamese offensive, on 1 April 1972, the 20th Special Operations Squadron was inactivated and its UH–1N Huey helicopter gunships were returned to the US, thus ending USAF involvement in helicopter gunship operations in South-East Asia.

Close on the heels of the F–4D deployment from Korea, beginning on 3 April, in response to the massive invasion of South Vietnam, the USAF rapidly deployed a number of tactical squadrons under the nickname 'Constant Guard', to augment the depleted residual air units remaining in South-East Asia after the withdrawals of the previous years.

'Constant Guard' movements were to become . . . well, constant. 'Constant Guard I' was the move of F–105G Thunderchiefs and F–4E Phantoms from stateside bases to Korat and Ubon in Thailand. On 5 April these USAF fighter-bombers began reinforcing units in Thailand. Also included in 'Constant Guard I' were several EB–66 electronic warfare aircraft.

On 6 April Marine aircraft began landing at Da Nang. The Chairman of the Joint Chiefs of Staff, Admiral Thomas W. Moorer, announced a resumption of aerial attack and naval bombardment against North Vietnam. This was a limited undertaking but Moorer and other advisors to

A potent team. An OV–10 Bronco of the 23rd TASS equipped with the 'Pave Nail' night observation device accompanies two Vought A–7Ds of the 355th Tactical Fighter Wing. During combat rescues, the OV–10 increased the ability of rescue forces to operate at night while the A–7D replaced the Skyraider as the principal weapon used to cover an actual rescue attempt. (LTV)

President Nixon were talking seriously about renewing a prolonged campaign.

To go along with the 'Constant Guard' movements of tactical jets from the US to South-East Asia, Strategic Air Command began to deploy B–52D and B–52G Stratofortresses to Andersen AFB, Guam – in addition to those already on station – under the program names 'Bullet Shot I' through 'V'. Some bombers were flying missions within 72 hours of receiving deployment alert at their stateside bases. Early 'Bullet Shot' deployments were made by the 306th Bomb Wing at McCoy AFB, Florida, and the 96th Bomb Wing at Dyess AFB, Texas.

The abrupt build-up of the B–52 force in the Western Pacific for a conventional bombing role posed a mighty challenge to SAC General John C. Meyer and the men on the scene. At this juncture the B–52 remained the most important leg of the strategic triad aimed at the Soviet Union – the other legs behind the intercontinental ballistic missile (ICBM) and the submarine-launched ballistic missile (SLBM) – and it was no easy task to maintain readiness for nuclear war while freeing up more than one-third of all B–52s for Vietnam.

On 'The Rock', as B–52 crews called Guam – actually, it was the top of a 35,000ft (10,670m) mountain with its roots in the deepest part of the Marianas Trench – normal operations had to continue while the force of B–52s in residence grew in number. Included were 'Olympic Torch' U–2 missions, 'Combat Apple' RC–135 intelligence-gathering flights, and 'Giant Scale' SR–71 missions, some of them flown over Vietnamese soil. B–52s began to use parking slots, fuel and facilities hitherto reserved for other types. At the height of 'Bullet Shot' movements, Andersen AFB abruptly had 12,000 more men than it had billets for. Tent cities were a partial solution in an era of improvisation.

The B–52 had had a key role in striking enemy forces in South Vietnam all along. Bombing strikes against targets in North Vietnam by B–52s were resumed on 9 April. On the 11th the first strikes against the interior of the country were launched against Vinh. On the 15th major POL storage areas near Haiphong were hit.

General John D. Lavelle, who had followed General Clay as commander of Seventh Air Force in Saigon, was relieved of his duties on 11 April and replaced by General John W. Vogt, Jr. Lavelle was charged with falsifying reports of unauthorized air strikes against North Vietnam. Lavelle apparently had ignored a fundamental rule during the 1970–71 interim when only 'limited duration, protective reaction' strikes had been allowed up north: strikes were to be authorized in the north only when US warplanes were fired upon first.

An Loc

The battle for the town of An Loc in South Vietnam began in earnest on 13 April 1972, and two strong strikes were repulsed with the aid of continued air strikes. On the 15th the town was besieged by NVA forces, and a massive airlift to supply the defenders was conducted in coordination with close air support.

The airlift effort at An Loc was superhuman. From 15 April until ground supply routes were reopened on 23 July, a total of 763 sorties air-dropped 10,081 tons of supplies. Several cargo aircraft were lost during the An Loc operations. Heavy B–52 support contributed greatly to the defeat of the NVA forces. As happened all too frequently, the town was destroyed in order to save it. An Loc was reduced to rubble.

In spite of the dramatic escalation of the war, the United States held to its decision to withdraw. On 26 April 1972, in the midst of the North Vietnamese invasion, President Nixon announced plans to reduce 20,000 more personnel so that American strength in South Vietnam would fall to 49,000 by July.

'Constant Guard II', the next stage in the cycling of stateside tactical fighters back into South-East Asia to cope with the invasion and its aftermath, commenced on 26 April. In this stage, squadrons of F–4E Phantoms from two US locations were moved to Udorn, Thailand. A week later an entire wing, the 48th Tactical Fighter Wing from Holloman AFB, New Mexico, consisting of four squadrons of F–4D Phantoms, was moved to Takhli, also in Thailand. This 'Constant Guard III' movement was accompanied by the airlift of over 8 million tons of cargo, and combat operations began within

USS *Kitty Hawk* (CVA–63) was one of the aircraft-carriers which arrived to bolster the naval fleet in the combat zone when North Vietnam launched its 30 March 1972 offensive. The F–4 Phantom fought through the conflict to the end, producing aces up north and slowing the advance of enemy troops in the south. (USN)

Used primarily over North Vietnam but seen on occasion in the south, the General Dynamics F–111A Aardvark returned for its second South-East Asia combat tour in 1972 and – despite an unearned notoriety – proved very effective as a night and adverse-weather, low-level strike aircraft. (USAF)

24 hours of the arrival of the Phantoms. 'Constant Guard IV' came next, the movement of two squadrons of C–130E Hercules from the US to nearby Taiwan.

There was good reason for the reinforcements. The offensive had led to an especially hard drive by the enemy against the Dong Ha–Quang Tri area. The attacks began with heavy artillery and mortar fire; tank-supported infantry attacks followed. The NVA were coming on while gloomy weather hung over the battlefield and hampered air support.

On 28 April Dong Ha fell. On 1 May Quang Tri city fell to the North Vietnamese. The ARVN troops who mounted a defense were fighting as valiantly as ever did any of South Vietnam's troops, but in the immediate area of Quang Tri were 40,000 NVA who outnumbered the friendlies at least three to one. The weather continued to make air support virtually impossible.

The SA–7 man-portable, shoulder-launched SAM was introduced to South Vietnam in April with the invasion. Designed to home in on its target with an infrared heat-seeker, the SA–7 became at once a serious threat to all aircraft, especially to helicopters and slow-flying machines such as the A–1 Skyraider and AC–130 Spectre gunship.

Tactics had not really been developed to cope with a SAM that could be carried by a single infantry soldier and the first response – which was simply to fly missions at higher altitude – almost proved disastrous when pilots belatedly learned that the SA–7 was effective up to 5,000ft (1,524m). During April and May several A–1 Skyraiders, O–1 Bird Dogs and O–2 Skymasters fell victim to the SA–7, partly because they were too slow, partly because pilots had never been trained to evade the tiny lethal missile.

The first AC–130 Spectre ever be shot down in South Vietnam fell to the SA–7 on 18 June. The gunship was flying south-west of Hue – next after Quang Tri as a likely target of the communist assault – its crew believing that it was high enough to escape harm from the missile. Sergeant William B. Patterson was the lookout for the aircraft, which had the call-sign 'Spectre 11'. Patterson lay on the aft cargo door, actually hanging out into the airstream so that he could spot the telltale flash of light when a missile was fired.

Everything worked the way it was supposed to. Patterson gave the warning when an SA–7 was fired and came rushing up at the AC–130, its rocket motor burning with an eerie blue-white light – boring straight at the gunship rather than porpoising back and forth the way SA–7s usually did. The pilot fired a decoy flare and began an evasive turn but the SA–7 reached 'Spectre 11' anyway, colliding with the number three engine.

The violent, booming explosion shook the aircraft. The AC–130 bucked, threw its nose up, and settled again as the right inboard engine separated from the wing. There was a confusion of voices on the intercom as crew members reported the AC–130 heading downward and beginning to disintegrate.

When the North Vietnamese launched their invasion, the USAF had only four fighter squadrons in South Vietnam – three of F–4s and one A–37. Fighters like this F–4D Phantom were rushed to South-East Asia in a series of 'Constant Guard' deployments aimed at bolstering airpower to cope with the offensive. At the same time, although the war was escalating, the US stuck to its policy of withdrawing forces and reducing troop strength. (USAF)

Sergeant Patterson rolled back into the aircraft, unhooked the restraining strap which kept him from falling out, and reached for his chest-pack parachute. At about that time the right wing came off and the aircraft started into a cartwheeling roll. Patterson managed to hook only one side of his parachute to his body harness, in his haste attaching it backwards, when new explosions sent him hurtling into the black void outside.

Only three men survived this mid-air encounter between AC–130A Spectre 55-0043 of the 16th Special Operations. Patterson was one of them. The AC–130 Spectre, including the newer model AC–130E now in action, was an exceedingly potent weapon in the face of the North Vietnamese invasion, but every time an aircraft was lost it was a bitter blow to a small and tight-knit community.

Drive For Hue

Once Quang Tri had fallen, it appeared that the North Vietnamese were in an excellent position to drive on to Hue, the old imperial capital which had been the scene of heavy fighting during the 1968 Tet offensive. The weather continued to be generally bad but some aircraft were able to get into the fight against an enemy who had suddenly become capable of fielding tanks and missiles. An Air Force report quotes an OV–10 Bronco forward air controller, Lieutenant Colonel Ray Stratton, who described the new conflict between tanks and 'smart' bombs:

'I found two tanks just north of [a force of South Vietnamese] on the My Chanh River. It was at twilight. There was a PT–76 and a T–54. The PT–76 was trying to pull the T–54 out of a dry stream bed. They were just about a mile to the east of [the road] and about a mile and a half north of the town. I called for ordnance and there was none available. I waited and finally "Schlitz" and "Raccoon", two F–4s out of Ubon, showed up. They were equipped with a laser-illuminated bomb system known as Paveway One. "Raccoon" was the "illuminator", that is, he carried the laser gun used to direct the laser energy on to the target. "Schlitz" carried laser-guided bombs.

'They checked in with two or three minutes of "playtime" left – that is, they were running short on fuel. I briefed them on the way in to save time. I put the smoke down marking the target. By this time, the [laser] illuminator, "Raccoon", was in orbit, he asked me which tank we wanted to hit first. I suggested the one that was not stuck. Within about 30 seconds he said, "I've started the music," meaning the laser beam was on the target. "Schlitz" was already in position for the drop – the LGB (laser-guided bomb] hit right on that PT–76, blew the turret off and flipped the tank over. The blast covered the second tank with mud, so I put another smoke rocket down. "Raccoon" "started the music" again. "Schlitz" meanwhile had pulled right back up on the porch for another run. The whole operation was over in three minutes. Two bombs – two tanks destroyed. I logged them in at 6.18 and off at 6.21. That must be a record of some kind.'

Although the NVA mounted a full-scale assault and, again, made heavy use of tanks, South Vietnam's army was up to the task of containing the onslaught. The bulk of sorties flown in defense of Hue were flown by the VNAF. On the ground ARVN troops stood up to the advancing North Vietnamese in every encounter. Hanoi's finest were not able to overwhelm Hue, but in other sectors the onslaught persisted. And tanks kept coming.

Although the new laser-guided bombs were the most efficient air-delivered munition against tanks, most tanks were destroyed by 500lb (227kg) bombs of the older, 'dumb' variety. Many were released from VNAF A–1s and A–37s – more accurate than F–4s with the same bombs but

Employed since the big American build-up of 1965, the Grumman A–6 Intruder was a seasoned veteran by 1972 and no longer suffered teething troubles with its electronics systems. The KA–6D tanker was becoming increasingly important to the Fleet as older tankers were retired. KA–6D Intruder (151819), side No 522 of the 'Arabs' of VA–115 operating from the USS *Midway* (CVA–41), is seen making a landing approach. (USN)

With the Easter offensive and the assault on An Loc came the enemy's first use of numbers of main battle tanks. This Soviet-built T–54 tank (circle) sits in a street at An Loc – a town virtually devastated by fighting – after having been fired on and knocked out by an AH–1G Cobra gunship helicopter of the 79th Aerial Field Artillery. (USAF)

not as accurate as F–4s with LGBs. Surprisingly, the North Vietnamese tanks were also being outgunned by ARVN M48 main battle tanks, which were far from new.

To the pilot of a US Army AH–1G Cobra gunship, battling the newly fielded enemy tanks was a tougher proposition. CW2 Neal Thompson was at the controls of a Cobra when he came upon a PT–76 tank in the Que Son Valley, not far from Da Nang. Thompson attacked with 2.75in folding fin aircraft rockets (FFAR). Although these projectiles lacked the power and explosive force to penetrate the tank's armor, the hammering on the PT–76 hull killed the crew and halted the tank.

In general, ARVN troops on the ground were holding well against North Vietnamese might – including the tanks. The friendlies could not, however, prevent a communist attack in force on Kontum in the Central Highlands on 25 May 1972. As the enemy probed the outskirts of the city with massed infantry and tanks, all available air and gunship support was put aloft to help the defenders.

As the battle progressed and the North Vietnamese continued to attack and fight with their big guns, it was time for the first combat use of a small force of US Army helicopters equipped with TOW (tube-launched, optically tracked, wire-guided) anti-tank missiles. Three UH–1B Huey helicopters and crews along with mechanics and hardware for the TOW system had arrived in late April 1972, traveling via the much-used MAC C–141 StarLifter. The wire-guided missiles were released at close range and packed a substantial warhead.

At first light on the second day of the fight for Kontum, TOW engaged the enemy's

A–7E Corsair of the 'Mighty Shrikes' of VA–94, a squadron commanded by Commander David Moss, is given the 'go!' to launch from the USS *Coral Sea* (CVA–43) on 8 May 1972. The final version in the A–7 series, this E model Corsair is carrying anti-shipping mines to be airdropped in the region around Haiphong harbor. (USN)

With an enemy offensive and heavier fighting in both north and south, US tactical aircraft were rushed to South-East Asia in a series of deployments called 'Constant Guard'. One result was this kind of mixed formation of F–4D and F–4E Phantom fighters. The OC-coded F–4Ds belong to the 13th Tactical Fighter Squadron and were at Ubon, Thailand, all along. The ED-coded F–4Es belong to the 33rd Tactical Fighter Wing at Eglin AFB, Florida, and came to South-East Asia under one of the 'Constant Guard' deployments. (USAF)

tanks. Among the first 101 firings of the missile only twelve were evaluated as misses. Through 12 June the Army claimed 26 tank kills by the helicopter-borne TOWs, including no fewer than eleven formidable T–54s in the Kontum area.

'Linebacker'

It was inevitable that the Easter Invasion would draw a response. On 8 May 1972 President Nixon announced the mining of North Vietnamese ports and the bombing of rail lines to 'keep the weapons of war out of the hands of the international outlaws' in Hanoi. He also stated that the US would stop all acts of force if the enemy would agree to return all American prisoners of war and consent to an internationally supervised cease-fire.

The use of aerial mines in warfare had been a rare event since 1945 but one for which US forces had maintained a capability. The dropping of barrel-shaped anti-shipping mines in and around Haiphong was carried out by A–6 Intruders and A–7 Corsairs. Commander David Moss, skipper of the 'Mighty Shrikes' of VA–94 aboard the USS *Coral Sea* (CVA–43), led one of the first mining strikes and was surprised that the North Vietnamese did not mount even token resistance. No shore batteries, no SAMs, no MiGs. Rafael Iungerich, an intelligence officer with Seventh Air Force headquarters in Saigon, scrutinized the action reports of the mining missions and prepared a report for General Vogt, saying that the job had been carried out with incredible efficiency. 'We zipped up that port tight' says Iungerich. 'After the first few sorties, there wasn't going to be any merchant ship going in or out of the harbor, no matter what.'

Nixon's decision to send US warplanes back to North Vietnam in force evoked memories of the 1965–68 air campaign over the north, nicknamed 'Rolling Thunder'. The campaign had not been a success, had not forced Hanoi into reducing the flow of supplies or sitting at the conference table, or doing anything else. This time, said the men who planned the bombing of the north, it was going to be different.

'Linebacker' was the name given to the new air campaign against the north announced by Nixon. It was intended to stop the flow of supplies entering North Vietnam from allied countries and was a continuing effort involving USAF and Navy tactical airpower and naval gunfire support. It was directed against the entire North Vietnamese transportation system. This time, one of the differences was that precision-guided munitions – 'smart' bombs – were being used. Aerial bombardment had never been nearly as accurate as some of its strongest proponents said, but now it was far more accurate than before.

The 'Linebacker' campaign brought the biggest day of air combat over the north on 10 May 1972 when nine MiGs were shot down, strikes were carried out against bridges, marshalling yards, and other targets, and a Navy F–4J Phantom crew became the war's first aces. On 13 May 'smart' bombs destroyed the Thanh Hoa Bridge which had resisted bombing in the earlier campaign. A detailed account of the new war being fought up north appears in companion volume *Air War Hanoi*. Here, it is important to note that the fighting up north made it far more difficult for Hanoi to push the offensive in the south.

By June the number of B–52 Stratofortresses based in the western Pacific totalled 206 aircraft, the largest Strategic Air Command (SAC) bomber force ever assembled in the theater. The number of KC–135 Stratotankers reached 172 aircraft, the largest tanker force ever assembled.

It is almost impossible to exaggerate the importance of the KC–135 tankers, which faced an ever-growing workload. Besides being essential to the movement of newly arriving aircraft across the Pacific, they had to serve aircraft flying combat missions in a war zone which now encompassed four countries – Cambodia, Laos, North and South Vietnam. Until the enemy offensive, most B–52 missions had been flown from U-Tapao, the Thai air base from which any target could be reached without mid-air refuelling. Now, B–52s flying from Guam required en route refuelling, and a force of KC–135 tankers took position at Kadena for this purpose. With augmentations of US airpower under the 'Constant Guard' deployments, air refuelling requirements rose from a stabilized commitment of 36 per day to a peak of 130 daily. SAC positioned 46 tankers at U-Tapao and several other bases. Eventually, as noted, there were 172 KC–135s and 285 crews in South-East Asia.

On 29 June 1972 General Frederick C. Weyand replaced General Abrams as MACV commander. Still, there were continuing draw-downs. Weyand had earlier commanded the 25th Infantry Division in Vietnam and had been military advisor to the Paris peace talks in 1968–70.

Major Don Ellis of the 8th Special Operations Squadron does a final check of the ordnance load hanging under his A–37B Dragonfly before a combat mission in the lightweight attack aircraft operated by both Americans and Vietnamese. Here Ellis turns his attention to a 500lb (227kg) GP, or general-purpose bomb, and away from a CBU–57 cluster bomb unit consisting of a SUU–14 dispenser containing 132 BLU–69 fragmentation bomblets. When the North Vietnamese invaded on 30 March 1972, the USAF had only four fighter squadrons in South Vietnam, one of these being the A–37 unit. (USAF)

Fighting a newly escalated war, the US was nevertheless sticking to its firm decision to withdraw. On 27 June 1972 USAF C–123 Provider operations in South-East Asia came to a halt with the inactivation of the 310th Tactical Airlift Squadron at Tan Son Nhut and the transfer of its C–123s to the VNAF.

War at Home

No properly painted police car was available on the night of 17 June 1972 to respond to a routine complaint about a break-in at Washington's Watergate Hotel. Had a marked police cruiser responded, lookouts would have seen it coming, the thieves inside the

From an American viewpoint, the Vietnam war lasted sixteen years – but there were those who argued that all the issues were settled in the 'Eleven-Day War', the period between 18 and 29 December 1972 when B–52 Stratofortresses pounded North Vietnam and forced an agreement to end the war. This B–52D is similar to the 'Big Belly' D models which carried 108 bombs. (USAF)

building would have escaped, and the Watergate scandal – the worst in American history – would never have happened.

But it was an unmarked police car, with plainclothes officers, that was closest to the scene. The lookouts did not give a warning in time. James McCord, security chief of the Committee for the Re-election of the President, and four more 'plumbers' were arrested during their break-in of Democratic Party headquarters in the building.

It was not clear why President Nixon needed support from criminals in an election year when his opponent, Senator George McGovern, had virtually no chance of unseating the White House incumbent. Perhaps Nixon was busy with other things – a new approach to China, detente with the Soviets, and above all the Vietnam war – to notice that his subordinates were trampling over the electoral process. For whatever reason, it became known that Nixon's associates had thrived on 'dirty tricks', and a saga of political chicanery and double-dealing began to unfold.

Senator McGovern, a decorated B–17 Flying Fortress pilot in the Second World War, ran against Nixon on only one issue – the Vietnam conflict. McGovern was among those who wanted Americans out, now, regardless of the cost, including the cost to South Vietnam's people. A decent and straightforward man, he lacked broad foreign policy experience. In spite of popular opposition to the war, McGovern was never a serious threat to the man occupying the White House. Nixon, however, had sorely damaged himself by allowing Watergate to happen – although the full consequences would not be felt until two years hence.

More Withdrawal

As of 12 August 1972, all US combat troops had departed South Vietnam. Some 43,500 Americans remained in the country in advisory and adminsitrative roles. It was announced on 29 August that 12,000 more troops would be withdrawn by 1 December, leaving authorized strength at 27,000.

On 29 August President Nixon announced that US troop withdrawals would reduce troop strength in South Vietnam to 27,000 by 1 December.

On 16 September South Vietnamese troops recaptured Quang Tri city, but most of Quang Tri province remained in communist hands.

The next step in the continuing movement of US aircraft into South-East Asia was 'Constant Guard V' on 28 September, when

Those versions of the B–52 Stratofortress powered by water-injected J–57 engines created enormous clouds of smoke when they took off. At Andersen AFB, Guam, and at U-Tapao where bombing missions were launched during the 'Linebacker II' campaign, this became a recurring sight. (USAF)

Boeing B–52D Stratofortress (56–0670), probably belonging to Strategic Air Command's 307th Wing, releases a string of bombs. This view of 750lb (340kg) HE bombs was taken on a mission over South Vietnam, but B–52s operating in three-ship cells performed similar work up north in the December 1972 'Linebacker II' campaign. (USAF)

two F–111A squadrons from Nellis AFB, Nevada, arrived at Takhli. They relieved the F–4D Phantom squadrons of the 49th TFW which had deployed under 'Constant Guard III' in May.

Beginning on 10 October in 'Constant Guard VI', two squadrons of Vought A–7D aircraft (not given the Corsair nickname assigned to Navy versions) deployed to Korat to replace the F–4E Phantoms of 'Constant Guard II'. This was the first appearance in the combat zone of the USAF version of the A–7. Combat missions by the A–7Ds began in South Vietnam on 16 October 1972, and plans were finalized to use the A–7D as a replacement for the A–1 Skyraider in the Sandy role as the escort for combat rescues.

It was a difficult period. On balance, far more men and materiel were being withdrawn than were being rushed into the area to counter the effects of the Spring invasion. By late in the year the invasion had clearly fallen short of bringing about the final victory Hanoi had sought, but it had also shattered any notion that the enemy might be willing to allow the war to peter out. 'Linebacker' operations against North Vietnam were halted on 23 October when bombing north of the 20th Parallel was curtailed. Termination of 'Linebacker' resulted from the secret talks between Kissinger and Le Duc Tho and from an American perception

that progress was being made in the negotiations. Like all previous partial or full bombing halts, it was a mistake.

'Peace is at hand,' Kissinger said. This, too, was a mistake. The United States embarked on Project 'Enhance Plus', designed to build up the VNAF to a level adequate to conduct operations after a cease-fire or withdrawal by US forces. Between September and November in a rush effort, no fewer than 288 additional aircraft had been transferred to the VNAF (116 F–5A/Bs, 90 A–37s, 28 A–1s, 22 AC–119Gs and 32 C–130As). There could no longer be any doubt that the VNAF, now the world's third largest air force, had far more aircraft than it could possibly use. Some of the F–5s delivered to Saigon's air arm had been aircraft originally slated for Taiwan and South Korea.

VNAF Numbers

The VNAF had year-end strength of 1,817 assigned aircraft, with a total of 1,297 formed aircrews. Major aircraft types included 246 A–37s, 135 F–5s and 540 UH–1 Huey helicopters.

Overstocking the VNAF was a conscious decision. Although neither side had tabled the proposed text of an agreement to end the war, US leaders felt that any such armistice might include a prohibition against introducing new combat aircraft into Vietnam. (Such a prohibition was part of the 1953 Korean cease-fire and was abrogated in 1958 not by the communist side but by the US.) Even if they were not bound by such an agreement, Nixon administration leaders knew very well that the US Congress might prevent them from supplying military equipment to Saigon's armed forces in any future conflict – and, indeed, they were correct in their interpretation of Congress's intent.

On 22 November 1972 the first B–52 Stratofortress ever lost to enemy action fell prey to a SAM over North Vietnam. The aircraft made it to Thailand where the crew ejected and was recovered.

The peace Kissinger had predicted was elusive. On 18 December 1972 the third and final campaign over North Vietnam was launched. 'Linebacker II' was directed against military targets in the Hanoi/Haiphong area. The message to field commanders minced no words: 'You are directed to commence . . . a maximum effort, repeat maximum effort, of B–52/Tacair strikes in the Hanoi/Haiphong areas . . . ' The largest number of B–52s ever assembled – now between one-third and one-half of SAC's worldwide force – was to carry the brunt of 'Linebacker II' strikes against the North Vietnamese heartland. For once the restrictions which hamstrung American airmen over the north were removed. 'Linebacker II' was to be an all-out effort.

To those who supported the effort it was the 'Eleven-Day War'. To those who opposed it, including folksinger Joan Baez who was on the ground in Hanoi, it was the Christmas bombing – although the campaign was briefly halted on 25 December.

It is generally understood that 'Linebacker II' inflicted such a painful blow to Hanoi that Le Duc Tho was finally forced to ink an agreement with Henry Kissinger. (Fuller details appear in the companion volume on the war up north). In the south, the campaign heartened Saigon's leaders who were delighted to see a massive show of force.

A summary of the 'Eleven-Day War' from 18 to 29 December over North Vietnam shows 714 B–52 sorties, 830 USAF tactical sorties, and 386 US Navy/Marine sorties. Nineteen aircraft were lost to enemy action during 'Linebacker II' – fifteen B–52s, two F–4 Phantoms, and two F–111As. The North Vietnamese launched a total of 1,293 SAMs during the operation.

On 31 December 1972 there were only 7,600 USAF personnel in South Vietnam.

The USAF's Vought A–7D attack aircraft, never given the Corsair II nickname of its US Navy version, arrived in South-East Asia in October 1972. Immediately assigned to replace the A–1 Skyraider in the Sandy rescue-escort role, the A–7D went on to participate in the 'Linebacker II' bombing. (LTV)

1973 SETTLEMENT

Combat operations in South Vietnam resumed on 1 January 1973 after a 24-hour New Year's break. Air strikes against North Vietnam resumed the following day. Within a fortnight, citing progress in talks between Henry Kissinger and Le Duc Tho, President Nixon ordered missions up north to be halted on 15 January.

Depending upon point of view, either the North Vietnamese or the Americans finally had what they wanted – although it was not clear that South Vietnam had anything at all. Officially, Saigon's diplomats had a full role in negotiations, as did the Viet Cong. In fact, both were pretty much ignored by Kissinger and Tho. On 23 January in a surprisingly public event, Kissinger and Tho initialed an agreement to end the war, bring about complete US withdrawal, and return American prisoners.

Hanoi would now confront the south without Americans standing in the way. Washington would get its POWs back and domestic opposition to the war, hopefully, would be silenced. In Saigon, as one ARVN officer put it, it was time 'to suck in our breath, hold it, and wonder what happens to us'. American CIA official Frank Snepp charged that the US was doing nothing more than assuring a 'decent interval' between its departure and the gobbling up of South Vietnam by the North.

Many, including Saigon's leaders, ARVN officers and Snepp, believed that the US' master negotiator, Henry Kissinger, had settled for too little. Long before the 'Eleven-Day War', Kissinger had dropped a demand that any removal of American forces from South Vietnam would have to be accompanied by a withdrawal of NVA troops above the 17th Parallel. North Vietnam's regular forces were already firmly in control of a number of locations in the south, were entrenching themselves, and had no obligation under the agreement to pull out.

The NVA had suffered terrible losses in Hanoi's 1972 Easter invasion and the North's supply of manpower was far from inexhaustible. After the invasion failed, the North Vietnamese then suffered the devastation wreaked by the 'Linebacker II' bombings. Skeptics were always able to find something wrong with this employment of American airpower, but captured documents proved that Stratofortresses, Phantoms, and F–111s had a damaging impact on NVA morale and materiel. Hanoi had been

As part of the 1973 deal which ended the US role in the war, Operation 'End Sweep' was to remove mines from North Vietnamese harbors – the same mines that had been laid by US warplanes the previous year. RH–53D Sea Stallion helicopters (predecessors of the more advanced MH–53E version shown here) were designed to tow an electronic mine-detector in trail through the water. When discovered, mines were destroyed. (USN)

This C–130E Hercules (62–1834) of the 50th Tactical Airlift Squadron is identical to the first American aircraft to land at Hanoi's Gia Lam airport following the cease-fire, piloted by Lieutenant Colonel Philip J. Riede. Americans visiting North Vietnam in connection with the truce and the return of prisoners saw bomb damage everywhere from the December 1972 campaign. (VIA JERRY GEER)

battered by a double whammy and was in no immediate position to exploit its gains from the Kissinger–Tho accord.

Hanoi was punished, too, by the inexorable impact of time. Although Ho Chi Minh's followers had been struggling for more than a generation to take over South Vietnam, in 1972 they were no closer to achieving this goal than in 1965. So Kissinger got less than he should have asked for – a bad deal, critics said. Kissinger got the POWs plus an easy way out, they argued. With tougher negotiations, or a prolonging of the 'Eleven-Day War', or both, Kissinger might have gotten much, much more . . .

Many years earlier Vermont's Senator George Aiken had proposed a simple solution to the deepening American involvement in Vietnam. Aiken's solution: 'We'll just tell everybody we won, then leave'. This kind of thinking might well have been attributed to Defense Secretary Melvin Laird when, on 8 January, he announced that Saigon could now defend itself (the logical conclusion being, then, that the US could leave). 'From a military viewpoint, the Vietnamization program has been completed,' said Laird, adding he was certain the South could now defend itself.

President Thieu, as if on a different planet, called for an invasion of North Vietnam. Thieu was making other utterances as well, some of them more realistic in recognizing the plight of his regime and his country, but only a few arch-conservative US leaders were listening and they lacked the clout to drum up support for military aid. Of his proposed invasion, Thieu said, 'Had we bombed North Vietnam continuously, had we landed in North Vietnam, the war would be over by now'. More than a few people believed Thieu was right, but he was at least ten years too late.

On 20 January 1973 Richard M. Nixon was inaugurated for the second time in a low-key ceremony. Nixon had swept the election the previous November with little serious challenge from South Dakota's Senator George S. McGovern – despite the Senator's appeal to anti-war sentiment. (Curiously, McGovern never made it well known that his distaste for war was based on experience: in the Second World War Nixon was a naval officer in an administrative slot and was best remembered for his shrewdness at poker; McGovern was the highly decorated pilot of a B–17 Flying Fortress in Europe.)

If never popular or well liked, Nixon had always been respected for his command of foreign policy and he was appreciated for opening a new American initiative towards China while the Vietnam situation worked itself out. Were it not for growing domestic scandal, Nixon might by now have carte blanche from almost every portion of the electorate.

Whether Nixon had any role in it or not, his victory at the polls had been accompanied by a slew of supporters' 'dirty tricks', loosely defined under the term Watergate. Within months South Carolina's feisty Senator Sam Ervin would be holding televised hearings on the Watergate scandal and cover-up, drawing attention away from other matters, including the President's success in ending the American role in the war.

Air Stand-down

Air action over South Vietnam continued until 27 January 1973, the agreed date for the end of the American role in the conflict. The last B–52 'Arc Light' strikes against targets in South Vietnam, which had been continuous since 1965, recorded a TOT (time over target) of 6.28 a.m. on 28 January.

On 28 January the Kissinger–Tho accord, called 'The Agreement of Ending the War and Restoring the Peace in South Vietnam', was formally signed in Paris. Signatories of this cease-fire agreement were the US, North Vietnam, South Vietnam, and the Provisional Revolutionary Government (PRG) – the Viet Cong. Within 60 days from the signature date, all US and Allied personnel, except those authorized under the peace accords, were to be withdrawn from South Vietnam.

With the signing of the cease-fire for South Vietnam, all US air operations over North and South Vietnam ended. Virtually all US tactical aircraft were out of South Vietnam anyway, but the milestone had little meaning for US Air Force and Marine Corps fighter pilots at bases in Thailand, or for Navy men on carriers at sea. Although public support was largely lacking, American aircraft were to continue bombing in Laos until 22 February and in Cambodia until 15 August.

Prisoners

Under the terms of the cease-fire, American prisoners were to be released and the last 23,700 American troops withdrawn from South Vietnam within sixty days. Pulling out American troops was something the USAF was getting very good at – more than a decade earlier, the practice of sending American soldiers overseas by ship had ended – but the new situation meant that Military Airlift Command would have to fly some new and unique missions.

Lieutenant Colonel Philip J. Riede, commander of the 345th Tactical Airlift Squadron equipped with C–130E Hercules, drew the precedent-setting job of taking two C–130s from South Vietnam to Hanoi to pick up the communist delegations to the joint military commission, a newly formed group intended to police the agreement. Piloting the second C–130 into Hanoi was Captain Theodore C. Appelbaum. As the USAF describes their mission:

The two C–130s took off from Tan Son Nhut on the morning of 29 January. Upon reaching Da Nang, both crews circled for nearly an hour awaiting clearance to enter communist territory. The planned flight route was mostly over water, but new instructions called for westward flight to a point well inland, then northward to Hanoi.

With strong reservations, the C–130 crews set forth on the new routing. Back in Saigon, General Vogt monitored the progress of the historic mission. Fifteen minutes before reaching Hanoi the crews established radio contact with Gia Lam airport and obtained landing instructions. Colonel Riede flew the arranged approach using the low-frequency radio beacon and breaking out from the clouds at about 3,000 feet (almost 1,000m). Before landing, the C–130 crewmen were able to look over bomb damage to the bridges around Hanoi. They landed on a patched surface, of which a runway length of about 6,000 feet (almost 2,000m) was usable.

On the ground at Hanoi's principal airport, buildings were in shambles from the recent American bombings. Hundreds of civilians came to look at the Americans and their C–130s, but kept a respectful distance at the end of the ramp. Conversations were cordial and an English-speaking official invited the crewmen to a small building for tea. Carrying the delegations, both planes took off shortly after noon, landing at Tan Son Nhut three hours later.

The only hitch came midway in the flight when the Americans asked the communists to fill out visa forms. After landing at Tan Son Nhut, the communists remained on the C–130s for more than 24 hours while a dispute about visas was thrashed out. There was a principle involved: applying for a visa would mean recognizing South Vietnam as a sovereign state, something the communists would not do.

The C–130 mission was the beginning of numerous MAC flights into communist North Vietnam, a new experience for those involved.

The Hanoi Hilton was one of several camps which served as home for American prisoners of war in North Vietnam, some for as long as six or seven years. The agreement which ended American participation in the conflict also resulted in the release of all the POWs. (USAF)

Cooper–Church

The 15 August cut-off date was determined by Congress's Cooper–Church Amendment, which in effect stripped the President of authority to commit forces into Vietnam, Laos and Cambodia. This included a congressional ban on use of aerial weapons in South-East Asia – a fact not appreciated by most observers over the next two years. Further, now that US troops were out of South Vietnam, Congress voted to stop all spending on military activities in or over South-East Asia.

The law passed by Congress simply reaffirmed what public sentiment had already decided. Opposition to the war in the US now made it exceedingly unlikely that South Vietnam would receive the financial and other aid necessary to guard the peace.

More important, the Cooper–Church Amendment and the sentiment which created it eliminated a major means of leverage to deter North Vietnam from launching a major offensive. In advance of any decision it might take, the US was broadcasting that it would not fight.

The day after the cease-fire took effect, 28 January 1973, the US opened its Defense Attache Office at the embassy in Saigon (and later at Tan Son Nhut). It would be like no other such office in the world, for the defense attache would be, in effect, the commander of the military personnel who remained. Military Assistance Command Vietnam (MACV) was disestablished on 29 March 1973, and Headquarters Seventh Air Force ceased to exist.

As part of the agreement between the Americans and North Vietnamese – the other two signatories, South Vietnam and the Viet Cong, were not really full partners in the accord – the US agreed to clear North Vietnamese ports of the mines sown by Navy A–6 Intruders and A–7 Corsair aircraft the previous year. Called Operation 'End Sweep', the mine-clearing operation was carried out by RH–53D helicopters of US Task Force 78. The helicopter carried an

Among aircraft which had been rushed to South-East Asia during the heavy fighting in 1972 were the F-4E Phantoms of the 4th Tactical Fighter Wing at Seymour-Johnson AFB, North Carolina, like aircraft 72–0141. When the cease-fire took effect, a large number of American fighters remained in Thailand to police the situation. (JIM SULLIVAN)

electronic mine-detector, designed to trail behind it in the water.

RH-53D pilots had been trained to fly their mine-clearing mission under combat conditions. But even with no one shooting at them, the chore of cleaning up the deadly munitions was far from easy. 'We had to operate without an infrastructure in place to support us,' says Commander George Timil. During the period beginning at the end of January, the USS *America* (CVA-66), *Constellation* (CVA-64), *Coral Sea* (CVA-43), *Enterprise* (CVAN-65) and *Ranger* (CVA-61) provided logistic support for 'End Sweep' and provided air cover for the operations. But conditions for the RH-53D helicopters remained difficult.

The helicopters, along with CH-53s specially configured for the mine-clearing mission, came from one Navy and two Marine squadrons (HM-12, HMH-463, and HMM-165) which operated from the decks of two amphibious assault ships, USS *Inchon* (LPH-12) and USS *New Orleans* (LPH-11). Mine-clearing operations ended on 27 July 1973 after CH-53 and RH-53D helicopter pilots had devoted more than 1,100 flying hours to the operation.

Laos Cease-Fire

The 30-year civil war in Laos officially ended on 21 February and a cease-fire took effect. US air strikes were halted. A coalition government embracing all three warring factions was to be formed a year later.

Inside South Vietnam there was a lull. Both sides were vying for advantage with troop movements, but actual fighting was at a standstill. North Vietnam's continuing expansion of its air force had only an indirect effect on the south, but Saigon's planners knew that MiGs or Ilyushins could appear in their skies at any time. South Vietnam's expansion of its air arm had gone as far as it could. There were a few improvements that could be made, but the basic composition of the VNAF was to remain unchanged for the next two years.

One of the improvements came in the airlift area. When the VNAF received 32 C-130A Hercules cargo aircraft, this was deemed to make 55 C-123K Providers surplus to its needs. These aircraft were distributed to other countries in Asia, including sixteen to the Philippines, sixteen to Korea, and eight to Thailand. President Nixon directed that VNAF aircraft losses be replaced on a one-for-one basis in order to maintain in-country strength levels as they existed on the cease-fire date, 27 January. The USAF found this assignment an 'onerous burden' which had a negative affect on its own readiness.

The problem that faced the VNAF and its American supporters was simple enough to understand: while the ink was still drying on the cease-fire agreement, Ho Chi Minh's successors were planning to take over the South. The failure of their 1972 Easter invasion had been a major setback, but with the Americans leaving, conquest of the South seemed a realistic goal after – to re-use Snepp's term – a decent interval.

No longer worried about defending their own airspace from B-52s or anything else, the North Vietnamese could now move anti-aircraft defenses and missiles farther south, to help them in any future thrust towards Saigon. Jet-capable airfields were being paved in the southern portion of North Vietnam to counter the VNAF. Khe Sanh, where American Marines had made a stand, now belonged to Hanoi's forces and was being enlarged so that its runway would have limited accommodation for jet aircraft.

For the departing Americans, the major event of 1973 – after the cease-fire itself – was the homecoming of the POWs. The release of American prisoners of war began when the first group of 116 were freed by Hanoi on 12 February 1973.

One American who visited Hanoi's Gia Lam airport where the prisoner release took place, Colonel William Hubbell, recalls that Gia Lam was European in character, as it was built by the French: 'a normal, small airport with no shops or anything like that, very bland'. Few people were seen doing routine business at the airport, although Hubbell did see 'plenty of the Russian version of the Boeing 727 (Tupolev Tu-154)'. Between the city and the airport was a rickety bridge, crossed by a few vehicles and countless

This view of Lieutenant Mike Anderson's A–6A Intruder aboard the USS *Coral Sea* (CVA–43) was taken on 27 January 1973, the day that marked the end of American participation in the South Vietnam war. Several US carriers were on station when the war ended – each with several men who claimed to have flown the last mission of the war – and the situation remained tense even after the fighting was over. (TOM PATTERSON)

people on bicycles. When the bridge was blocked off, to other traffic, it meant special treatment was taking place. The bridge was blocked off when the prisoners were bussed to the airfield.

On the first C–141A StarLifter bringing the men out from Hanoi, Colonel John Flynn, the courageous commander of the men in captivity – the Fourth Allied POW Wing, they called themselves, their slogan, 'Return with honor' – pulled rank on Commander Everett Alvarez, the longest-held

Happier than anyone at what it meant for him when the US role in Vietnam ended, Major Philip E. Smith (center, foreground) is escorted out of China at Hong Kong by American Red Cross Field Director Eugene Guy. Smith, of the 436th Tactical Fighter Squadron, was flying Lockheed F–104C Starfighter 56–0883 on a Vietnam mission on 20 September 1965 when he was shot down by Chinese MiGs over Hainan. Because he was held by the Chinese rather than the North Vietnamese, Smith had no companions during his eight years in prison. He was released at the same time as the POWs set free by Hanoi. After the release shown here, Smith boarded a Douglas C–9A Nightingale in Hong Kong to be returned to the US. (HONG KONG GOVERNMENT INFORMATION SERVICES)

prisoner (since August 1964), and so Flynn became the first released POW to step out of the C–141A at Clark Field in the Philippines. When Alvarez did step out, he expressed thoughts which sounded simple but were deepfelt for this man of conviction who had been a captive for nearly eight years: 'God bless the President and God bless you, Mr and Mrs America, you did not forget us.'

The releases were to continue into March. March was also the first month since July 1963 that no combat losses were recorded by the US in an entire month.

In addition to agreeing to release American prisoners, Hanoi had taken on an obligation to account for all missing Americans about whom it possessed knowledge. Many Americans whose names did not appear on the roster of POWs were officially listed as missing in action (MIA), yet the communist side had knowledge of them – and in the opinion of some, even held some against their will.

A classic case was an F–100 Super Sabre pilot who had gone down in the Mekong Delta region on a routine close-support mission years earlier. His wingmen knew that he had ejected safely and reached the ground alive. He was never listed as a prisoner. No remains were ever found. Yet a casual conversation with a North Vietnamese made it absolutely clear that Hanoi knew exactly what had happened to the man. He had died in a crossfire between NVA troops pursuing him. Because Hanoi never revealed what it knew – until much later, when it happened more or less by accident – his family spent years wondering what had happened.

Hanoi was to give conflicting signals on the issue of accounting for the missing in action. Yet there was never any doubt that the North Vietnamese knew far more than they were saying. RF–101C Voodoo pilot Captain Vincent J. Connolly was another of the missing, shot down in his reconnaissance aircraft on 4 November 1966 and listed as MIA. The community of men who flew the sleek, powerful RF–101C was small – and its losses high – and all the men wanted to know what had happened to Vince. Surely with the war ending, the North Vietnamese would tell what they knew?

They did not. Connolly's widow, Honey, went through years of suffering and uncertainty, never able to find whether her man was dead or alive. When he was not listed among the POWs and was presumed

The war was over for the Americans, if not the Vietnamese, but the F–4 Phantom remained on guard aboard US Navy carriers in the region. Although Congressional restraints might have prevented them from going in to help, even if the President had wanted to do so, the Navy's carrier battle groups off the Vietnamese coast remained on a combat footing throughout 1973, even past the 15 August 1973 cut-off of bombing of Cambodia. (USN)

RF-101C Voodoo pilot Captain Vincent J. Connolly, finally brought home from Vietnam in 1984, is laid to rest at Arlington National Cemetery. Had the North Vietnamese abided by the 1973 cease-fire agreement, Connolly's widow could have learned of his fate and he could have gotten a proper burial years earlier. (H. C. BAKER)

dead, Honey Connolly kept searching for someone who could tell her, at least, how Vince had died. RF-101C Voodoos often flew alone. There were no American witnesses. No one knew.

Yet a short time after the end of the conflict, an individual named Trung H. Huynh published a letter in a western magazine claiming that Connolly had become disconcerted when he discovered that he was flying into a narrow valley being flooded – in a unique defensive measure – by NVA weather balloons. According to Huynh, no sooner had Connolly found a way to avoid the balloons than he was felled by anti-aircraft fire.

The North Vietnamese possessed this kind of information in almost excruciating detail, yet Honey Connolly could learn nothing of what had happened to Vince. During the period after his death, while the North Vietnamese knew that he was dead, Connolly was listed as MIA and promoted to major, then to lieutenant colonel. It was only in 1984 that Hanoi finally announced it was holding Connolly's remains and facilitated his return to the US and burial at Arlington National Cemetery. Honey Connolly subsequently married F-105 pilot Colonel Elmo (Mo) Baker, who had been a prisoner of war and the couple now reside in Weatherford, Texas. As late as 1990 Hanoi still possessed information about other MIA which it did not share. In this and many other respects, the North Vietnamese side simply violated the cease-fire agreement from the outset.

The last American troops left South Vietnam on 29 March 1973. Henceforth the only men in uniform would be assigned to the Defense Attache office, the DAO.

Beginning in 1973, the US had to cope with Hanoi's unwillingness to share what it knew about the missing in action (MIA). From the time he was shot down in 1966, the North Vietnamese knew that RF-101C Voodoo pilot Captain Vincent J. Connolly had been killed – and were in possession of his remains. But the communists never revealed what they knew and released Captain Connolly's remains only in 1984. (USAF)

Revolutionary Spirit

In October the North Vietnamese Central Committee's 21st Plenum adopted a resolution stating that the path of revolution in the south left no alternative but to conduct a revolutionary war and liberate the south. Ironically, events of the past decade had given Hanoi complete control of the Viet Cong apparatus in the south which, in the earliest days of US involvement, had begun as an indigenous insurgency. The North Vietnamese began a series of raids against selected targets during the first week of November.

Although the US land presence in South Vietnam had ended, the naval presence off the coast remained. Gary Wright was an ordnanceman on the USS *Oriskany* (CVA–34) on the last cruise made by that ship, from 5 June 1972 to 30 March 1973. Things were tense enough on the carrier when the war was still on and the ship was on station a surprisingly scant 18 miles (28.8km) south-west of Hanoi – a 55-minute flight by F–8 Crusader or A–7 Corsair.

'It was no holiday pushing around 250lb [113kg] bombs on a cart,' Wright recalled. 'It was a bitch. Everything had to be done by hand.' *Oriskany* apparently was not as well equipped with support equipment as the older vessels. The HLU–196 loading device hooked up to the pylon of an A–7 and preload MERs (multiple ejector racks) and TERs (triple ejector racks), but the actual loading of the bombs had to be done with 'our sweat and our muscle'. It was also necessary to be exceedingly careful. Apart from the fact that *Oriskany* had already suffered one major fire during the Vietnam war, 'The gunner [ordnance chief] just doesn't like it when bombs roll across the deck.'

A sailor on a carrier had a compact living space 3–4 feet wide, with bunks stacked three high, no room to sit, a locker under the bunk, a small light. At the end of each bunk was the OBA (oxygen breathing apparatus) if a fire should again fill the interior of the ship with smoke. Like many, Wright obtained canvas and safety wire from the ship's parachute riggers and used it to fashion a privacy curtain. He was never comfortable: others slept when he was awake and vice-versa.

Oriskany flew missions until the end. There have been numerous conflicting claims to have flown the last mission in Vietnam, and the carrier had some of the claimants – but no certain holder of this dubious honor has ever been identified. With the end of bombing over both North and South Vietnam, a mood of celebration was noticeable on the ship, but not for long. Although combat had ended, pilots and crews on the carrier continued to stand alert, fly defensive missions, and maintained readiness.

Before the cease-fire, there were the inevitable mishaps at sea. Wright was standing in the arm, de-arm area between catapults one night just after the cease-fire when an F–8 Crusader veered off course and passed within a few feet. The F–8 went over the side and its pilot was killed. This happened on 27 September 1972 with F–8J Crusader 150325 of squadron VF–194.

Three Americans received the Medal of Honor for their conduct while prisoners of war in North Vietnam. One of these was US Navy Rear Admiral James Bond Stockdale, who was held in Hanoi from September 1965 to March 1973. Here Stockdale receives other awards earned during his stay in Hanoi from Secretary of the Navy J. William Middendorf II. (US NAVY)

The next night as Wright remembers it (he has the date wrong) he was on his way forward carrying a MER when the carrier's Air Boss shouted 'Heads up!' on the loudspeaker. The right landing strut of an F–8 Crusader broke. The jet fighter ripped its

Colonel (later Brigadier General) Robinson Risner was another of the heroic prisoners of war who were held for years by Hanoi and whose release was essential to the agreement ending the war. Risner was an air ace in the Korean War with eight MiG kills in the F–86 Sabre. In Vietnam he was shot down twice and became a prisoner the second time. After his March 1973 release, Risner wrote a book, *The Passing of the Night*, and presented a copy to President Nixon. (USAF)

tailhook from the cable and came careering straight at Gary:

'I dropped that MER. A lot of guys ran to starboard. I ran towards the numbers [the large 34 for the carrier's hull number, painted on the forward deck]. I'm gonna jump, gonna jump, I told myself, ready to heave myself over the side as the Crusader came at me.

'There was a big explosion. Everything stopped. The blast knocked me over and there was a rip across the front of my flight deck vest. A piece of the ship's antenna went sailing over my head. I knew I wasn't dead and as everything started again, I wondered why I had been saved. Another guy leaped into the port net [on the side of the carrier] and the Crusader went right over top of him, missing by inches. The port strut of the Crusader had caught in the port catwalk and hit a red round fire main. There was water spewing up, a geyser. The Crusader went into the drink.'

Wright did not see it but the pilot ejected safely. The incident occurred on 26 November 1972 with F–8J 150887 of VF–191.

Attaché Office

Perhaps the strangest office belonging to any American embassy in the world was the Defense Attaché Office (DAO) located in the former MACV building at Tan Son Nhut airport. In almost any other country, the DAO was a small office inside the embassy chancery, preoccupied with protocol matters and the gathering of intelligence. In Saigon, however, the DAO existed to manage continuing resupply, local maintenance and contractor support for South Vietnam's armed forces. The DAO was initially authorized no fewer than 50 military and 1,200 US civilian personnel slots. When Vietnamese employees were added, the DAO became an organization of 4,750 individuals. Its first boss was Major General John E. Murray.

Murray was in a 'no win' situation. If South Vietnam found some way to achieve stability, he would go unnoticed. If Saigon fell, he would be the goat. An army officer in a slot many felt should go to an airman, Murray had a realistic view of events around him, and they were not encouraging.

On 30 September 1973 in a periodic report, General Murray set forth a grave warning that the North Vietnamese were gathering strength. He reported that the Vietnamization program was not succeeding. VNAF problems were especially vexing. In Saigon's air arm, training was inadequate, operational readiness was almost a joke, and performance of airlift – particularly the C–130A Hercules – was dismal.

The VNAF still lacked high-performance aircraft that would be able to cope with the north's MiGs if a direct challenge should come. Saigon's air arm was also without sophisticated ECM (electronic countermeasures) equipment and precision-guided munitions ('smart' bombs) needed for operations in high-threat areas and to interdict enemy supply lines along the Ho Chi Minh Trail. These deficiencies apparently had not been given much thought, but they were to make life easier for the North Vietnamese as they planned a recovery from their losses in the 1972 invasion and a new effort to take over the entire country.

The VNAF had brave men and men of

President Nixon, here with wife Pat emerging from the Boeing VC–137C known as Air Force One, was basking in praise for withdrawing US troops when Watergate troubles clouded his presidency. Nixon intended to continue providing military aid to South Vietnam but could not find support in Congress. (USAF)

ability, but many of the best had died during endless years of a war which gave its Vietnamese participants no rest and recuperation holiday, no rotation date, no home to go back to. Undoubtedly some men of great courage had reached the point of despair by now and were no longer trying. But the real problem was that many newer VNAF personnel were poorly trained, ill-equipped and unmotivated.

War Powers

On 7 November 1973 the US Congress overrode President Nixon's veto and passed the War Powers Resolution, making it illegal to commit US forces for more than 60 days without congressional approval. Coupled with the earlier ban on bombing, these limitations assured the North Vietnamese that the US was practically powerless to intervene in Vietnam any longer. In Saigon leaders knew that Congress had a strong anti-war sentiment and that the President was increasingly tied up with domestic reactions to the Watergate scandal.

General Murray continued to report to his superiors that Saigon's air force could not cope. By now, given political reality in the US, there was nothing his superiors could do about it.

Despite the cease-fire, some combat activity continued in South Vietnam as both sides sought advantages. The VNAF, with only limited US advice and assistance, possessed a total of 2,075 aircraft by year's end and flew 458,468 sorties during the year. VNAF aircraft losses reached 185, including 91 UH–1 Huey helicopters, 265 O–1 Bird Dogs and 22 A–37Bs.

Price of War

For the American services 1973 was the year to tot up what the war in Vietnam had meant and what it had cost.

In the war the US Navy had employed seventeen attack carriers, ten from the Pacific Fleet and seven from the Atlantic – indeed, every carrier in its inventory with the sole exception of the USS *John F. Kennedy* (CVA–67). These capital ships had spent 8,248 days on the line during 73 combat cruises between August 1964 and August 1973.

In its loss column, the Navy could list 530 fixed-wing aircraft (most of them carrier-based) and thirteen helicopters downed by the enemy. 317 Navy aircrews lost their lives.

During its long years of combat operations in South-East Asia – including operations in South Vietnam from October 1961 to March 1973 – the US Air Force had suffered 2,118 deaths, 3,460 wounded and 599 missing. 2,257 aircraft had been lost in combat or to operational causes in 5,226,701 sorties, representing a loss rate of 0.04 per cent (compared with 2.0 per cent in Korea and 9.7 per cent in the Second World War).

Were the Air Force's number-crunchers certain that the number of sorties in a seemingly endless war was not 5,226,700 or 5,226,702? Apparently so. Losses included 445 F–4 Phantoms, 397 F–105 Thunderchiefs, 243 F–100 Super Sabres and 30 B–52s. Somehow, the number experts knew that the lost aircraft had cost a total of $3,129,948,000.

1974 DECENT INTERVAL

American veterans came home from the war in Vietnam but did not receive the tickertape parades, the recognition, the thanks of a nation that had bestowed all three to veterans of earlier wars. The men came home and were ignored – or worse. Major Don Kilgus, who had flown F–100s and F–105s in the conflict, was walking down the sidewalk of a West Coast city in uniform and was spat on. Another fighter-bomber pilot was upbraided by a neighbor who called him a 'baby killer', furthering the fiction that Americans had bombed indiscriminately.

Men who left the armed forces to return to civilian life found that mentioning Vietnam combat service did not enhance a resume. Those who went to the Veterans Administration for benefits, such as help with educational costs, found that unlike survivors of previous wars they had few benefits to collect. Men who remained in uniform found the services being wrenched apart by racial conflict.

The war to defend South Vietnam killed the citizen army which had defended American interests since 1940. By 1974 the wheels were in motion to end it forever. The following year the armed forces would become 'all volunteer' – ending forever the role of the draft in American life.

1974 was the year of preoccupation with Watergate. President Nixon might have fulfilled his promise to end American involvement in the war – he had also opened the door to China and achieved detente with the Soviet Union – but his administration's cover-up of the irregularities of the 1972 election was the only issue on the public's mind. Nixon was heading for a fall.

It was still possible to arrive at Tan Son Nhut airport outside Saigon, see tourist billboards praising the joys of travel to sunny Vietnam, and perhaps observe the occasional A–37B or F–5E taking off with a bombload. Small-scale fighting was taking place regularly in the north-west portion of South Vietnam, and a battle occasionally broke out elsewhere while both sides pretended that it was not a shooting war – not at the moment.

1974 was also to be the year of the 'decent interval' granted to the Saigon regime by the American departure. Like an unwelcome dinner guest, it seemed that the Americans had stayed too long, then left too abruptly. USAF officers at the Defense Attache Office in Saigon felt they had been left behind in the lurch – and given an impossible task. How, indeed, could they help South Vietnam's air arm to defend itself when there was no equipment or materiel to help with?

While it was important for the United States to show its intention to stand fast and not betray its South Vietnamese ally, every American embassy and consulate abroad was required to have an 'E & E' (emergency and evacuation) plan to cover the withdrawal of private American citizens and government civilians in the event of earthquake, flood, or (as in Saigon) war. In 1974 an evacuation plan named 'Talon Vise' set forth details of how the American embassy and consulates in South Vietnam would be evacuated – with combat support, if necessary, from A–7s, F–4s, F–111s, and OV–10s stationed in Thailand.

The escape plan called for close contact between the embassy and airlines serving Saigon. By 1974 the various airline companies which flew into the Vietnamese capital – Northwest, Pan American, World – were virtually an extension of the US mili-

The Lockheed SR–71 Blackbird was the USA's principal strategic reconnaissance aircraft during and after the war in South Vietnam. It was widely rumored, but never confirmed, that some SR–71 missions continued while North Vietnam recovered from 1972 and prepared for 1975. (USAF)

tary, most of their payloads being the limited numbers of parts and equipment that could still be supplied to the South Vietnamese. To be ready for an evacuation, embassy consular officers conferred with airline officials and made contingency plans.

By the time it became necessary to implement 'Talon Vise', it was to be renamed 'Frequent Wind'. But in 1974 evacuation was still a prospect covered only in files and file folders. The planners of both 'Talon Vise' and 'Frequent Wind' had given much attention to saving American civilians and almost no attention to the thousands of South Vietnamese who had been directly employed by the US.

VNAF Aid

Although the mood in the US remained strongly against providing assistance to Saigon, eight more F–5E fighters were delivered to the VNAF in March 1974. This final delivery was a holdover, arranged before Congress cracked down. It was increasingly clear to leaders in Saigon that they were not going to get much from their American allies, especially since Washington was preoccupied with Watergate and the Arab oil embargo.

US aid to South Vietnam, limited to $1 billion by Congress for fiscal year 1975, was reduced when stricter accounting procedures under a single Department of Defense audit agency were adopted on 1 July 1974. Audits disclosed that amounts some $296.3 million in excess of the limit had been scheduled.

The amount of aid to be received by South Vietnam was further reduced following President Nixon's resignation in August, to a ceiling of $700 million. On 9 August 1974 Gerald Ford inherited the job of president with virtually no options left that would permit aid to the Saigon government.

In fact, financial assistance to Saigon was so far below what had been anticipated that there was no choice but to continue to store aircraft which the VNAF lacked the means to operate. In 1974 over 200 aircraft were retired to flyable storage, including nearly all A–1 Skyraiders, O–1 Bird Dog observation craft, and C–7, C–47 and C–119 transports. In addition, a significant number of helicopters were taken out of use and set aside. The capacity of the Vietnamese armed forces to carry out helicopter missions was cut back by no less than 70 per cent.

To make matters worse, the thirty-two C–130A Hercules of the VNAF were suffering from fuel leaks, wing cracks, parts shortages and cutbacks in flying time. Only four to eight C–130As were flyable at any given time.

Facing a solid wall of resistance to providing aid to the Saigon government, US officials in South Vietnam urged conservation measures on the VNAF. Eleven squadrons were grounded, flying hours and bombing missions were reduced, and other stringent measures taken to conserve funds. As USAF leaders saw it, 'Congress seemed intent on making [South Vietnam] a military invalid' even though 'further cuts in military aid to South Vietnam could be equated with real estate lost to North Vietnam'. Aid cuts took effect just at the time that North Vietnam launched a series of strategic raids.

The storage of aircraft which could not be used tied up some 500 people who had to inspect and maintain them. Still, the result was greater efficiency in the employment of the aircraft that remained. In 1974 the VNAF had 1,484 aircraft in service, having lost 299 to combat, operational causes, or transfers. The VNAF had 62,585 personnel on duty.

Return of the A–1

At some point in 1974 – the record is unclear when – the VNAF took some of its prop-driven A–1 Skyraiders out of mothballs and began using them again in limited skirmishes against the NVA. Virtually all battles were with NVA regular troops now that the Viet Cong had been swallowed up by its supporter in the north. Apparently someone had decided that the Skyraider was more effective for some missions than the F–5E and A–37B jets which had entered inventory more recently.

It has been argued that American failure to bolster South Vietnam was a kind of

Among the last American combat units in South-East Asia were the USAF squadrons which operated the Vought A–7D Corsair, introduced to the conflict only in October 1972 and kept on station in Thailand after the cease-fire. At one time there had been discussion of providing A–7Ds to the VNAF but no easy way could be found to spare them and they were thought too advanced for Saigon's air arm. (LTV)

The US Navy continued to stand guard off the Vietnamese coast, but Congressional restrictions made it unlikely that the US would ever 'go back in'. Some electronic patrol missions were carried out by the Grumman EA-6B Prowler, which had been introduced into the combat zone in July 1972 and remained on duty through the final withdrawal in 1975. (US NAVY)

dereliction of duty, that the United States abandoned an ally it could have saved with just a little more financial and material help. Certainly it is true that the VNAF had sharply to reduce its combat missions. Troop reinforcement, resupply and medical evacuation were all seriously affected.

In fact, however, by 1974 there was probably nothing anyone could do to save South Vietnam. In all likelihood, additional aid or equipment would only have prolonged the end. North Vietnam had thirteen divisions already in South Vietnam and seven in

No longer endangered by US warplanes, the North Vietnamese built up their country and their infra-structure during 1973–75, while also girding for another intended full-scale invasion of the south. Bridges, like this one at the Canal de Rapides just east of Hanoi, were rebuilt and returned to service quickly. (USAF)

reserve. Partly thanks to aid from the Soviet Union, Hanoi possessed the supplies for a 15- to 20-month campaign.

In August 1974 Major General Homer D. Smith replaced Major General John E. Murray as head of the Defense Attache Office (DAO) headquartered at Tan Son Nhut airfield. Again, there was the problem of reduced appropriations to be dealt with. The program of military assistance to South Vietnam had been planned at $1.4 billion for the fiscal year begun just before his arrival, but Smith ended up receiving less than half this amount.

Like his predecessor, Smith reported that shortfalls in financial aid had robbed South Vietnam's armed forces of both the initiative and the means to conduct offensive operations. The VNAF, he reported, was in especially bad shape even though the spirit of many Vietnamese combatants remained high. The South Vietnamese were *trying*, General Smith told his bosses, but only American economic power could save the situation.

Exit Nixon

Unfortunately people in Washington had other things on their minds. In August 1974, brought down by the weight of the Watergate scandal, President Nixon became the first American chief executive ever to resign. Fortunately for the world at large, Nixon's original vice president, Spiro Agnew, had already left office in an unrelated scandal, and had been replaced by Gerald Ford, the former Michigan congressman.

Ford moved to the White House promising the American people 'a little straight talk among friends', and a return to honesty in government. He provided both. He could not, however, save South Vietnam. Neither the American electorate nor Congress wanted to save South Vietnam if it was going to cost money.

In a sense, the Vietnamese people were misled. As late as the end of 1974, remnants of American airpower were still located next door in Thailand – B–52 bombers and KC–135 tankers at U–Tapao, A–7s, AC–130s, F–4s and F–111As at Korat. In Saigon the well-informed citizen might be forgiven if he deduced that the warplanes next door had a purpose. Given the mood of the American public, there was no possibility of American ground soldiers ever again fighting in Vietnam. But while no one had ever actually said so, American leaders had strongly hinted that American airpower was available in case of trouble.

Likewise, US Navy aircraft-carriers remained on station near South Vietnam, fully able to return and help South Vietnam's armed forces if the need arose. But public sentiment was against providing that help.

By late 1974, although actual combat was scattered and sporadic, it was clear that

A few American military personnel remained in South Vietnam with the Defense Attache's Office (DAO). They were explicitly forbidden from engaging in combat – with North Vietnam licking its wounds, there was very little combat anyway – but they did practise defending themselves, as shown here. (USAF)

For Americans, including prisoners of war, the end of the Vietnam conflict meant a flight home on a commerical airliner, called a 'Freedom Bird', or on a C–141A StarLifter like this one crossing San Francisco's Golden Gate. During 1973–75 the C–141A was also the backbone of airlift efforts in support of South Vietnam. (USAF)

North Vietnam's forces – strengthened and rebuilt since Hanoi's reverses in 1972 – were getting ready for something. With SA–2 surface-to-air missiles located farther south than ever before (although still in North Vietnam), and with ground troops carrying SA–7 missiles around on their shoulders, the effectiveness of the VNAF was markedly reduced without a shot being fired. South Vietnamese intelligence remained good and many in Saigon were warning that trouble was coming.

The NVA began making trouble at the airstrip at Song Be, a scant 100 miles (161km) north of Saigon, the critical point of entry for men and supplies in Phuoc Long Province. The NVA heavily shelled and then seized an adjacent hilltop, set up mortars on the peak, and forced the ARVN and VNAF to evacuate the much-needed airfield.

Thieu Meeting

President Thieu visited Da Nang in late 1974 to confer with military advisors about how to handle increasing NVA military action. A few leaders, including VNAF commander Lieutenant General Tran Van Minh, were courageous enough to tell Theiu bad news. Several recommended that a future withdrawal from the Central Highlands would be essential to any defense of the remainder of South Vietnam. This idea of giving up some territory to preserve the rest was utterly wrongheaded, but no one could see so at the time.

The officers argued that shortening their supply lines would ease the task of logistic supply. Defending a smaller area of turf would also help to conserve men and machinery, supplies and ammunition. Given the uncertainty of future US aid, this kind of conservation had to be a part of South Vietnamese planning.

Robert C. Mikesh points out that the VNAF employed an unusual method to test their ability to supply ground forces with airdrops by C–130 Hercules. Aware that anything dropped during aerial resupply tests could fall into NVA hands, the South Vietnamese searched for something of no value to use as a simulated parachute cargo. Their choice was ice! This could be shaped to represent the weight and ballistic effect of a cargo package and was totally expendable. The North Vietnamese must have scratched their heads wondering what the parachute had carried to the ground when they did recover parachutes after their cargo had melted.

In December 1974 an intelligence report noted that the North Vietnamese were probing around Phuoc Binh. This was to become the first provincial capital in more than two years faced with possible enemy seizure. This was the first move in what was to become the final push by Hanoi's forces.

1975
END OF A CONFLICT

On 6 January 1975 Phuoc Binh, the capital of South Vietnam's Phuoc Long Province, fell to North Vietnamese troops after a week of heavy fighting. President Ford asked Congress for an additional $300 million for aid to South Vietnam. On Capitol Hill the mood was strongly against any such spending. The funds were not forthcoming.

North Vietnamese forces launched an offensive in the south on 28 February 1975. Again, Hanoi's troops were attacking with everything they had – as they had done without success in 1972 – but this time resistance was uneven. On 14 March the NVA captured Ban Me Thuot. The seizure of this vital city turned over another airfield and a number of aircraft to the communists. President Thieu made the tactical decision which had been recommended to him by some subordinates the previous December – to withdraw some of his forces from the highlands. The idea had been, and was, a mistake. It proved to be a disastrous mistake. It precipitated a rout.

The city of Hue had to be abandoned on 26 March. More than $1 billion worth of US-supplied arms were abandoned by retreating South Vietnamese troops. On 31 March a C–130 Hercules evacuated the nuclear fuel from the 250kW atomic reactor at Da Lat, in Tuyen Duc Province, to keep it from falling to the North Vietnamese.

Da Nang was perhaps the best known Vietnamese city – and port, and airfield – next to Saigon and by 25 March 1975 it was clear that North Vietnamese forces were massing to overrun the city. On that date Al Francis, the American consul general in Da Nang, ordered the evacuation of all American citizens in the area, plus a few South Vietnamese who had worked for the US and warranted assistance. Ed Daly, head of World Airways, which did a considerable amount of military contract flying for the US, was even more certain than Francis that Da Nang was about to fall – and after Da Nang, all of South Vietnam. Without any assurance that anyone would reimburse him for it, Daly decided to increase the number of World Airways airliners assisting in the evacuations.

Apart from the North Vietnamese, who were now unleashing the 1975 version of their 1972 invasion, Da Nang was filled with bands of South Vietnamese troops who had lost all discipline, were shooting wildly, and were looting shops.

On the evening of 26 March one of Daly's Boeing 727s landed at Da Nang to bring out American citizens and, possibly, a few Vietnamese. Suddenly panic was let loose. While evacuees scheduled to fly on the 727 climbed aboard, a nervous crowd surrounded the aircraft. Some Vietnamese seeking to delay its departure blocked the Boeing's path with vehicles, then tried to force their way aboard. While the World Airways flight crew looked on with disbelief, many people who were not manifested began

As the pace of North Vietnamese activity increased in 1975, it seemed that the USAF's Military Airlift Command was bringing more supplies and people out of South Vietnam than it was bringing in. In Operation 'Babylift' a C–5A Galaxy carrying Vietnamese orphans out of Saigon crashed shortly after take-off in one of numerous tragedies in the final days of the war. Other C–5A Galaxies brought what little equipment and materiel could be made available to South Vietnam in the final days. (USAF)

forcing their way aboard, filling the aisles, the toilet, the galleys.

By some miracle, this Boeing 727 and others on 27 March were able to get out of Da Nang in spite of the overcrowding. In one tragic incident a Vietnamese citizen seeking escape from the coming communist onslaught hid inside the landing gear well of an airliner – and fell to his death shortly after take-off. By air and by sea, a mass exodus emptied Da Nang by 28 March, allowing the NVA to come in and take over the city with only sporadic fighting.

Just as South Vietnam seemed to be 'going down the tubes', as one US airman put it, Cambodia went first. President Lon Nol left Cambodia on 1 April. On the 12th Operation 'Eagle Pull' brought out the remaining American embassy staff and some private American citizens by helicopter. The principal means of getting the job done was the Sikorsky CH–53A Sea Stallion, the same craft which had served so many other purposes during the conflict. 'Eagle Pull' was, unfortunately, not the last helicopter evacuation to occur in South-East Asia.

Airlift Effort

No one was yet acknowledging in public that the end was near, but by 1 April 1975 the largest fixed-wing evacuation in history was under way. Contract airliners, C–141s and C–5As hauled people out of Saigon. An embassy planning group struggled mightily to figure out who was entitled to evacuation – what about a Vietnamese who had worked for the embassy? a Vietnamese whose brother was an American citizen? the Vietnamese wife of an American soldier? – and to get people notified and readied. Later there was to be much criticism of this process, but in general it was handled efficiently.

Brigadier General Richard M. Baughn, who served under Major General Smith in the thankless position of Deputy Defense Attache, ordered provision to be made to evacuate 100 employees per day, then 200. This figure covered most Americans who needed to get out, but failed to help the immediate families of many Americans. A number of career diplomats who had served earlier in Saigon now returned in their own time, at their own expense, to locate people who had worked with them, as well as Vietnamese relatives. Some virtually forced the Air Force to carry out the people they wanted to save. In later years these men were to be commended for acting on their own.

On 4 April schedulers at Tan Son Nhut noted that a C–5A Galaxy was coming in with a shipment of 105mm howitzers for beleaguered South Vietnamese forces. Some 37 civilian employees of the Defense Attache office were rounded up to escort 250 Vietnamese infants who would be taken out in Operation 'Baby Lift'. In later years this aspect of the evacuation would draw fire because the infants, billed as Vietnamese orphans heading to the US for adoption, were for the most part not orphans at all. In the meanwhile, however, it seemed a sterling humanitarian deed. TV and news crews assembled to record the departure of the giant C–5A for the US.

On 4 April 1975 the fully loaded C–5A Galaxy (aircraft 68-0218) took off from Tan Son Nhut. The C–5A had just begun this very first flight in Operation 'Baby Lift' with its crew convinced they were leaving a country now rapidly falling apart. Pilot Captain Dennis Traylor leveled off at 23,000ft (7,010m) some 10 miles (16km) off the Vietnamese coast when the giant aircraft – at the time, the largest aircraft type in the world – underwent a massive structural failure in the rear cargo door area.

Captain Traylor exerted considerable airmanship but could not get the Galaxy back to Tan Son Nhut. The C–5A grazed the earth east of the Saigon River, bounced, and came to rest a half-mile away on the west side. 175 survivors and the crew were able to get out. 206 people aboard the C–5A, including most infants and their escorts, were killed.

The C–5A Galaxy was the biggest aircraft loss, with the greatest loss of life, of the Vietnam war. In later years some people, including other C–5A pilots, have suspected that the catastrophe was set off by an SA–7 shoulder-launched missile or even that the C–5A may have been hit by small-arms fire. Colonel Dennis Traylor, now located at Maxwell AFB, Alabama, insists that he suspects no such thing.

The loss of the 'Baby Lift' C–5A cast a pall over evacuation plans. Those seeking to be ready for a final pull-out also faced obstacles because of Ambassador Graham Martin's firm refusal to acknowledge that anything was wrong. Despite problems, workers began identifying locations where UH–1 Huey, CH–46 Sea Knight and CH–53 Sea Stallion helicopters would be able to land if they were needed.

On 21 April President Thieu resigned, charging that the US was an untrustworthy ally. The end came just over a week later.

Evacuation Plans

Brigadier General Leroy Swenson, who arrived to replace General Baughn as Deputy Defense Attache, watched the 'Eagle Pull' evacuation from Cambodia to get ideas for the much larger 'Frequent Wind' pull-out from Saigon. Swenson was now urging retired American military personnel and civil contract Americans to get out of South Vietnam without delay.

Although many were able to leave South Vietnam by sea up until the final days, the period 20-28 April 1975 (culminating with the communist seizure of Tan Son Nhut airfield) saw the largest fixed-wing evacuation undertaken. During this period, Ed Daly of World Airways made a Douglas DC-8 available to some evacuees without proper authorization, an act which made him an instant hero. At one point twenty C-141s were moving out at thirty-minute intervals. A similar number of C-130s brought people out daily. Although Ambassador Martin still denied that it was happening, Operation 'Frequent Wind' was under way and the long American presence was nearing its end.

It was as clear to VNAF pilots as anyone else that the sky was falling in. Some pondered how to escape their home country with their families. One remarkable flier eventually got out of South Vietnam in an A-1 Skyraider with five people aboard!

A few changed sides. On 8 April a VNAF Northrop F-5E dropped two 500lb (227kg) bombs on the presidential palace, apparently hastening President Thieu's decision to hit the road. On the evening of 28 April – when everyone except US Ambassador Graham Martin could see that the end was near – a tower operator at Tan Son Nhut airfield queried three approaching Cessna A-37 Dragonflies as to their identity and purpose. The approaching A-37 flight leader gave a vague reply, stating that his was an 'American-built aircraft'.

No other information was needed when the A-37s began releasing bombs on the airfield. Their approach had been calculated to enable them to strafe Tan Son Nhut's flight line, then turn north. Six bombs exploded on the ramp, damaging several C-47s and AC-119s. Shells flew around the scene of devastation.

F-5 fighters scrambled to intercept the A-37s but were unable to catch them. The A-37 attack was unique: it was the first and only time that airpower was used against the South Vietnamese. Whether the A-37 pilots were turncoats or North Vietnamese using captured machines scarcely seemed to matter. The attack had a devastating effect on the morale of the few South Vietnamese who where still willing to fight.

For the Americans who increasingly felt themselves under siege in their classy new embassy building in Saigon, and in the defense attache's office at Tan Son Nhut, it was apparent that North Vietnamese troops were coming down the pike and that South Vietnam's forces were not going to stop them. US Information Agency chief Alan Carter began telling Ambassador Martin that it was time to make practical plans for an

The US Navy's capability to muster a helicopter task force at sea made it possible to evacuate the Americans who remained in Phnom Penh and Saigon. That capability was enhanced by helicopter assault carriers such as the USS *Guam* (LPH-9), shown in this post-war view. Although the North Vietnamese were in the process of seizing Saigon on 29 April 1975, they did not seriously challenge the effort to get Americans out safely. (US NAVY)

During the evacuation of Saigon in April 1975, combat air patrol (CAP) missions from the nuclear-powered USS *Enterprise* (CVAN–65) were flown by a new fighter-interceptor, the Grumman F–14 Tomcat. These aircrewmen of the 'Wolfpack' of squadron VF–2 were among those who introduced the Tomcat to Vietnam. (US NAVY)

evacuation. Martin kept telling Thieu that the United States would not evacuate, would not abandon its ally.

Martin, who clearly believed it himself, kept saying that the US would stand fast, even after the communists had overrun Da Nang. No one else believed it. A few brave Foreign Service and military officers began plotting to evacuate those South Vietnamese citizens who had worked most closely with Americans; their leaders in Washington had given almost no thought to what might happen to individual Vietnamese closely identified with US interests.

Most of the embassy staff did not believe Ambassador Graham Martin's repeated assertions that the end was not near. On the morning of 28 April, junior diplomat Peter Orr glanced out of the window of the embassy to see Marine guards cutting down trees with chainsaws. He leaned out, 'What are you guys doing?'

'Sir, we're creating landing zones for helicopters.'

At about that time the last flights left Tan Son Nhut, NVA troops stormed the airfield, and fixed-wing aircraft were no longer an option for anyone wanting to leave.

On 29 April Operation 'Frequent Wind' evacuated 395 US citizens and 5,205 foreign nationals from Saigon. Three aircraft were lost and two US Marines killed during the evacuation. The Saigon government surrendered on 30 April 1975 and the long war was over. A number of people looked askance when, a few days later, there was revealed a 5 June 1973 letter from Nixon to Thieu promising to 'take swift and severe retaliatory action' if North Vietnam violated the peace accords.

Air Support

The US Air Force in Thailand and the US Navy at sea off the Vietnamese coast flew support for the evacuation of Saigon. A few of these missions were flown by a new aircraft type, the Grumman F–14A Tomcat, which was making one of its first operational cruises aboard the USS *Enterprise* (CVAN–65). No air opposition met US aircraft in the Saigon area.

The tales of harrowing escapes from Saigon would fill a book. An O–1E Bird Dog pilot got out with several people aboard his two-seat ship and landed safely aboard the USS *Midway* (CVA–41). Some helicopters filled with escapees landed aboard American carriers at sea and had to be dumped overboard to make space for more. A VNAF pilot flew a C–130 to Thailand and found he had to park in a sea of A–37Bs, A–1 Skyraiders, and other warplanes gotten out by intrepid VNAF pilots.

Beginning in April 1975, Americans assisted in the evacuation of up to 160,000 Vietnamese refugees. Some were 'boat people' who washed ashore in Singapore, Malaysia, the Philippines and Hong Kong. Some were picked up by American vessels and taken to Guam. In early May 1975 the author of this volume, State Department officer Andrew F. Antippas, and Immigration Service boss General Leonard F. Chapman sat around a table and hurriedly created the guidelines under which tens of thousands of these refugees were permitted to enter the United States. Refugee processing camps were set up at Eglin AFB, Florida, Indiantown Gap, Pennsylvania, Fort Chaffee, Arkansas, and Camp Pendelton, California.

15
MARINES

Key to the successful helicopter evacuation of American personnel remaining in South Vietnam was the Marine Corps CH–53 Sea Stallion helicopter, which had already served valiantly in the conflict and now served as the means for the last Americans to get out. Because US Ambassador Graham Martin did not want to broadcast a signal of weakness, detailed plans for Operation 'Frequent Wind', the final evacuation, were not completed until the last minute. (USMC)

The end of the American dream in South Vietnam. Embassy officer Andrew F. Antippas leads evacuees from a Marine Corps CH–53A Sea Stallion on the deck of the USS *Hancock* (CVA–19). It is 29 April 1975 and Operation 'Frequent Wind', the final pull-out, is in high gear. To the end, US Ambassador Graham Martin insisted that the Americans would not leave. (USMC)

Vietnamese Air Force (VNAF) aircraft which escaped to US Navy ships offshore in the final moments on 29–30 April 1975 are lined up at Guam while American authorities ponder what to do with them. Similar line-ups appeared at American bases in Thailand and the Philippines. Visible here are 45 UH-1 Hueys, 27 A-37B Dragonflies, three CH-47 Chinooks, and an O-1E Bird Dog. These VNAF aircraft were eventually re-absorbed by US forces. (USAF)

It has been argued that the Vietnamese who escaped with American help were not always those who deserved it the most, while many other Vietnamese who labored on the anti-communist side were left behind. Once North Vietnamese troops seized Saigon on 30 April 1975, one of their first steps was to assign thousands of former South Vietnamese officials to 're-education' camps in the north. This turned out to be the first of many cruelties the new regime embarked upon.

The Vietnamese Air Force, which had fought so valiantly for so many years, was swallowed up by its North Vietnamese enemy. Vietnam now became one nation (the Socialist Republic of Vietnam) and its new communist rulers operated a few of the F-5s, C-130s, and other American aircraft types seized from the VNAF – without a lot of success and without a flow of spare parts. In later years the new Vietnam's Soviet ally would fly 'Bear' reconnaissance aircraft and MiG-23 fighters from the magnificent airfield built by the Americans at Cam Ranh Bay.

The cruelties inflicted by communist conquerors on South Vietnam are outside the scope of this work – suffice to say that many critics of the US role in Vietnam, among them folk singer Jaon Baez, later softened their views when the harsh truth was known – and our story really ends with the evacuation of Saigon. It was then that the air war in the south, and the American role in it, reached its final denouement.

Last Stand

On that last day for the city of Saigon – the wonderful capital which had been the Paris of the Orient and which was now to slide into a long dark night under its new name, Ho Chi Minh city – a few men made the ultimate decision, to fight to the end. In a final moment of futility and courage, a VNAF AC-119G gunship flanked by two A-1H Skyraiders took off from Tan Son Nhut as communist troops were coming through the wire on the airfield perimeter. Weaving through gunfire and criss-crossing SA-7 missiles, the gunship and the two Skyraiders made a last-ditch stand within view of much of the population of Saigon.

Repeatedly the VNAF warplanes flew into enemy fire in order to unleash their own shells and ordnance and slow down the NVA advance. Finally, the AC-119G and one A-1H were blown out of the sky by SA-7 missiles. The remaining A-1H Skyraider – the last aircraft seen to fly in combat in South Vietnam – was last observed heading up the Saigon River, in the direction of more enemy, trailing smoke. There are those who say that the Skyraider is still flying and fighting out there in some eternal combat zone in the sky, destined to continue flying so long as men believe it worth the price to lay their lives on the line in defense of freedom.

For everybody else, the long air war in South Vietnam had finally ended.

INDEX